A Stovall Museum Series Publication

CLASSICAL ANTIQUITIES

CLASSICAL ANTIQUITIES

THE COLLECTION OF THE STOVALL MUSEUM OF SCIENCE AND HISTORY

THE UNIVERSITY OF OKLAHOMA

EDITED BY A.J. HEISSERER

Contributors:

Frederick L. Brown
Mario A. Del Chiaro
Barbara L. Gunn
A. J. Heisserer
A. Jamme
Daniel C. Snell

University of Oklahoma Press : Norman and London

By A. J. Heisserer

Alexander the Great and the Greeks: The Epigraphic Evidence (Norman, 1980)
Classical Antiquities: The Collection of the Stovall Museum of Science and History, the University of Oklahoma (editor; Norman, 1986)

Library of Congress Cataloging-in-Publication Data

Stovall Museum.
    Classical antiquities.

    "A Stovall Museum publication"—P.
    Bibliography: p. 155
    Includes index.
    1. Classical antiquities—Catalogs.   2. Mediterranean Region—Antiquities—Catalogs.   3. Stovall Museum—Catalogs.
I. Heisserer, A. J.
DE46.5.N678S76   1986   938′.0074′016637   86–40074
ISBN 0–8061–1993–4

Publication of this book has been made possible in part by grants from the University of Oklahoma Associates Research/ Creative Activity Funds and the University of Oklahoma Foundation, Inc.

For Harriet Peterson
with respect and gratitude

Contents

Editor's Preface

For many years a small but significant collection of classical antiquities has been housed in the Stovall Museum of Science and History of the University of Oklahoma. Our goal in this volume is to bring a substantial portion of this collection to the notice of both scholars and the general public and to share with others the results of our research on these objects. Only a few have been published previously. With this volume we initiate a full presentation with discussion and photographs.

The classical collection had its inception in the academic year 1939–40, when H. Lloyd Stow, professor of Greek and the first curator of the museum, and his wife, Hester, began assembling and later exhibiting various artifacts from the ancient world. Through their efforts the Fogg Art Museum of Harvard University and the Boston Museum of Fine Arts were induced to make donations of small objects and to lend more impressive ones. Joe Smay, a member of the faculty of the School of Architecture, lent ancient sculptures, terra-cottas, and vessels to the Stovall Museum for periodic displays. In 1941, Stow and Henry S. Robinson, professor of classics in the University of Oklahoma, were influential in instituting a vigorous policy of purchase and gift solicitations that added dramatically to the number and quality of the objects in the collection. Professor and Mrs. Stow had already donated various items that they had acquired in their travels, and to their generosity was added that of Professor and Mrs. Robinson, who became closely associated with the American excavations in the Athenian Agora. By 1945 the purchasing program was proceeding apace with funds provided primarily by the Alumni Development

Fund of the University of Oklahoma Foundation, and from this time into the mid-1950s the most important pieces were obtained. In 1953, Robinson became curator of the collection, energetically continuing the program of purchase and successfully persuading various individuals to donate objects to the museum. Rebecca Robinson was also active in these concerns. In 1958, Robinson left the University to become director of the American School of Classical Studies in Athens, and thereafter for many years the collection languished for lack of attention. In 1976, owing to the interest of Candace Greene, curator of collections in the Stovall Museum, I was invited to become involved in the collection. Activity has revived in recent years, especially with the addition of some excellent donations. The primary credit for this renewed spirit belongs to Candace Greene, who, among other things, made it possible for William Kamp (with the aid of a grant from the Institute of Museum Services) to organize the collection systematically during the summer of 1979. In the last few years Julie Droke, collections manager in the museum, has given unselfishly of her time and energy to help bring about this publication.

The artifacts in the classical collection have been used for many years in general undergraduate and graduate education in the University of Oklahoma. Lloyd Stow conceived of it originally as a teaching collection, and so it has remained to the present day. In years past students were encouraged by Stow and Robinson in the study of archaeology through study of the objects themselves, and I have followed their lead. At one time or another students have studied the museum's specimens of Greek pottery, glassware, terra-cotta lamps, and Roman coins, usually in directed readings under my direction, as doubtless previously under the direction of earlier curators. I have conducted tours of the collection both for my own classes in the university and for high-school classes in the Norman—Oklahoma City area; periodically I bring replicas from the collection into the classroom to stimulate curiosity and further study, and during the spring of 1980, I offered a seminar on the Greek pottery in the collection.

Exhibitions of portions of the classical collection have been offered periodically to the university community, the residents of the Norman area, and to the general public of the state and region—for it is certain that the collection in its entirety is unique to the Southwest. There are (imperfect) records of displays presented in the years 1946, 1948, 1954, 1973, 1975, 1977, 1980, and recently we have arranged for a continuous display of the collection through rotation of its various components. We look forward to the time when we may be able to display for the public the entire collection as one whole.

For specialists in the different disciplines we wish to call attention to some of the most important and interesting pieces in this catalogue, of which the ceramics clearly form the majority. For example, the Mycenaean stirrup jar (no. 53) shows a Cypro-Minoan character painted in red above its base. The decoration on the Geometric high-rimmed bowl (no. 73) exhibits careful technique and lavish ornamentation. Among the classical pieces unquestionably the Attic eye cup (no. 84) and the Diosphos vase (no. 85) occupy a place of prominence; their beauty is self-evident, and the eye cup is a rare specimen of a subclass of Attic vases. Another fine Attic piece, whose incised decoration and intact condition mark it as exceptional, is the black-glazed stamped amphoriskos (no. 104). The Apulian crater fragment (no. 96) is the only ceramic known to date which depicts a scene of Peleus and Phoenix. The Etruscan bronze figurine of Apollo with lyre (no. 122) is also in a class by itself. The recent gift of two tall female terra-cottas from south Italy (nos. 137, 138) adds an important dimension to the collection; to date we have found no precise parallels for them. The inscriptions in Greek and Latin on a terra-cotta lamp (no. 153) appear to be unique. Several pieces of glassware are noteworthy for their charm: the small toilet bottle (no. 167), the double-head flask (no. 174), and

the cosmetic tube (no. 177). The coin collection has one exceptional group: the superb bronzes donated by Cornelius Vermeule (nos. 236, 238, 240, 242, 245, 251–54, 311, and 323). Most of these coins come from the early Roman Empire and are distinguished by their state of preservation; that of Nero (no. 242) is the most striking. The pieces described above are the prizes of the collection of classical art and archaeology in the Stovall Museum, those of which we are most proud.

In the description of each object we have attempted to give an adequate delineation of its appearance, the appropriate typology, and the correct date; wherever possible we have drawn attention to similar artifacts. Instead of appending a bibliography at the end of each description, a practice especially prevalent in cataloguing pottery, we have placed the major bibliographical references at the heading of each section and incorporated other references within the commentary on the individual entry. This procedure permits a minimum of repetition and should cause the reader no discomfort. Although care has been taken to show the reader where to find further information relating to the object under discussion, we have made no endeavor to cite all pertinent literature. Indeed, since approximately 80 percent of the articles and books used in writing this volume came into our hands for a limited time through Inter-Library Loan Service, it was impossible to do more than cite the most important works for the items in each section, e.g., the books by J. D. Beazley on Attic vases. Despite this limitation, considerable discussion of alternative theories and proposals will be encountered, with sufficient bibliographical notation. In this way we hope that the specialist will find our accounts satisfactory and the general reader will gain a stimulus for further reading.

The heading of each section or subsection shows the person(s) responsible for the research on the items within that section. There are, however, some exceptions. In the South Arabia section I, not A. Jamme, wrote the brief note on the lithics (no. 39). The same applies for the Attic Geometric fragment (no. 74) and three of the four sherds from Elche (nos. 76–78). I revised the description of one Iron Age Cypriote vase (no. 64) and wrote the accounts of two Hellenistic vessels (nos. 105, 107). Barbara Gunn compiled the information on the small terra-cotta horse and rider (no. 131) and the votive egg (no. 133), to which I added further notes and bibliographical references. I did the reports on an Italian lamp (no. 154) and a Roman Imperial lamp (no. 160) and added references and made modifications in the discussion of all the lamps. Frederick Brown wrote the account of the Tarentine didrachm (no. 185) and that of the bronze apparently from Ascalon (no. 222). In typing the final manuscript, I have made alterations for almost all sections. These are the only exceptions with regard to the authorship of individual entries, but it should be publicly acknowledged that in many of our descriptions I have followed the lead of the two former curators. Often a correct identification of an object depended on a note written by either of these scholars in our accession records. We also wish to recognize the splendid cooperation and scholarship provided by those who wrote reports on, or communicated with me about, very specialized topics: Daniel C. Snell, assistant professor in the Department of History, University of Oklahoma, for his description and translation of our cuneiform tablets, based on a previous study of these by Albrecht Goetze, of Yale University; Gary Beckman, assistant curator of the Babylonian Collection at Yale University, for his work on the opisthographic stone stele (no. 31); John A. Brinkman, director of the Oriental Institute in the University of Chicago, for that on the Neo-Babylonian fragment (no. 29); William Horwitz, formerly associate professor of classics in the University of Oklahoma, for that on the small Elamite fragment (no. 30); A. Jamme, a member of the faculty of the Catholic University of America, for that on the South Arabian objects; and Mario A. Del Chiaro, of the Department of Art History, University of California at Santa Barbara, for that on the three Etruscan bronzes. To them and to the former curators of the classical collection at the Stovall Museum we express our heartfelt gratitude.

Cedric Boulter, my former professor in the Department of Classics in the University of Cincinnati, first suggested to me the idea of preparing this catalogue. For his suggestion and for his reading of many reports on the Geometric, Archaic, and Classical pottery, I tender my profound appreciation. My thanks goes also to Gerald Cadogan and Gisela Walberg, of the Department of Classics in the University of Cincinnati, for their helpful comments concerning, re-

spectively, the descriptions of the Greek Bronze Age and Cypriote Iron Age vases. I wish to thank also Dietrich von Bothmer, the well-known expert in the Metropolitan Museum of Art, for comments on the Diosphos vase (no. 85); Sidney M. Goldstein, chief curator at the Corning Museum of Glass, for assistance on a piece of Syrian glass (no. 177); Lawrence Richardson, Jr., of Duke University, for general suggestions regarding information on certain glass pieces; Rosina Kolonia, for permission to study Black-figured vases in the National Archaeological Museum, in Athens; F. W. Hamdorf, of the Antikensammlungen in Munich, for providing photographs and information about several Attic head vases and Red-figured lekythoi in his museum; Rosemary Puszkajler, of Vienna, for her comments on the Apulian fragment (no. 96); and, finally, Leslie F. Smith, professor emeritus in the University of Oklahoma, for his constant encouragement in this endeavor, assistance with many reports on the coins, and advice on countless other objects. We acknowledge our debt to these individuals but in no way hold them accountable for any errors in text or interpretation.

David A. Burr, vice-president for University affairs in the University of Oklahoma, has been largely responsible for seeing this volume come to light, through his unstinting encouragement and assistance in securing financial support. The Office of Research Administration of the Norman campus of the university provided financial assistance for summer research on the catalogue but, above all, made possible the grant from the Associates Research/Creative Activity Funds for the purpose of publication. A generous grant from the University of Oklahoma Foundation, Inc., was for the same purpose. I hereby recognize their immeasurable support.

All the black-and-white photographs were taken by me, and those of the coins represent actual size or extremely close approximations. The color photographs are the effort of Gil Jain, chief photographer in the university, who also developed all the black-and-white negatives. He advised me for many weeks on matters photographic, and I express my appreciation for his expertise.

A. J. HEISSERER

Norman, Oklahoma

Abbreviations used for th...
material described in eacl
at the beginning of that
Each catalogue entry has
ber, placed on the left ma
scription of that entry; th
following the date and
object, is the accession nui
seum of History and Scie
tions used in this book ar

Ancient Near East

Mesopotamia
  Sumerian Civilizatic
  Third Dynasty of U
  Old-Babylonian Pei
  Neo-Babylonian En
South Arabian Civiliza
early centuries A.D.)
Persian Empire (ca. 5

Ancient Greece

Bronze Age (ca. 3000
  Minoan Civilization
  Mycenaean Civiliza
  Greek Mainland
Dark Age (Iron) and
500 B.C.)
  Homeric Greece
  Geometric Culture
  Greek Colonies in S

Acknowledgments

We acknowledge the generosity and assistance provided by the individuals and families named below, who either directly donated objects to the Stovall Museum or helped in one way or another in augmenting our classical collection.

Professor Edgar J. Banks
William Bennett Bizzell
Dr. Stephen Borhegyi
Dr. and Mrs. Albert Bothe
Dr. David A. Burr
Professor Lacey D. Caskey
Gerald Chase
Professor George H. Chase
Professor Lloyd W. Daly
Professor Mario A. Del Chiaro
Brigadier General Robert L. Denig
Professor Franklin Fenenga
Alison M. Frantz
Allan Gerdau
The Reverend Gregory Gerrer, O.S.B.
Mickey Gibson
Lawrence E. Gichner
Elgin Groseclose
Nick Horn
Jane Howe

Mrs. Minnie M. Howe
Professor Oscar B. Jacobson
Professor Allen C. Johnson
Justin Jones, O.S.B.
Mrs. Shaun Kelly, Jr.
Mr. and Mrs. Russell L. Long
Dr. Arthur McAnally
Charlie Mooney
Harriet Peterson
Mrs. Jessie Newby Ray
Professor and Mrs. Henry S. Robinson
Herbert D. Seabourn
Gerald W. Shivers
Professor and Mrs. Joseph E. Smay
Professor Leslie F. Smith
Juanita D. Spiva
Harry P. Stiely
Professor and Mrs. J. Willis Stovall
Professor and Mrs. H. Lloyd Stow
Frances Sudderth
Professor Cornelius Vermeule
Malcolm A. Via, Jr.
Rick and Cindy Watson
E. E. Westervelt
The Woodruff family

CLASSICAL ANTIQUITIES

INSCRIBED MATERIALS

Cuneiform Inscriptions

DANIEL C. SNELL

At the end of the last century and the beginning of this one clandestine diggers exported from southern Iraq thousands of cuneiform inscriptions. The collection amassed slowly by the Stovall Museum was bought from antiquities dealers in the United States and presents a representative group of texts from the earlier periods of ancient Mesopotamian history. The catalogue entries below were prepared by Daniel C. Snell, assistant professor of history in the University of Oklahoma, on the basis of notes made by the late Albrecht Goetze of Yale University. Gary Beckman, assistant curator of the Babylonian Collection at Yale University, prepared the scholarly data on no. 31; John A. Brinkman, director of the Oriental Institute in the University of Chicago, identified no. 29; and William Horwitz, formerly associate professor of classics in the University of Oklahoma, provided the information on no. 30. Snell will publish the inscriptions fully elsewhere.

Cones

Clay cones must have been produced by the hundreds; they were apparently used as plaques to ensure that future rebuilders of a temple would know to whom the temple was dedicated.

1 Cone of Gudea of Lagash

Ca. 2100 B.C.
20 × 13.5 cm, respectively, diameter and length (C49–50/6/1)

Translation: For Nindara, the exalted king, his king, Gudea, the city-governor of Lagash, built his house in Girsu.

2 Cone of Gudea of Lagash

Ca. 2100 B.C.
21.5 × 15 cm (C49–50/6/4)

This cone duplicates the inscription of the previous one.

3 Cone of Gudea of Lagash

Ca. 2100 B.C.
18 × 11.5 cm (C49–50/6/2)

Translation: For Ningirsu, the strong hero of Enlil, Gudea, city-governor of Lagash, produced the fitting thing and built the House of Fifty of the shining Anzu-bird and restored it to its place.

4   Cone of Gudea of Lagash

Ca. 2100 B.C.
19.5 × 9 cm (C49–50/6/3)

This cone duplicates the inscription of cone 3.

5   Cone of Gudea of Lagash

Ca. 2100 B.C.
19.5 × 14.7 cm (C49–50/6/5)

Translation: For Ningizzida, his god, Gudea, the city-governor of Lagash, client of Gatumdu, built his house in Girsu.

6   Cone of Lipit-Ishtar of Isin

Ca. 1930 B.C.
15 × 10.5 cm (C43–44/1)

This king of Old Babylonian Isin left many duplicates commemorating the building of the house of justice.

Translation: I am Lipit-Ishtar, the humble shepherd of Nippur, the upright farmer (of Ur), the tireless one of Eridu, the fitting lord of Uruk, king of Isin, king of Sumer and Akkad, the favorite of Inanna. When he had established justice in Sumer and Akkad, in Namgarum, the eminent place of the gods, the house of justice, he built.

Economic Documents from the Third Dynasty of Ur (2112–2004 B.C.)

7   Receipt for oxen and sheep from Puzrish-Dagan

Ca. 2030 B.C.
3.2 × 3 × 1.5 cm, respectively, height, width, and depth (C43–44/2)

Translation: 2 western, speckled oxen, 1 grain-fed sheep, 1 lamb, dead; 26th day, from Dudu Šulgi-urumu received. Month: (Puzrish-Dagan ii), year: (Šū-Sîn 5).

8   Receipt for grain from Umma

Ca. 2030 B.C.
4.2 × 4 × 1.4 cm (C43–44/3)

Translation: 60 quarts of grain of Lu-X, from Nig-urum, seal of the city-governor. Month: (Umma viii), year: (Šū-Sîn 6).
Seal: Fragmentary, but mentioning Šū-Sîn and Aa-kala, city-governor of Umma.

9   Receipt for four sheep from Puzrish-Dagan

Ca. 2030 B.C.
2.7 × 2.4 × 1.3 cm (C43–44/4)

Translation: 4 sheep [——], 28th day, from Abba-šaga, Šulgi-a'amu took in charge. Month: (Puzrish-Dagan xii), year: (Amar-Suen 5).
Left edge: 4.

10   Rations for messengers from Umma

Ca. 2020 B.C.
3.7 × 3 × 1.4 cm (C43–44/5)

Translation: (Quantities of beer of various qualities, bread, oil, alkali, onions for various persons.) [Day:] 6th, month: (Umma iv), year: (Ibbi-Sin 2).

11 Receipt for reed bundles from Umma

Ca. 2030 B.C.
4.5 × 3.6 × 1.6 cm (C43–44/6)

Translation: 150 reed bundles, craftsmen, 11th day; 390 reed bundles, craftsmen, via Lugal-kala; 508 reed bundles, Ir, Šeš-kala's son, 12th day. Month: (Umma xi), year: (Šū-Sîn 7).

12 Receipt for a priced copper object from Umma

Ca. 2030 B.C.
3.7 × 3.3 × 1.5 cm (C43–44/7)

Translation: 4 pounds of a copper [——], its price being one-half sheqel, from Ur-šakidu, Ninuma, the wife of Šeš-šeš, the doorkeeper of the god Šara, received. Month: (Umma v), year: (Šū-Sîn 3).

13 Receipt for a dead sheep from the city of Umma

Ca. 2030 B.C.
4.8 × 4.6 × 1.6 cm (C44–45/1)

Translation: 1 male sheep unshorn, milk-fed (?), dead, from Šeš-kala, seal of Lukala. Month: (Umma xii), year: (Šū-Sîn 6).

Seal: Lu-kala, scribe, son of Ur-e'e.

14 Receipt for 10 animals from Puzrish-Dagan

Ca. 2040 B.C.
3 × 2.8 × 1.3 cm (C44–45/2)

Translation: 1 grain-fed lamb, 7 *alum*-sheep, 2 goats, fourth day, from Abbašaga, Nalu took in charge. Month: (Puzrish-Dagan i), year: (Amar-Suen 4).

15   Receipt for 10 oxen from Puzrish-Dagan

Ca. 2040 B.C.
3 × 2.7 × 1.4 cm (C44–45/3)

Translation: `10 oxen, 17th day, from Lugal-
amar-ku, Uta-mišaram took in charge. Month:
(Puzrish-Dagan iv), year: (Amar-Suen 8).
Left edge: 10.

16   List of field areas and workers, from Umma

Ca. 2030 B.C.
7 × 5 × 2 cm (C56–57/17)

Translation: 1230 (area) SAR to be cleared of
thorn bushes (at the rate of) 10 SAR each (man).
Wages therefor (amount to) 121 man-days. 930
(area) SAR grass carrying (at the rate of) 10 SAR
each (man). Wages therefor (amount to) 93 man-
days. 1 workman for 25 days chasing off the
crows, field of Šulpae, 6 workmen for 6 days to
travel from Umma to Eduru-Kudda. 6 workmen
for 6 days to travel from Eduru-Kudda to Umma,
and to go to cross the river. Wages for the two
(journeys). Foreman: Šeškalla. Year: (Šū-sîn 4).
Seal: Kuggani.

A. Goetze, "Two Ur-Dynasty Tablets Dealing with
Labor," *Journal of Cuneiform Studies* 16 (1962):
14–16.

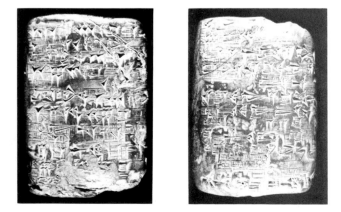

Documents from the Old Babylonian Period (2004–1595 B.C.)

17   Allotment of barley issued

Undated, perhaps from the Larsa Dynasty, ca. 1760 B.C.
6.5 × 4 × 2 cm (C49–50/5/1)

18   List of metal objects and their weights, one price

Undated
4 × 3.5 × 1.6 cm (C49–50/5/2)

19   Contract for loan of grain, a case tablet

Ca. 1740 B.C.
4.6 × 4.3 × 2.4 cm (C49–50/5/3)

Translation: 1 gur 60 quarts grain [——] with normal interest to be added, from Ilšu-ibbišu, Ibni-Dagan received. At the time of harvest he will repay the grain and its interest. Before (named witnesses). Month: (ix), day: 10th, year: (Samsuiluna 7).

Illegible sealings on all sides.

20   Account of barley for various purposes

From the Larsa Dynasty
7 × 4 × 2 cm (C49–50/5/4)

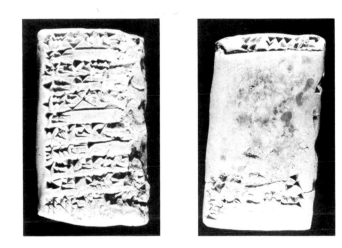

21   Contract for loan of grain, a case tablet

5.5 × 4.2 × 2.4 cm (C49–50/5/5)

Translation: 2 gur 120 sila of prime (?) grain, with the usual interest to be added, from Ilšu-ibišu, Ili-idinam [——] received. At the time of the harvest the grain and its interest he will repay. Before (named witnesses). Month: (xii), day: 7th, year: (perhaps Samsuiluna 7 from simi-

lar personal name in no. 19, which is dated to that year).

Illegible sealings on all sides.

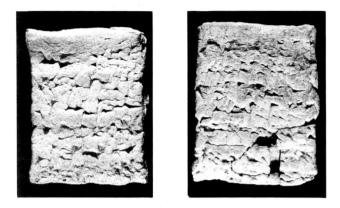

22   Contract? Mostly illegible

4 × 3.1 × 1.5 cm (C49–50/5/6)

23   Multiplication table

Fragment A: 2.4 × 4 × 2 cm
Fragment B: 2 × 5 × 2 cm
Fragment C: 2.5 × 4 × 2 cm
(C49–50/5/7)

Fragments A and C are probably from the same tablet, but fragment B is not clearly related. C is partly erased.

**24   Record, perhaps of grain, badly
       preserved**

3.6 × 4.1 × 1.4 cm (C49–50/5/8)

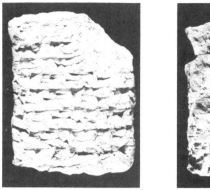

27   Extract from a syllabary

5.4 × 3.8 × 2 cm (C49–50/5/11)

A list of signs used by an apprentice scribe to
learn signs by copying them over. Two holes in
obverse.

25   List of payments in silver

Undated
6.7 × 4.6 × 1.8 cm (C49–50/5/9)

**26   Contract for loan of silver, badly
       preserved**

Date destroyed
4.8 × 3.6 × 1.5 cm (C49–50/5/10)

Translation: Two-thirds sheqel silver, interest
per sheqel (so much silver), he shall add, from
Itur-X and Ur-kuga, Ṣilli-[——] Sin-[——]'s son,
received [——].

28   Account of barley

Date broken
12.6 × 7 × 3 cm (C49–50/5/12)

Six columns of figures and personal names.

Other

29   Neo-Babylonian brick fragment

605–562 B.C.

Maximum height of surface, 10 cm; maximum width of surface, 14 cm; thickness, 8 cm (C75/1)

The surface shows remains of a royal inscription of King Nebuchadnezzar II (the Biblical Nebuchadnezzar), who reigned from 605 to 562 B.C. The first partly legible line contains this king's name. Obverse shows that some type of seashell (perhaps mussel) became imbedded when mixed accidentally with the builder's clay. Provenance of the fragment is Hilla, near Basra, Iraq.

30   Elamite cuneiform fragment from Persepolis

Height, 12 cm; width, 12.7 cm (encased within a brass binding) (C54–55/4)

This small fragment, which contains only two symbols, is likely part of a trilingual inscription, perhaps from the reign of Darius (ca. 521–486 B.C.). Provenance of the fragment is Persepolis.

31   Fragment of a stone stele

Second millennium B.C.

Height, 10.4 cm; maximum width, 16.2 cm, inscribed width, 13.7 cm; preserved thickness tapers from 6.8 to 5.8 cm (C54–55/1)

A thick fragment of a multicolumned stone stele inscribed in cuneiform characters. The reverse was inscribed but the lettering is heavily abraded. Possibly it was a boundary stone. Nothing is known about its provenance or origin, but it is probably from Mesopotamia. Gary M. Beckman, of the Babylonian Collection in Yale University, has prepared a copy of the text and informs us that this will appear in the *Journal of Cuneiform Studies* under the "Texts and Fragments" section.

This stone has a fascinating modern story. It was found by chance in the back of a file-cabinet drawer in the Treasure Room of the Bizzell Memorial Library at the University of Oklahoma during the fall of 1954; nothing was known or ascertainable about its appearance in the university library. Henry S. Robinson, then curator of Classical Art & Archaeology at the Stovall Museum, requested of Arthur McAnally, then director of the library, that the document be transferred to the museum; and by early December it was in the classical collection. Within days Robinson wrote to Albrecht Goetze at Yale University, a scholar known for his many publications of cuneiform texts. Not long afterward this stone fragment and some 27 cuneiform clay tablets were sent to Goetze for examination. Eventually he returned the 27 tablets with his description of their content but apparently had overlooked this stone fragment, which was forgotten in time and assumed to be lost. Then during the fall of 1982 correspondence between A. J. Heisserer, Daniel Snell, and Gary Beckman revealed that the stone, indeed, was still present at the Babylonian Collection in Yale University, located by its old accession number. In November, 1982, Beckman returned the stele with his comments about its general nature (given above). We express our appreciation to Beckman for his assistance in working on the text and in seeing that this errant stone, after a twenty-eight years' absence, was returned to the Stovall Museum.

South Arabian Pre-Islamic Antiquities

(A. JAMME)

The proscynemas and slabs described below were all collected from the east edge of the present country of Yemen. For general information on ancient objects from South Arabia, see Richard LeBaron Bowen, Jr., and Frank P. Albright, *Archaeological Discoveries in South Arabia* (Baltimore, Md., 1958); and R. L. Cleveland, *An Ancient South Arabian Necropolis: Objects from the Second Campaign (1951) in the Timma^c Cemetery* (Baltimore, Md., 1965).

32 Proscynema

Fourth century B.C.
Height, 30.6 cm; width, 16.4 cm; thickness, 13.4 cm (C84/4/5)

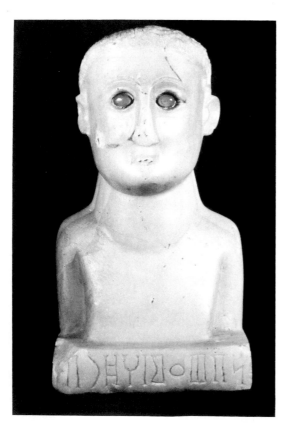

A monolith proscynema or funerary stele composed of a male bust and its base; this type of proscynema is unusual in that only the upper section of the arms is shown. The eyes are modern.

nbṭ^cm/ḥḏrb Nabaṭ^camm [of the family] Haḏrab.

nbṭ^cm is a well-known Qatabanian personal name, e.g., Ja 184/1 and 372/2. Cf. A. Jamme, *Pièces épigraphiques de Ḥeid bin ʿAqîl, la nécropole de Timna^c (Hagr Kohlân)* (Louvain, 1952), pp. 74, 213. *hḏrb* is a new family name. For other types of a human bust on a base as a proscynema, cf., e.g., TC 1557; R. L. Cleveland, *An Ancient South Arabian Necropolis: Objects from the Second Campaign (1951) in the Timna^c Cemetery* (Baltimore, Md., 1965), pl. 45 and pp. 23B–24A; and A. Jamme, *Notes on the Published Objects Excavated at Ḥeid bin ʿAqîl in 1950–1951* (Washington, D.C., 1965), p. 63.

33 Base of a proscynema

Fourth century B.C.
Maximum height, 5.5 cm; width, 16.5 cm; maximum thickness, 5 cm (C84/4/9)

A very well-known example of the base of a proscynema. Cf., e.g., TC 1527 in R. L. Cleveland, *An Ancient South Arabian Necropolis: Objects from the Second Campaign (1951) in the Timna^c Cemetery* (Baltimore, Md., 1965), pl. 80, center of the upper line, and pp. 68–69; and A. Jamme, *Pièces*

épigraphiques de Ḥeid bin ʿAqîl, la nécropole de Timnaʿ (Hagr Koḥlân) (Louvain, 1952), p. 113: Ja 244.

ġsnm/ršm   *Ġasnum [of the clan] Rašam.*

ġsnm is a new personal name. ršm is a well-known clan name of the Qatabanian capital. Cf. ibid., pp. 126–29: Ja 265–68.

34   Proscynema

Second century B.C.
Height, 15 cm; width at base, 11.6 cm; thickness, 5.7 cm (C84/4/8)

A very well-known type of a monolith proscynema without any decoration on the upper section. Cf., e.g., TC 1872 in R. L. Cleveland, *An Ancient South Arabian Necropolis: Objects from the Second Campaign (1951) in the Timnaʿ Cemetery* (Baltimore, Md., 1965), pl. 75, upper left corner, and p. 50B; for the inscription of TC 1872, cf. A. Jamme, *Notes on the Published Objects Excavated at Ḥeid bin ʿAqîl in 1950–1951* (Washington, D.C., 1965), pp. 72–73. The Arabic number "60" is painted on the back of the antiquity.

nʾdm/ḏrḥn   *Naʾdum [of the clan] Ḏarḥân.*

nʾdm, e.g., Qatabanian RÉS 4116/1–2, and Sabaean Ja 2776 d, and Ḥaḍrami Ja 915. ḏrḥn, a well-known clan of the Qatabanian capital. Cf., e.g., A. Jamme, *Pièces épigraphiques de Ḥeid bin ʿAqîl, la nécropole de Timnaʿ (Hagr Koḥlân)* (Louvain, 1952), pp. 40–62: Ja 138–67.

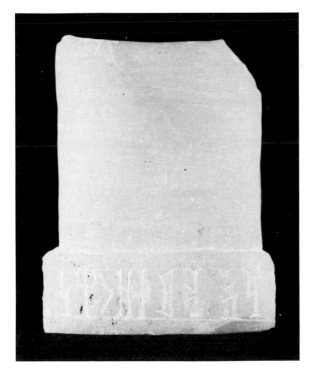

35   Base of a proscynema

First century B.C.
Height, 6.5 cm; maximum width, 18.2 cm; maximum thickness, 6 cm (C84/4/10)

Same type of base as the proscynema in no. 33.

bʾnm/hnʿmt   *Baʾnum [of the clan] Hunaʿamat.*

bʾnm is a Sabaean name in G1 1591/5. hnʿmt is the well-known name of a secondary clan of the Qatabanian capital. Cf. A. Jamme, *Pièces épigraphiques de Ḥeid bin ʿAqîl, la nécropole de Timnaʿ (Hagr Koḥlân)* (Louvain, 1952), pp. 101–106: Ja 225–33.

36   An undated proscynema

Height, 14.8 cm; width, 16 cm; maximum thickness, 5.8 cm (C84/4/6)

An uninscribed rectangular proscynema with the eyes, nose, and mouth in relief from the excised center of the plaque. A large forehead serves as the superior rim; the width of the rim on the three other sides is half that of the forehead. Cf., e.g., TC 1822; R. L. Cleveland, *An Ancient South Arabian Necropolis: Objects from the Second Campaign (1951) in the Timnaʿ Cemetery* (Baltimore, Md., 1965), pl. 37, upper left, and p. 18A.

37   An undated plaque

Maximum height, 20 cm; maximum width, 16.5 cm; thickness, 2.5 cm (C84/4/7)

The upper part of a polished plaque with a bucranium. The bull was the main symbol of the lunar deity; it is mostly represented by the bucranium. The present antiquity was the top of either a simple ex-voto without any inscription (cf., e.g., TC 1686 and 2076 in R. L. Cleveland, *An Ancient South Arabian Necropolis: Objects from the Second Campaign [1951] in the Timna⁽ᶜ⁾ Cemetery* [Baltimore, Md., 1965], pls. 65 and 66, top, and pp. 41 and 42B) or a proscynema. Cf., e.g., TC 1519 in ibid., pl. 64 and p. 40A.

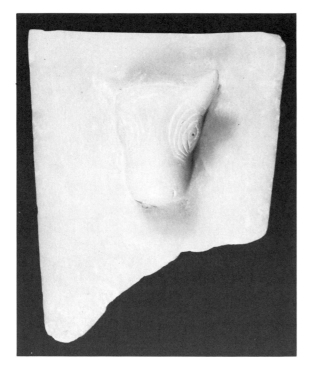

38   An undated slab

Maximum height, 15.8 cm; maximum width, 20 cm; thickness, 3 cm (C84/4/1)

A fragmentary slab with a graffito hand-pecked on the back before the original was broken. The front being polished, the fragment could belong to a stele, such as, e.g., no. 37 or no. 34. Graffito: nr⌈w⌉ *Naraw.* The upper half of the last letter is broken off; name of a Sabaean god who may be identified as the Venus-god ⁽ᶜ⁾Aṭṭar. Cf. A. Jamme, "Le panthéon arabe préislamique d'après les sources épigraphiques" in *Le Muséon,* 60 (1947): 100.

39   Prehistoric small lithics

(C84/4/15)

A total of 257 prehistoric arrowheads, spearpoints, and flints, collected north of the Hadhramaut Valley but on the south edge of the Rub al-Khali north of Say'ūn city. Very little research appears to have been done on prehistoric implements from the Arabian peninsula. For some discussion with references see H. A. McClure, *The Arabian Peninsula and Prehistoric Populations* (Coconut Grove, Fla., 1971), pp. 81–82.

Roman *Columbarium* Inscription

(A. J. HEISSERER)

40 Inscription and translation

Third century A.D.
(C47–48/8)

Text (obverse)

1   D(is)·M(anibus)
MIN·DI·O
PHI·LA·DEL·FO
QVI·BI·XIT·ANNIS
5   L·V·D(iebus)·III·CAECILIA
PRI·MA·CO(n)IVCI

INCONPARABI-
LI·B(ene)·M(erenti)·FECIT

Translation: To the gods of the underworld. For Mindius Philadelphus, who lived 55 years and 3 days, Caecilia Prima made (this) for her incomparable spouse, who deserved well of her.

Text (reverse)

1   D(is) M(anibus)
BOLVSIVS·FL-
AVIANVS QV-

I VIXXIT·ANN-
5   IS·L·M(ensibus)·II·CO(n)-
    IVC(i)·B(ene)·M(erenti)·F(ecit)

Translation: To the gods of the underworld. Volusius Flavianus, who lived 50 years and 2 months. (His wife) made (this) for her well-deserving spouse.

The measurements vary slightly for each side, since all edges of the stone were shaved off at an inward angle from the surface of the obverse. The measurements for the obverse show approximately: height, 25 cm; width, 22.3 cm; thickness, 2.2 cm. The base of the obverse is the top of the reverse. The obverse has been so designated on the grounds that the style of its lettering seems to be a bit earlier than that of the other surface. The letters on the reverse show considerable traces of red paint (*minium*), but both surfaces reveal poor workmanship and irregular spelling (e.g., *vixxit* in line 4 of the reverse). Letterforms and historical considerations (names ending in *-ianus*, as Flavianus here, are common as *cognomina* for freedmen and their descendants only in the mid-Empire) suggest a date in the third century A.D. for the inscribing of both sides of the stone.

There is a minor palaeographic problem with the text of the reverse. The name of Volusius Flavianus occurs in the nominative with customary life span but no name of his spouse. The most obvious interpretation is that *co(n)iuc(i)* and *m(erenti)* both refer to Flavianus, who alone is the decedent, and that the stonecutter omitted inscribing the name of the wife in the nominative. On the other hand, an emended text can be supplied on the assumption that the mason mistakenly engraved a single letter: *D.M. Bolusius Flavianus, qui vixit annis L mensibus II. Coiux bene merenti fecit* ("Volusius Flavianus, who lived 50 years and 2 months. His spouse made (this) for him, well-deserving it"). This emendation overcomes the irregularity of the absence of the name of the wife, for a dedicant need not be named in an epitaph. A final possibility is that Flavianus was both decedent and dedicator, that is, he may have stipulated in his will or indicated to his friends that he wished a sepulchral marker set up for his spouse should he predecease her; accordingly, even though care was taken to have a plaque placed for the wife, her name is not given. With this interpretation, the text may be translated, "Volusius Flavianus, who lived 50 years and 2 months, made (this) for his spouse, well-deserving it." Since, however, it is most likely that *co(n)iuc(i)* is to be taken as a normal dative, of a type very common in epitaphs, and that it refers to Flavianus, it is best to conclude that the name of his spouse was inadvertently omitted; the text has been translated with this in mind.

This Latin inscription is of a type that the Romans termed *columbarium*. The name comes from the large rectangular burial chamber that was shared as a common tomb by members of the same family or of the same association. The chamber was built partly above and partly below ground, with its inner walls filled with horizontal rows of small recesses or niches having the appearance of pigeonholes (*columbarium* in Latin = "dovecote"). These niches were used to hold vases, or cinerary urns, containing the ashes of the dead. Frequently this type of tomb contained the ashes of men and women of the lower classes, such as freedmen and slaves, and usually was constructed by Roman social associations known as *collegia* ("guilds") or *societates* ("fellowships"), in order that their members might be assured a final resting place for themselves and their families. Once a *columbarium* was built, the total number of niches was sometimes divided equally by lot among all the members, so that each was the proprietor of one niche in each division. Each member indicated his own place by inscribing his name upon a marble tablet, which was fastened above or below the recess, or by writing his name on the wall of the building. When the individual died, his fellow members either added the customary sepulchral information to the tablet or replaced it with a more ornate stone. In either case the stone came to be called, from its place of location, a *columbarium* inscription. If one member contributed a larger amount to the association than his fellows, he was allowed to have more than one niche; and those niches that he did not require for his own use, he could assign to his friends.

It is clear that the Stovall Museum's inscription is a characteristic specimen, for it records the names of unknown persons, who were very likely freedmen or their descendants. The absence of the first names (*praenomina*) for the males indicates, most likely, such a status. The plaque is inscribed on both sides ("opisthographic"), showing that space within many chamber-tombs became scarce, which in turn necessitated assigning old niches to new owners; and this seems to have happened in this instance. The obverse was obviously incised first, then turned over for a second use by another, apparently unrelated, individual. Source: A. J. Heisserer, *La Parola del Passato* 36 (1981): 385–92.

GREEK POTTERY

Bronze Age

(BARBARA L. GUNN)

Little more than a century ago Bronze Age Greece was known largely through legend and myth, and these tales were generally discounted by most scholars. Since then, however, archaeological excavations have revealed the remains of several highly developed civilizations in the Aegean area. Archaeological remains, especially pottery, are particularly important for the reconstruction of Bronze Age history simply because they are almost the only contemporary record left by the civilizations of that time. Pottery indicates different elements of a given culture. Since pottery often had a specifically funerary purpose, or even at times depicted religious or funerary scenes, it often can reveal a great deal about the religious customs of a people. The technique of pottery is an indication of the mechanical skills of a culture, and the decoration on vases is evidence both of the artistic ability of a people and of certain customs of their culture. Pottery, through its shape and decoration, may indicate external influences, such as trade relationships, on a settlement or it may illustrate the development of an indigenous craft in an isolated area. Pottery shapes may also reveal the types of products important to a culture either for its own use or for export. In addition, the distribution of specific vessels is one key factor in determining interarea commerce and emigration patterns. Finally, pottery is crucially important because, after it is arranged by style and the succession of periods determined, it provides a chronological framework within which to view other archaeological evidence. As these instances demonstrate, ancient pottery, because it is used for so many purposes and is virtually indestructible, is critically significant to archaeology and to the reconstruction of both Bronze Age and Iron Age history.

The Bronze Age Cypriote vases in the Stovall Museum are interesting for several reasons. These vessels as a whole represent almost every major pottery style of the Cypriote Bronze Age, including Red Polished ware, Black Polished ware, Black Slip ware, Red-on-Black ware, White Painted ware, Base Ring ware, and White Slip ware. They date from ca. 2000 B.C. to ca. 1100 B.C., spanning much of the Cypriote Bronze Age, and illustrate certain developments in the history of Cyprus. For example, the black-topped Red Polished II bowl, which is probably from the region near Lapithos in northern Cyprus, bears near its perforated lug a small straight mark that is common to such bowls and is similar to the numerals of the Minoan hieroglyphic system. Such marks may indicate limited Cypriote adaptation of a foreign writing system during the late Early Bronze Age. The Cypro-Minoan character painted in red on the Mycenaean stirrup jar is an instance of the Cypro-Minoan script, which is still undeciphered. This syllabic script, which first appears ca. 1500 B.C., seems to be a Cypriote adaptation of Minoan Linear A, another syllabic script also undeciphered. This Mycenaean stirrup jar, found in Cyprus, itself illustrates the pervasive character of Mycenaean trade and civilization in the Late Bronze Age. Thus, the Bronze Age vases from Cyprus in the Stovall Museum, though few in number, give an overall picture of the development of Cypriote pottery and civilization, at the same time reflecting some of the foreign influences at work in Cyprus.

The following abbreviations are used throughout the section on Bronze Age pottery:

Furumark, *MP*	Arne Furumark, *The Mycenaean Pottery: Analysis and Classification* (Stockholm, 1941).
Myres, *Cesnola*	John Myres, *Handbook of the Cesnola Collection of Antiquities from Cyprus* (New York, 1914).
SCE IV (1A)	Porphyrios Dikaios and James R. Stewart, *The Swedish Cyprus Expedition*, vol. IV, pt. 1A, *The Stone Age and The Early Bronze Age in Cyprus* (Lund, 1962).
SCE IV (1B)	Paul Åström, *The Swedish Cyprus Expedition*, vol. IV, pt. 1B, *The Middle Cypriote Bronze Age* (Lund, 1957).
SCE IV (1C)	Paul Åström, *The Swedish Cyprus Expedition*, vol. IV, pt. 1C, *The Late Cypriote Bronze Age* (Lund, 1972).

Cypriote Bronze Age Chronology
(Ashmolean Museum Guide)

Early Cypriote (2300–2000 B.C.)
EC I	2300–2200
EC II	2200–2100
EC III	2100–2000

Middle Cypriote (2000–1600 B.C.)
MC I	2000–1850
MC II	1850–1750
MC III	1750–1600

Late Cypriote (1600–1050 B.C.)
LC IA	1600–1450
LC IB	1450–1400
LC IIA	1400–1300
LC IIB	1300–1230
LC IIIA	1230–1190
LC IIIB	1190–1150
LC IIIC	1150–1050

Mycenaean (Late Helladic) Chronology (Furumark)
Mycenaean I	1550–1500 B.C.
IIA	1500–1450
IIB	1450–1425
IIIA:1	1425–1400
IIIA:2(early)	1400–1375
IIIA:2(late)	1375–1300
IIIB	1300–1230

IIIC:1(early)	1230–1200
IIIC:1(late)	1200–1125
IIIC:2	1125–1100

Vases

41   Cypriote Black Polished bottle

EC II to MC II (ca. 2200–1750 B.C.)
Preserved height, 11.4 cm; diameter, 7.6 cm (C53–54/18)

This small handmade bottle of Cypriote provenance is made from coarse, soft, light orange clay that has been fired black and polished on most of the surface, but misfired to buff on the lower portion of the body and the upper part of the neck. It has a double convex shape and a long, narrow, cylindrical neck. The decoration, which is incised and was originally filled with a white substance, consists of groups of parallel lines encircling the neck and body with a break in the pattern where the two ends of the line groups would meet. The decorative motifs include horizontal straight lines, horizontal wavy lines, a dotted line, and lines with pairs of concentric semicircles drawn around them.

Black Polished ware was made by a variation of the Red Polished ware technique: by restricting the admission of air during firing, the potter changed the color from red to black. These polished wares were polished with a pebble or a

large tooth. There was a gradual development of concentric circles during the Early and Middle Bronze Ages in Cyprus, with the concentric semicircles drawn around a line or lines. Myres, *Cesnola*, pp. 18–20. Compared to the Red Polished series, Black Polished ware is confined to small shapes, almost always incised, and never very common. The Stovall bottle is very similar to a Red Polished ware flask, dated to Early Cypriote II–Middle Cypriote II, illustrated in fig. CI.5, *SCE IV (1A)*. Another bottle, similar both in shape and decoration, is illustrated and dated to the Early Bronze IB period (= EC II or EC III, 2200–2000) in Tony Spiteris, *The Art of Cyprus* (New York, 1970), p. 26.

42 Cypriote Red Polished II or III jug

EC II to MC III (ca. 2200–1600 B.C.)
Height, 21.9 cm; diameter, 11.1 cm (C53–54/17)

This jug of Cypriote provenance is made of rather coarse, soft, yellowish-buff clay, which has a small amount of foreign matter; it carries a polished red-brown slip. The jug is globular,

with a knobbed base, handle from neck to shoulder, and cutaway spout.

This vessel, of a type labeled Red Polished ware, appears in the Early Cypriote Bronze Age and continues for centuries. *SCE IV (1A)*, p. 225. As with many common wares, the shapes and fabric of Red Polished ware seem to be fairly unchanging. The buff and clay and lightly polished slip of our jug are found in Red Polished III ware, but the technique of the Red Polished wares varies considerably in Red Polished II and Red Polished III. Ibid., pp. 227–28. With its cutaway spout, this piece should be placed in Stewart's Type IA. Ibid., p. 303. The jugs shown in ibid., figs. LXI–LXII, are especially similar to the Stovall jug (except for their lack of a knobbed base), but this observation is of little help since these jugs are both Red Polished I–II and Red Polished III. The classification and date for this jug, therefore, are necessarily only tentative, and the period assigned to it spans the existence of both Red Polished II ware and Red Polished III ware.

43 Cypriote Red Polished II bowl

Late EC III or MC I (ca. 2100–1850 B.C.)
Height, 8.5 cm; diameter, 14.5 cm (C53–54/16)

A handleless, handmade bowl from Cyprus, this object is made of rather fine, hard clay with much foreign matter intermixed. It is approximately hemispherical with the sides incurving toward the lip and with a horizontal perforated lug projecting outward below the lip. The bowl has been fired black on the interior and on the upper one-third of the exterior. This black color on the exterior fades into a purplish-red band, and this then changes into the normal orange-

red color of the fabric on the bottom half of the bowl. There is a short horizontal mark on the right of the lug in line with the perforated area of the lug, which seems to be a potter's mark, a common feature in black-topped Red Polished II bowls like this one. It is actually one of a group of horizontal and vertical slashes and U-shaped crescents that seem to have been local to Lapithos in northern Cyprus, though they are occasionally found elsewhere. Ellen Herscher in Noel Robertson, ed., *The Archaeology of Cyprus: Recent Developments* (Park Ridge, N.J., 1975), p. 44. These marks are like the numerals of the Minoan hieroglyphic system and may have been used as potters' memoranda to denote the number of pots produced at a particular time. Virginia Grace, *AJA* 44 (1940): 40–43; John Daniel, *AJA* 45 (1941): 261, 265–66. According to one scholar, a straight horizontal mark stands for the number 10. The Minoan numerical system apparently followed the same general lines as the Roman. W. French Anderson, *AJA* 62 (1958): 363 with n. 2. Black-topped Red Polished II bowls have been found to date to the late Early Cypriote III and the Middle Cypriote I periods.

44   Cypriote Red Polished IV bowl

MC (ca. 2000–1600 B.C.)
Height with handle, 9.6 cm, without handle, 6.3 cm; diameter, 11 cm (C53–54/19)

Composed of hard, fine, light reddish-brown clay and fired to a deep red, this hemispherical bowl from Cyprus has considerable lime incrustation. A wishbone handle projects upward from the rim; three very small lugs project slightly above the lip. The brown clay and the mat finish are one indication that the bowl belongs to the

class of Red Polished IV ware. *SCE IV (1B)*, p. 78. In addition to its fabric, the wishbone handle shows that it is Red Polished IV ware rather than an earlier Red Polished class, since in figs. CXXIX–CXLVIII in *SCE IV (1A)* showing hemispherical bowls from the Early Cypriote Bronze Age there are no bowls with wishbone handles. Red Polished IV ware first appears in the Middle Cypriote I and continues throughout the Middle Cypriote period. *SCE IV (1B)*, pp. 274–77. The wishbone handle of this bowl is somewhat similar to that of ibid., fig. XIX.2, a Red Polished IV hemispherical bowl.

45   Cypriote Red-on-Black jug

Early MC III (ca. 1750–1700 B.C.)
Height, 23.8 cm; diameter, 12.8 cm (C53–54/5)

This jug of Cypriote provenance (ex Kolokasides coll.) is handmade from very hard, compact, and brittle clay. It has a convex shoulder that is set off from its ovoid body by a sharp angle, a small flat base, a slender neck with a flaring lip, and a broad flat handle attached at the midpoint of the shoulder and neck. With a black slip it is decorated horizontally and vertically in red paint with groups of five parallel, wavy, rather broad lines. The parallel line groups in this kind of fabric usually were painted with a multiple brush or comblike instrument. J. Boardman, *Antiquity* 34 (1960): 85; also *SCE IV (1B)*, p. 117.

Since Red-on-Black ware is a regional technique of eastern Cyprus, this jug likely came from that area. V. Karageorghis, *The Ancient Civilization of Cyprus* (New York, 1969), pp. 134–35. Broad wavy lines in Red-on-Black ware usually indicate a relatively early date in the fabric; Åström in *SCE IV (1B)*, pp. 117 with n. 29, 276–77, states that early varieties of Red-on-Black ware appear during the period ca. 1750–1700, and that the style becomes fully developed in the following century. Since this example seems to be of a relatively early variety, it probably dates from the early MC III. Fig. XXXIV.4 in ibid. is very similar to this jug, except that the specimen there does not have a horizontal five-line band just below the shoulder.

46   Cypriote White Painted jug

MC III (ca. 1750–1600 B.C.)
Height, 13.2 cm; diameter, 6.5 cm (C53–54/4)

Made from fine, soft buff clay, this small ovoid handmade jug is also from the Kolokasides collection. The curved neck is molded as one with the body, and the lip has been greatly elongated and shaped as a pouring spout; a small handle extends from the shoulder to the middle of the lowest point of the neck and mouth. Two perforated lugs or string holes are attached on either side of the neck, two smaller ones on the handle itself, one at its base and the other near the top. The jug is decorated in gray paint, bands encircling the neck. At the point where the neck becomes the body, double lines are painted down to the base, while a diamond pattern is painted on the slope of the shoulder. From the bottom of the diamond two lines run to the base, and there is a wavy line from one side of the diamond that continues down to the base. This general pattern is repeated, with some variation, around the jug.

This specimen is probably best categorized as belonging to the White Painted III–V String-Hole style, as it has several string holes, and the clay seems to fit the description in *SCE IV (1B)*, p. 34. On the other hand, the decoration is simpler than is usual for the String-Hole style, which exhibits a general preference for horizontal decoration, although vertical elements, whenever they appear, are usually found on vessels such as this one. Ibid., p. 48. This decoration is somewhat similar to the White Painted III–IV Pendent-Line style (though the diamond pattern on the shoulder is not mentioned), which is an eastern Cypriote product and appears on vases of the same clay as the String-Hole style. Ibid., pp. 27–29. It is possible, therefore, that the Stovall jug may be a combination of these two decorative elements. Both styles appear in the period ca. 1750–1700 and become common in the period ca. 1700–1600. Ibid., pp. 275–76. Although the String-Hole style continues into the LC I period, after 1600, it is most likely that this Stovall flask belongs to the Middle Cypriote III period.

47   Cypriote White Painted IV (?) bottle

MC III (ca. 1750–1600 B.C.)
Height, 10.2 cm; diameter, 6 cm (C53–54/20)

Made from rather fine, soft, buff clay, this small handmade flask from Cyprus (ex Kolokasides coll.) is ovoid and has a small flat base, a neck that tapers in and then flares out below the lip, and a single vertical pierced lug at the juncture of the neck and body. The decoration is painted in black, though it is reddish from overfiring, and is composed of encircling horizontal bands on the neck, a wide vertical band of crosshatched lines on either side running from the neck-body juncture to the base, and an alternating series of three extended zigzag lines and bands. This small bottle is probably White Painted IV ware, a type that flourished during the Middle Cypriote Bronze Age. It has the characteristic soft and floury consistency of that ware, and bottles in White Painted IV ware are usually decorated vertically like this one. *SCE IV (1B)*, pp. 48, 58, 63. Fig. XXXIV.4 in ibid. shows a similar pattern of zigzag lines. If this bottle is of the White Painted IV style (or, as is possible, of White Painted III or V styles), it dates to the Middle Cypriote period. Ibid., p. 276.

48   Cypriote Black Slip II amphora

MC III (ca. 1700 B.C.)
Height, 23.2 cm; maximum diameter, 16.5 cm (C53–54/10)

A handmade amphora from Cyprus (ex Kolokasides coll.), this vessel is made from soft, buff or pinkish-buff clay and is covered with a black slip. The body is in the shape of a flattened sphere, the neck wide and cylindrical with an everted rim. Two vertical string-hole projection handles, which are not perforated, are placed at the junction of the neck and shoulder. Decoration consists of narrow raised ridges of clay on the body, neck, and lip; these are predominantly horizontal alternating straight and wavy lines, but vertical straight ridges run from near the handles down to the base. This particular shape represents the characteristic form of amphorae in the Black Slip fabric. G. Buchholz and V. Karageorghis, *Prehistoric Greece and Cyprus: An Archaeological Handbook* (London, 1973), p. 149. Furthermore, the string-hole projection handles, whether pierced or unpierced, are a frequent decoration on this shape. Myres, *Cesnola*, p. 23.

Since Black Slip II ware was often decorated at Lapithos, but usually rendered plain in eastern Cyprus, it is possible that this vase originates from the area around Lapithos. In addition, the pinkish-buff or buff clay generally indicates an early variety of Black Slip II. *SCE IV (1B)*, pp. 89–90, 103. Åström observes that Black Slip II fabric appears ca. 1750–1700 and reaches its peak in the period 1700–1600. Ibid., pp. 275–76. Since this example probably is of an earlier variety, as suggested by the clay, the date for it may be placed somewhere near 1700 B.C. Similar examples of Black Slip II amphorae of our shape will be found in ibid., fig. XXIX.9; Myres, *Cesnola*, no. 152; and Buchholz and Karageorghis, *Greece and Cyprus*, no. 1552.

49 Cypriote Red-on-Black tankard

Middle or late MC III (ca. 1650–1600 B.C.)
Height, 19 cm; maximum diameter, 13.6 cm (C53–54/13)

This handmade jug from Cyprus, which is of a shape usually labeled tankard, is made of rather soft and coarse salmon-pink clay intermixed with much foreign matter (ex Kolokasides coll.). Covered with a brownish-black slip, it has a spherical body with concave shoulder and a wide cylindrical neck, an everted lip, a rounded base, and a flat, horned handle that is attached at the lip and the shoulder. The exterior is covered in an overall decoration of groups of short parallel lines and bands encircling the vase, executed probably with a multiple brush. J. Boardman, *Antiquity* 34 (1960): 85; also *SCE IV (1B)*, p. 117. The style of decoration, which is a favorite one on tan-

kards, is known as *horror vacui* and consists of an overall system of parallel lines and short strokes. *SCE IV (1B)*, pp. 117–18. The *horror vacui* style is late in the Red-on-Black ware fabric, which reached its full development in the years between 1700 and 1600; this tankard, therefore, probably dates to the middle or late MC III, perhaps ca. 1650 or later. Ibid., pp. 117, 276–77. Red-on-Black ware also represents an eastern Cypriote regional technique for Bronze Age styles. V. Karageorghis, *The Ancient Civilization of Cyprus* (New York, 1969), pp. 134–35.

50 Cypriote Base Ring I juglet

LC I (ca. 1600–1400 B.C.)
Height, 12.8 cm; diameter, 7.3 cm (C53–54/21)

A handmade juglet from Cyprus, this specimen is made of fine, hard, brittle, dull gray clay and fired brownish-black—a typical Base Ring fabric. It has a flattened piriform shape, an extremely long cylindrical neck, a low base ring, a flaring rim, and a strap handle attached to the neck and shoulder. Only vestiges remain of an ornamentation in two rings where the handle connects with the neck; there is no painted decoration.

Base Ring ware is so named because it is the earliest Cypriote fabric that habitually provides a distinct standing base for its vessels. This fabric

may have been of foreign, perhaps Syrian, origin. Myres, *Cesnola*, pp. 36–37. One author has speculated that these juglets were so shaped in order to overcome the language barrier of the export trade and to promote the sale of their contents, which, it is claimed, was opium (their shape closely resembles an inverted poppy capsule); the author has made a strong case that this resemblance was deliberate and was utilized for advertising and communication. Thus, this shape is also called a "poppy flask." R. S. Merrilles, *Antiquity* 36 (1962): 287–92. Another possibility is that Base Ring ware shapes were designed to imitate metal or leather forms.

Base Ring ware is usually divided into two phases: I is usually ornamented in relief, while II is normally decorated with white paint, although a few examples of relief ornamentation are known from the later period. Also, Base Ring II juglets are often squatter and larger than their Base Ring I counterparts. *SCE IV (1C)*, pp. 170–71, 195–96. The shape of the Stovall juglet is much like that of three illustrated in ibid., fig. XLIX.3–5, which are all assigned to Base Ring I. The shape, fabric, and decoration of our specimen all suggest strongly that it is Base Ring I ware.

51 Cypriote Base Ring I tankard

LC I (ca. 1600–1400 B.C.)
Height with handle, 16.4 cm, without handle, 13.3 cm; diameter, 11.1 cm (C53–54/12)

Composed of hard, fine, dark gray clay and covered with a polished black slip, this tankard from the Kolokasides collection has a relatively small, base ring foot, a horizontal ridge on the carinated midbody, a high, wide, slightly concave neck with a rather flat rim, a strap handle extending from the rim to the shoulder, and a thumbgrip. Two parallel bands in relief decorate the neck, a wavy band encircles the shoulder, and a straight band encircles the midbody.

A number of features assign this Stovall tankard to Base Ring I ware. The quality of the clay and slip are indications, as is the fact that the surface is evenly burnished to a smooth luster, the burnishing being executed vertically on the neck and horizontally on the body. Additionally, the relief decoration is common to this type of ware. *SCE IV (1C)*, pp. 137, 170–71. Finally, the tankard may be classified as an example of Åström's Type VIIB1cO, the characteristics of

which are precisely those listed above. Ibid., pp. 162–63.

52 Cypriote White Slip II bowl

LC II (ca. 1400–1230 B.C.)
Height, 11.1 cm; diameter, 19.4 cm (C53–54/9)

This handmade bowl (ex Kolokasides coll.) is made from hard, gritty, reddish-brown clay and covered with a buff-white slip on the interior and upper third of the exterior. Hemispheric in shape, with a slightly incurving rim, it has a wishbone handle, with a rather triangular shape on its inner surface, attached below the rim. The rather crude decoration is in reddish-brown paint. It consists of two horizontal bands of lattice bounded by heavier solid bands; similar bands extending radially from the bottom up the sides to meet the horizontal bands; bands of paint on the edges of the handle; and two horizontal bands of short vertical slashes, one around the rim and the other between the two horizontally framed lattice bands. This form was once believed to have been derived from leather work, but according to M. Popham in *SCE IV (1C)*, p. 431, it developed out of earlier Cypriote wares. Cf. Myres, *Cesnola*, p. 32. This type of ware was used for finer tableware, and apparently was widely exported, since it has been found in large quantities in Syria and Palestine.

The Stovall bowl, whose shape gives it the name "milk bowl," is an example of White Slip II (normal stage) ware. In respect to technique, this classification is indicated by the coarse clay and buff slip; the shape of the handles, with a triangular form on the inner face, is another sign. Elements in the decoration, notably the thick outer strokes of the lattice and the dashes around the rim and between the lattices, further confirm this classification. *SCE IV (1C)*, pp. 447–48, 454. The normal stage of White Slip II was a mass-produced ware, whose rapid production led to the use of timesaving methods such as the multiple brush. J. Boardman, *Antiquity* 34 (1960): 85; *SCE IV (1C)*, p. 431. The decoration on our specimen is similar to pattern HH (pl. 41) and bowl BL29 (pl. 16) in J. L. Benson, *Bamboula at Kourion* (Philadelphia, Pa., 1972), as well as to the bowl illustrated in *SCE IV (1C)*, fig. 54.5.

No. 53, Mycenaean stirrup jar (*above*). *Below*: underside of jar.

53   Mycenaean stirrup jar

Myc. IIIB (ca. 1300–1230 B.C.)
Height, 9.4 cm; diameter, 14 cm (C53–54/7)

This stirrup jar of Cypriote provenance (ex Kolokasides coll.) is made from a fine, hard buff clay. It has a low ring foot and a broad, shallow body with an almost horizontal shoulder; the stirrup handle is centered on the shoulder with the true neck set off-center. The decoration is in brownish paint with groups of broad and narrow bands on the body and shoulder. On the top of the handles and on the shoulder appear triangular hatched patterns, but one side of the triangle is missing. Concentric circles decorate the top of the false neck. A Cypro-Minoan character is painted in red above the base.

The stirrup jar first appeared in Middle Minoan III. Furumark postulates that the extra spout was invented to facilitate emptying the vessel and to eliminate the need for removing the stopper each time after use. The low stirrup jar developed later; indeed, Mycenaean stirrup jars are rare before Myc. IIIA. The Stovall example seems to be an angular version of a squat, globular, biconical-shaped stirrup jar in Furumark's typology, FS 179. Cf. F. Stubbings, *Mycenaean Pot-*

tery from the Levant (Cambridge, 1951), fig. 8g. Angular jars, such as this specimen, are all from Myc. IIIB horizons and are representative of the tendency toward the simple, well-defined outlines characterizing this period. The flat disk on the false spout and the strap handles also indicate a Myc. IIIB date. Furumark, *MP*, pp. 19, 45, 85–86, with figs. 6, 12, and 23. The decoration on the body is common, that on the shoulder similar to the concentric segment pattern on a jar illustrated on pl. 22.5 in V. Karageorghis, *CVA, Cyprus Museum*, fasc. 1 (Nicosia, 1963).

The most interesting feature of the Stovall jar is its secondary decoration of the Cypro-Minoan character on the body just above the base. Cypro-Minoan characters derive from Linear A directly, and when painted on pots are called *dipinti*. The characters are known to have been painted with a daub different from the paint on the pot itself and at a moment after the decoration had been painted, but it is still debated whether they were applied before or after baking. Consequently, their specific purpose is still unknown, although it is speculated that they represent potters' notations, marks of ownership, or merchants' monograms. J. Daniel (*AJA* 45 [1941]: 251, 265–66) argues that these marks on pottery are not Cypro-Minoan but a cognate script, while others such as Stubbings (*Mycenean Pottery*, pp. 42, 45, 50) believe that there is not enough evidence of the Cypro-Minoan script to warrant any conclusion. A Cypro-Minoan character that seems to be the same or similar to ours has been found at Kition on Cyprus on a pot recovered from a Myc. IIIB context. V. Karageorghis, *View from the Bronze Age* (New York, 1976), no. 7. A Cypro-Minoan character on a vessel from Old Paphos is also similar. T. Mitford, *Kadmos* 10 (1971): 94.

54 Mycenaean basket-handled pot

Myc. IIIC

Height with handle, 10.3 cm, without handle, 4.7 cm; maximum diameter, 9.2 cm (C57–58/6)

Made from buff clay and decorated with a reddish-orange paint, this handmade pot is of unknown provenance. It has a flat base, straight walls, and a rolled basket handle with a flat strap crossing the pot's mouth but contracting at each side so as to create an oval mouth. This shape seems quite unusual. The base is decorated with concentric circles, the innermost of which shows a cross. The walls are decorated with a pattern of

sequent triangles, with alternate triangle (filled with dots or triangles) within triangle. The interior is painted or glazed, while the handle carries a pattern of a dotted line between two bands.

In "Chamber Tombs at Mycenae," A. Wace (*Archaeology* 32 [1932]: 172, pls. 23 and 27) catalogued two basket-handled vases of a shape that he labeled typical to the mainland and unknown before Myc. III. These vases are similar in shape and size to the Stovall pot, but they have a more rounded base and a less elaborate handle. Furumark (*MP*, pp. 73–74) observes that basket vases such as Wace's have been found in mainland Myc. IIIA:2–IIIB contexts and states that they probably represent the Helladic tradition of basket-handled vases. In his catalogue of Mycenaean motifs there are two triangle patterns similar to part of the decoration on the wall (FM 61A.1 and FM 61A.2) consisting of triangles within triangles, both dated to Myc. IIIC:1–2. The pattern on the wall of our pot could represent a carelessly drawn or degenerate form of either pattern. The triangle does not appear in the Myc. IIIB style proper, but it is possible that it survived in stylistically retarded provincial areas. Furumark, *MP*, pp. 389–91. The monochrome interior may also indicate a date in the Myc. IIIC period. K. A. Wardle, *BSA* 68 (1973): 334. It is interesting, however, to note a similarly shaped basket-handled pot from the Geometric period published by Jean-Pierre Michaud in *BCH* 94

(1970): 903, fig. 36. Nevertheless, the design on the Stovall pot suggests strongly that it is provincial Mycenaean.

Mycenaean Sherds

The fragments grouped under this heading seem to be Mycenaean in origin; their provenance is unknown, except for no. 58, which was picked up on the surface at Mycenae. They are all made of the hard, fine, buff clay painted with the orange-brown glaze that is characteristic of Mycenaean pottery.

55   Rim sherd from a Mycenaean vase

Probably Myc. IIIB:2
3.4 × 4.6 cm (C39–40/1/4)

This small sherd is decorated with a diamond that has two of its corners spanned by curved concentric segments. Both inside and outside the rim there is a very thin line of paint, an element found elsewhere on Late Mycenaean IIIB:2 rim sherds and one that suggests a similar date for this fragment. K. A. Wardle, *BSA* 68 (1973), pl. 60(a) with pp. 297–348.

56   Rim fragment from a Mycenaean vase

Myc. IIIB or IIIC
4 × 5.8 cm (C57–58/11/1)

This fragment is decorated with a spiral (?) outlined by dots and a lily or palmette motif. The

Mycenaean fragments. *Left*: No. 58. *Right*: *above*, no. 56; *lower left*, no. 55; *lower right*, no. 57.

rim is decorated with a fairly wide band of paint on the outside and a smaller band inside. This sherd probably dates from the Myc. IIIB or IIIC period, to judge from the many examples illustrated in ibid., pl. 60(a)–(c).

57   Mycenaean sherd

Myc. III
2.8 × 2.7 cm (C39–40/1/1)

This small fragment is decorated with wavy lines outlined by dots. It is part of a motif labeled a whorl shell or murex shell. E. French, *BSA* 61 (1966):226; M. Mackeprang, *AJA* 42 (1938): 540. According to Mackeprang, the dots in this design are a stylized pattern derived from the articulated shell of the animal. This is a common pattern on late Mycenaean vases, especially kylikes; a closer dating does not seem possible.

58   Rim fragment of a Mycenaean deep bowl

Myc. IIIC
7.3 × 9.5 cm (C54–55/5)

This fragment of the rim and wall of a deep bowl has traces of a horizontal uptilted loop handle. The interior is completely painted, while the exterior has a wide band of paint around the rim, a vertical zigzag within two pairs of lines to the left of the handle, and paint on the base of the handle in the form of a leaf. The vertical zigzag between two pairs of lines is very close to Furumark's motif FM 75.38 (*MP*, p. 414), which is a Myc. IIIB triglyph motif, the difference being that the motif in Furumark has only one pair of vertical framing lines. Examples of the same or similar triglyphs are found in pl. 76d in A. Wace, *Mycenae: An Archaeological History and Guide* (Princeton, N.J., 1949); pl. 14(c)46 in P. A. Mountjoy, *BSA* 71 (1976); and pls. 18(c), 19(a)3 in E. French, *BSA* 64 (1969). The monochrome interior and the broad band of the rim suggest that the Stovall sherd may date from the early Late Helladic IIIC period. The shape also seems to indicate a rim profile much like that seen in fig. 21.251 and pl. 60(d) in Wardle, *BSA* 68 (1973).

Cypriote Iron Age

(BARBARA L. GUNN)

The following abbreviations are used in this section:

Birmingham, *Chronology* — Judy Birmingham, "The Chronology of Some Early and Middle Iron Age Cypriot Sites," *AJA* 67 (1963): 15–42.

Gjerstad, *CP* — Einar Gjerstad, *Cypriot Pottery from the Neolithic to the Hellenistic Period* (Mâcon, 1932).

Myres, *Cesnola* — John Myres, *Handbook of the Cesnola Collection of Antiquities from Cyprus* (New York, 1914).

SCE IV (2) — Einar Gjerstad, *The Swedish Cyprus Expedition*, vol. IV, pt. 2, *The Cypro-Geometric, Cypro-Archaic, and Cypro-Classical Periods* (Stockholm, 1948).

SCE IV (3) — Olof Vessberg and Alfred Westholm, *The Swedish Cyprus Expedition*, vol. IV, pt. 3, *The Hellenistic and Roman Periods* (Lund, 1956).

References are made to two kinds of pottery sequences for Cypriote Iron Age chronology:

Swedish Cyprus Expedition
(see *SCE IV (2)*, p. 427

Cypro-Geometric I	ca. 1050–950 B.C.
Cypro-Geometric II	950–850
Cypro-Geometric III	850–700
Cypro-Archaic I	700–600
Cypro-Archaic II	600–475
Cypro-Classic I	475–400
Cypro-Classic II	400–325

Birmingham, *Chronology*

Early Iron Age	ca. 1050–900 B.C.
Middle Iron Age I	900–725
Middle Iron Age II	725–600
Late Iron Age	600–Hellenistic

All the vases in this section are of Cypriote provenance, and the following are from the collection of Kolokasides: nos. 59, 60, 61, 62, 65, and 66.

Bichrome and Other Wares

59 Cypriote Bichrome III kylix

Cypro-Geometric III or Cypro-Archaic IA (ca. 850–650 B.C.)
Height, 10.5 cm; diameter, 13 cm (C53–54/11)

This object is a kylix, sometimes also called a goblet or stemmed bowl, made from hard, rather coarse clay. The clay is dull brownish-orange and is covered on the outside and the upper interior with a hard, dull, white slip. The kylix has a short, thick stem and a broad hollow foot, while its bowl is angular and deep and has horizontal handles that rise at oblique angles on each side. The bottom of the bowl is not flat and slopes down to the stem. A slight ridge is discernible bordering the rim of the kylix. The decoration is executed primarily in black paint, and in supplementary bright red paint on a broad band on the inside rim. On the outside the kylix is painted in black on the foot, on the stem with two narrow bands, and on the underside of the bowl with a broad streaky band. The handles are painted black, and two sets of five vertical lines in the

handle zone form a panel, within which is a swastika. The rim has a broad band, then three narrow bands, and finally another broad band. On the inside there are two narrow bands, then a very broad band in bright red, and a series of narrow black bands. The center of the bottom is decorated in black with a spiral pattern.

The Stovall kylix is assigned to Bichrome ware because it is decorated with two colors of paint. Cypriote Bichrome ware is a technique that apparently resulted from Syro-Palestinian influence. *SCE IV (2)*, p. 287. Several features indicate that this vessel should be classified as Bichrome III ware. For example, according to Gjerstad (*CP*, pp. 33, 41) the very bright red paint with which it is decorated was often used in Bichrome III; in addition, the slight ridge below the rim also is characteristic of Bichrome III ware. The shape of the kylix is another important index for determining its classification. Iron Age Cypriote kylikes developed from the Mycenaean form through the Cypro-Mycenaean stage, and in general the kylikes became broader and more angular as they developed. Myres, *Cesnola*, p. 74. The angular outline of the bowl, the sloping bottom of the bowl, the broad foot, the widening rim, as well as the lack of ridges on the stem, all strongly suggest that our kylix should be classified as Bichrome III. Gjerstad, *CP*, pp. 33, 44; also *SCE IV (2)*, pp. 52–54. By the time of Bichrome IV the sides of deep bowls are almost vertical and the rims slightly turned inward, unlike the sides and rim of this one. *SCE IV (2)*, p. 62. The decoration further points to this classification. As a rule, Cypriote Iron Age

ceramic decoration can be divided into three different ornamental systems: the zone style, the panel style, and the plain-bodied style. In the zone style the vase is decorated in horizontal or vertical zones separated by encircling bands and lines. In the panel style the zones are divided into segments that are either plain or filled with a single ornament. In the plain-bodied style the body is left undecorated except for encircling lines on the rim, neck, and base. Gjerstad, *CP*, pp. 28–29. This kylix is decorated in the panel style. In White Painted and Bichrome I wares the vertical panel lines are composed of broad filled bands or bands of zigzag lines, dotted lozenges, or similar ornaments framed by parallel lines. Beginning in White Painted and Bichrome II ware these vertical separating ornaments are gradually simplified, and by the time of White Painted and Bichrome III wares groups of rather widely spaced parallel lines, such as on this Stovall kylix, are the most common ornaments employed to separate panels. *SCE IV (2)*, p. 53. The swastika, which according to Myres (*Cesnola*, p. 73) first appears in Cypriote art in the Early Iron Age and disappears before the fifth century B.C., was a popular filling ornament in panels by the time of White Painted and Bichrome III. But the swastika was one of the few Cypro-Geometric ornaments not derived from predecessors in Late Mycenaean and Sub-Mycenaean ornamentation. *SCE IV (2)*, p. 286. In sum, all its elements, including shape, paint color, decoration, and the rim ridge, combine to indicate that this kylix should be assigned to the Bichrome III class of Cypriote Iron Age vases.

Under the chronology of the Swedish Cyprus Expedition, Type III appears late in the Cypro-Geometric IIIB. Then in the Cypro-Geometric IIIA, Type III becomes much more common, and finally by the time of the Cypro-Geometric IIIB it is the predominant ware. Type III continues to be numerous in the Cypro-Archaic IA, but thereafter becomes less frequent until it disappears early in the Cypro-Archaic IIA. Thus this kylix probably belongs in the Cypro-Geometric III or the Cypro-Archaic IA periods, ca. 850–650 B.C. Ibid., pp. 202–203, 427. According to the alternative chronology proposed in Birmingham, *Chronology*, pp. 40–42, our kylix would be placed in the Middle Iron Age I, ca. 900–800 B.C.

60   Cypriote Bichrome III or IV amphora

Cypro-Geometric III, Cypro-Archaic I, or Cypro-Archaic
  IIA (ca. 850–550 B.C.)
Height, 23.4 cm; diameter at rim, 12.5 cm (C53–54/14)

Made of a fine, hard clay buff or pinkish-buff
in color, this piece is covered with a rather pow-
dery self-slip and decorated in black and violet-
red paint. It has a somewhat rounded biconical
shape, a hollow broad base, a short, thick, cylindrical neck, vertical handles attached at the
shoulder and the rim, and a very slightly flaring,
everted lip. The outside decoration is composed
mainly of narrow and broad bands of black
paint. The line just below the attachment of the
handle to the body is red, as is the base and a
broad band just inside the rim. On each side of
the shoulder there are three vertical linear patterns composed of parallel lines framed by solid
bulges, or excrescences, as they are often labeled. The neck is decorated with a pair of very
short, rippled, wavy lines on each side and the
rim with three concentric circles. The exterior
side of each handle is painted solid except for
several alternating blank spaces, perhaps indicating that a wavy line was painted on the handle

and then the edges were painted, the paint
sometimes covering part of the wavy line.

This amphora, classified as bichrome because of the two colors of paint, may be either Bichrome III or IV. In White Painted and Bichrome I the amphora with handles from rim to
shoulder has a concave neck and flaring mouth.
By the period of Bichrome III this type of amphora has handles less curved than in earlier
examples, a rim with a decreased flare, and a
neck less concave and sometimes nearly straight.
Small Type III amphorae with handles from rim
to shoulder often have a foot, and sometimes
have bodies that are much depressed. In Type
IV amphorae with handles from rim to shoulder, the neck remains cylindrical or at times
widens upward, the rim usually is ring shaped
and flat or swollen, the body at times shows a tendency to be biconical in shape, and often the
amphorae have a low foot. *SCE IV (2)*, pp. 53–
55, 64. This vase, with its almost flat rim and
its somewhat biconical shape, seems most like
the Type IV amphorae, but it could belong to
Type III. In fact, to judge from illustrations, Bichrome III examples resemble ours more than
do those of Bichrome IV. Ibid., figs. XXIV.2–3
and XXXVI.2–6, respectively. This is especially
true in the case of fig. XXIV.3, which appears
very similar in shape to ours except for a wider
neck and a short stem.

Elements of the decoration also suggest
that this amphora should be assigned to either
Bichrome III or IV. The wavy line, which is
probably a degenerate remnant of the Cypro-
Mycenaean false spiral, is common in the Cypriote Iron Age, but the extremely short ripples
on the Stovall vase do not appear until White
Painted and Bichrome III and continue into
White Painted and Bichrome IV. Gjerstad, *CP*,
p. 35. The vertical pattern on the shoulder is a
form of the panel style. As this style developed,
the panels were often left unfilled, and beginning in White Painted and Bichrome II the separating bands became broader and the panels
narrower, sometimes to the extent that the bands
or dividing ornamentations were broader than
the empty panels. Bands of parallel lines with
lateral excrescences began to be used in White
Painted and Bichrome III, and continue to be
employed in later wares. Ibid., pp. 34–35. Both
of these elements, the variation of the panel style
and the parallel bands with lateral excrescences,

decorate this Bichrome amphora. In addition, no. 669 of the Cesnola collection is similar in shape to ours, especially in the upper body, including the neck, handles, and rim. Myres, *Cesnola*, p. 82. Amphora no. 182 in Fairbanks's catalogue is also analogous in shape to ours, except that it has a short stem. A. Fairbanks, *Catalogue of Greek and Etruscan Vases in the Museum of Fine Arts, Boston* (Cambridge, Mass., 1928), pl. 13.

Type III appears in the Cypro-Geometric IIB, according to the Swedish Cyprus Expedition's chronology, is common until the end of the Cypro-Archaic IA, and eventually disappears early in the Cypro-Archaic IIA. Type IV appears in the Cypro-Geometric IIIB, is common until the end of the Cypro-Archaic IIA, and disappears in the Cypro-Archaic IIB. *SCE IV (2)*, pp. 202–203, 427. The Stovall amphora, therefore, should be placed in the period from the Cypro-Geometric III to the Cypro-Archaic IIA, ca. 850–550 B.C. Under Birmingham's *Chronology* (pp. 40–42), however, it would be assigned to the Middle Iron Age I or the early Middle Iron Age II, ca. 900–700 B.C.

61 Cypriote Bichrome IV oinochoe

Cypro-Archaic I or Cypro-Archaic IIA (ca. 700–550 B.C.)
Height, 21.4 cm; diameter, 15.7 cm (C53–54/2)

This oinochoe with spherical body is made of rather hard, fine clay very light buff in color and is covered with a whitish slip. It has a ring foot, a short cylindrical neck, a trefoil mouth with broad, flaring nozzle, and a double-rolled handle that is attached at the rim and shoulder; but the double rolls are not completely joined at some points. The decoration consists of black paint on the outside edges of the handle, a band on the trefoil lip both inside and outside, two bands around the upper neck that break under the handle, a band around the point of junction of the neck and body, two large vertical circles, one on each side, painted in reddish-brown and outlined in brownish-black, and two smaller concentric circles on each side in the middle of the large circles. Within the large concentric circles four smaller concentric circle groups are arranged around the central concentric circle group on each side of the vase. The inner central concentric circle groups have thick outer bands, but the smaller surrounding concentric circle groups have thick inner circles. In the middle zone, three small concentric circles are lined up ver-

tically. The general execution of the painting on this oinochoe is poor, but this fact gives little indication of the date or class of the vase since, as Myres (*Cesnola*, p. 90) has pointed out, "at all periods the Cypriote potter was capable of surprisingly unskillful work." Concentric circles were painted using compasses with a row of small brushes attached so that one rotation produced a set of circles. Ibid., p. 75.

The spherical shape of the body and the short, wide neck indicate that this vase should be classified as Bichrome III or IV ware. Although the smooth, thick, white slip is a feature more characteristic of Bichrome III, the wide and rounded lip with rim turned inward is characteristic of Type IV oinochoai. Gjerstad, *CP*, pp. 33–34, 42; also *SCE IV (2)*, p. 54. Type III oinochoai have pinched rims that are nearly straight and nonflaring, in contrast to the rounded, flaring nozzle of the Stovall vase. *SCE IV (2)*, pp. 54, 63. Furthermore, elements in its decoration as well as its shape strongly urge attributing this vase to Bichrome IV ware. In Type IV decoration, concentric circles are often connected in vertical or horizontal rows, as on the front vertical zone here, while in Type III decoration, concentric circles are never connected. Also, in Type IV decoration, the outer line of the concentric circles is often thicker than the other lines, as is the case with the inner circles on our oinochoe. Ibid., pp. 55, 65. Finally, this oinochoe is similar in shape to a Bichrome IV example illustrated in fig. XXXIV.8 in ibid.

Under the chronology of the Swedish Cyprus Expedition, Type IV appears in the Cypro-Geometric IIIB, is the predominant ware in the Cypro-Archaic I and IIA periods, and disappears near the end of the Cypro-Archaic IIB. Ibid., pp. 202–203, 427. This oinochoe probably should be assigned to the Cypro-Archaic I or Cypro-Archaic IIA periods, ca. 700–550 B.C. Again, in Birmingham's alternative scheme (*Chronology*, pp. 40–42), Type IV belongs in the late Middle Iron Age I or early Middle Iron Age II, ca. 800–700 B.C.

62   Cypriote Bichrome IV jar

Cypro-Archaic I or Cypro-Archaic IIA (ca. 700–550 B.C.)
Height, 25.5 cm; 26.9 cm (C53–54/1)

The shape of this vase has been labeled variously as a crater, jar, or pyxis. Although it does not have a lid, the groove below the rim suggests that it may have had one at some time, and thus may actually have been a pyxis. But since its shape is the same as that of a jar, it is classified primarily on the basis of that shape. It is made from hard, fine, brittle, light brown clay that is covered with

a buff slip. Its shape is globular, but it has a somewhat angular transition from the body up to the rim and from the body down to the base ring foot. There is a hole near the base. The jar is neckless, with a flattened lip and a groove below the rim on the outside; two vertical strap handles are placed low on the shoulder. The paint is brownish-black and faded brownish-red, while the decoration is panel style with a series of broad and narrow bands framing a broad band on the body that is divided into panels by groups of vertical lines; the panels are filled with a large leaf pattern that has reserved ribs. Groups of vertical lines decorate the top of the lip, and horizontal lines, framed by vertical lines, decorate the handles.

Because it is decorated in black and red, this jar must be assigned to a Bichrome ware. According to Gjerstad in *SCE IV (2)*, p. 286, the depressed biconical or pyriform-shaped jar with vertical handles on the shoulder was a Syrian form, introduced into Cyprus near the end of the Middle Bronze Age or in the early Late Bronze Age. Thus, the shape of our jar may have been derived from a Syrian prototype. Gjerstad also observes that the biconical jar with vertical handles on the shoulder is represented in White Painted I, and reappears in Type III. By the time of Type IV, such a vessel has a more evenly curved outline than in Type III, and the handles are on the shoulder or the belly. Our example is similar to the shape of a Bichrome III jar illustrated in fig. XXII.2 in ibid., but its neck motif finds a very close parallel on a Bichrome IV vase illustrated in fig. XXXV.20 of the same work. Unfortunately, the decoration does not define the category within which our jar should be placed. But in Walters's catalogue pyxis no. C765, which on the basis of its purple supplementary color probably belongs in the Bichrome IV class, has a leaf pattern very similar to that on the Stovall crater, which is likely, therefore, to be Bichrome IV ware. H. B. Walters, *Catalogue of the Greek and Etruscan Vases in the British Museum*, vol. 1, pt. 2, *Cypriote, Italian, and Etruscan Pottery* (London, 1912), p. 149. The rather widely spaced framing parallel lines on the panels indicate that it is at least no earlier than Bichrome II. *SCE IV (2)*, p. 53. If, as seems very likely, it is Bichrome IV ware, then it dates from the Cypro-Archaic I through the Cypro-Archaic IIA periods, when Type IV was the predominant pottery. Ibid., pp. 202–203, 427. This means that the jar dates from the period ca. 700–550 B.C., according to the chronology established by the Swedish Cyprus Expedition. Birmingham (*Chronology*, pp. 40–42), however, places Type IV in the late Middle Iron Age I or early Middle Iron Age II, ca. 800–700 B.C.

63   Cypriote Bichrome V oinochoe

Cypro-Archaic II or Cypro-Classic IA (ca. 600–440 B.C.)
Height, 22.5 cm; diameter, 18 cm (C52–53/1)

This vase seems to be made from fine, hard, light clay, covered with a light slip, which has changed to a grayish-brown, rough surface, perhaps because of burial and mineralization. The original surface is better preserved on the underside of the vase near the foot. The oinochoe is roughly spherical, with a ring foot, short, slightly tapering neck, trefoil mouth, and a double-rolled handle that rises slightly higher than the mouth. The decoration, painted in brownish-red and brownish-black, is composed of straight bands around the neck at the mouth and the junction of the neck and body, a wavy line on the lower neck, groups of two or three brownish-red horizontal lines on the handle, bands on the sides of the handle, and large inter-

secting concentric circle groups, one horizontal and two vertical. The reserved spaces are filled with many smaller circles. The vertical circles contain a medium-sized central concentric circle group, and five or six smaller concentric circle groups surround the central circle group. The front is decorated with a concentric circle group composed of one circle, then two side-by-side circles underneath the first, then the bands of the horizontal circle and then three more pairs of side-by-side concentric circles painted down the front of the vase. Underneath the handle there are three pairs of side-by-side concentric circles.

Owing to elements in its shape and decoration, this oinochoe should most likely be classified as a Bichrome V specimen. It has the spherical body and short neck often characteristic of one variety of Bichrome V oinochoai, and although it has the inward-turned pinched rim that is characteristic of Type IV oinochoai, it does not have the usual wide outlet. Type V oinochoai have pinched lips with narrower outlets than those in Type IV, lips that are often in the shape of "an inverted, truncated cone." *SCE IV (2)*, p. 66. Additionally, the slightly tapering neck and a handle that is higher than the mouth are both marks of Type V oinochoai. Ibid. Bichrome V is one of the first wares to show the beginning of the decadence of Cypriote painted wares. Its decoration is generally either impoverished or superabundant, as is the case here. The circle style is on the decline by the time of Bichrome V ware, even though some examples are found covered with circles; and the circle style disappears after Type V ware. Ibid., pp. 59, 67. The oinochoe illustrated in fig. XLVI.17 in ibid., which is actually an example of White Painted V ware, is similar in shape and to a lesser extent in design to this vase.

According to the chronology of the Swedish Cyprus Expedition, Type V appears in the Cypro-Archaic IB, is common in the Cypro-Archaic IIA, becomes the predominant ware in the Cypro-Archaic IIB, remains common in Cypro-Classic IA, and disappears early in the Cypro-Classic IB. Ibid., pp. 202–203, 427. This Stovall vase thus should be placed in the Cypro-Archaic II or the Cypro-Classic IA periods, ca. 600–440 B.C. But again, Birmingham (*Chronology*, pp. 40–42) assigns many vases of Type V ware to the period of the late Middle Iron Age II, ca. 700–600 B.C.

64   Cypriote White Painted II barrel jug

Cypro-Geometric II or Cypro-Geometric III (ca. 950–700
   B.C.)

Height, 26.6 cm; maximum diameter, 19 cm (C53–54/22)

This barrel jug is made of coarse, rather soft,
buff clay and is covered with a reddish-buff or
brown slip. It has an irregularly shaped body,
with one side noticeably larger than the other.
The body is elongated along an axis at right
angles to that of the neck and handle, a feature
accentuated by small bulges on the sides. As is
normal for this type of vessel, it has a single strap
handle, which is attached to the body and to
the funnel-shaped neck about one-third of the
length up the neck. At the point of junction of
the neck and the top of the handle there is a
ridge around the neck, which itself is slightly off-
center. The decoration is painted in red and
brownish-black paint, and in some instances, especially on the thin lines, the brownish-black
paint is considerably lighter than the rest of the
black paint. The decoration consists of encircling
bands of both colors on the funnel portion of the
neck, a band inside the lip, vertical strokes on
the outside of the lip, horizontal lines in black
on the handle, and two large concentric vertical

circles on either side of the vessel. The broad
bands of these two large circles are red while the
narrow bands are brown. There are central concentric circles of broad (red) and narrow (brown)
lines around a Maltese cross on each side within
the large vertical concentric circles, and both
a crosshatched lozenge pattern with two lines
(slanting on one side but straight on the other)
and a solid triangle decorate the reserved area
between the vertical circles.

The shape of the barrel jug is almost totally
peculiar to Cyprus; although it may have been
derived from wooden prototypes, it is more
likely that it developed from the lentoid jug of
the Late Cypriote Bronze Age. Myres, *Cesnola*,
p. 78; also, *SCE IV (2)*, pp. 283–84. The handle
ridge evolved from both the strapped handle of
the Late Cypriote Base Ring ware and the collar-
shaped mouth of earlier Cypro-Geometric jugs.
SCE IV (2), p. 285. The barrel-shaped jugs of
White Painted and Bichrome I often have collar-
shaped mouths with straight or concave sides
and are often decorated in the vertical zone style,
with a row of latticed lozenges in the upper part
of the reserved vertical zone. By the time of
White Painted and Bichrome II wares the collar-
shaped mouths have changed into a funnel,
which retains a remnant of the collar in the ridge
around the neck, and the jugs are more elongated along the axis perpendicular to the handle
and mouth than was the case in White Painted
and Bichrome I wares. In addition, in White
Painted and Bichrome II wares the angle lines of
triangles and lozenges are often elongated into
triangles and filled in. In White Painted and Bichrome III wares the funnel mouth becomes
wider and the barrel shape even more elongated.
Gjerstad, *CP*, pp. 27, 30–34. Although it is possible that our vessel is a Bichrome II jug as in fig.
XVI.3 in *SCE IV (2)*, it is more likely that it ought
to be classified as White Painted II ware on the
basis of its very close parallel to two White
Painted II vases illustrated in fig. XIII.6–7 in
the same work. It is unlikely to be either White
Painted I or III ware.

According to the Swedish Cyprus Expedition's chronology, Type II begins late in the
Cypro-Geometric IB and lasts until early in the
Cypro-Archaic IA; it becomes the predominant
ware in the Cypro-Geometric IIB and Cypro-
Geometric IIIA, but is common throughout the
entire Cypro-Geometric II and III periods. Ibid.,
pp. 202–203, 427. The Stovall barrel jug prob-

ably was produced during these last two periods, that is, ca. 950–700 B.C. But according to the alternative dating system Type II should be placed in the mid to late Early Iron Age, ca. 1000–900 B.C. Birmingham, *Chronology*, pp. 40–42.

65   Cypriote Black Slip II oinochoe

Cypro-Geometric II or Cypro-Geometric III (ca. 950–700 B.C.)
Height, 13.5 cm; diameter, 10.1 cm (C53–54/8)

Made from an orange-brown clay and covered with a rather mat grayish-black slip, this small oinochoe has an ovoid body tapering to a ring foot, a short neck, and a trefoil lip. The strap handle is attached slightly off-center at the rim and shoulder. The decoration consists of eight incised encircling bands around the shoulder, some of which have worn away. Vertical, slightly slanted lines run from the bottom of the lowest encircling line to near the foot.

Clay, slip, shape, and decoration all demonstrate that this Stovall vase is to be assigned to Iron Age Black Slip II ware. Black Slip ware is connected, with regard to its technique, with the "pseudo-bucchero" of the Late Cypriote III Bucchero ware and therefore is almost certainly derived from Cypriote Bronze Age traditions. *SCE IV (2)*, p. 287. The clay of Black Slip II ware is more often brown than is usual for Black Slip I, although there are local varieties, and Black Slip II is frequently covered with a mat grayish-black slip. The decoration on this ware is generally a

more carelessly drawn version of the Black Slip I parallel vertical furrows, which are apparently in imitation of the ribbed surface on metal models. Gjerstad, *CP*, p. 57; Myres, *Cesnola*, p. 55; *SCE IV (2)*, p. 78. By the time of Black Slip III ware, the surface of the vases is only occasionally decorated with careless ribbing, while in Black Slip IV the surface is always left plain. *SCE IV (2)*, pp. 77–79. The Stovall specimen is very similar to a Black Slip II jug illustrated in fig. XVII.1 in ibid.

Under the chronology of the Swedish Cyprus Expedition, Type II appears late in the Cypro-Geometric IB period and disappears early in the Cypro-Archaic IA period. Since within the Cypro-Geometric II and Cypro-Geometric III periods, Type II ranges from 25 percent to 70 percent of all pottery, this Stovall oinochoe is likely from either of these two periods, that is, ca. 950–700 B.C. Ibid., pp. 202–203, 427. In the alternative system Type II pottery is placed in the mid to late Early Iron Age, ca. 1000–900 B.C. Birmingham, *Chronology*, pp. 40–42.

66   Cypriote Black-on-Red II(IV) oinochoe

Cypro-Archaic I or Cypro-Archaic IIA (ca. 700–550 B.C.)
Height, 21.8 cm; diameter, 14.9 cm (C53–54/3)

This vessel is made of fine, hard, red clay and has a lustrous self-slip, although the surface was mistakenly fired black in an area near the base. It possesses a spherical body, ring foot, short, narrow neck, trefoil mouth, and double-rolled handle. The decoration, in black paint, consists in part of bands encircling the neck, vertical bands on the handle, and an encircling band at the base of the neck covering a slight ridge where the neck joins the body. The primary decoration is composed of groups of large horizontal and vertical concentric circles, comprising eleven and nine lines respectively, with smaller concentric circles all over the body in the reserved area. On the front shoulder there is an X-shaped pattern drawn with crossing diagonal lines, a single line passing through the center of this pattern vertically. Three concentric circle groups are present on each side of the line pattern; such circles were produced by means of a compass equipped with a row of small brushes. Myres, *Cesnola*, p. 75.

This oinochoe belongs to the Black-on-Red II(IV) class on the basis of both its shape and decoration. The classification II(IV) means that the second class of Black-on-Red ware is con-

circle style is believed to be a result of Syro-Palestinian influence and was employed even on older Cypriote wares such as White Painted and Bichrome vases. Ibid., pp. 71, 288, 315. The jug illustrated in fig. XXXIX.2 in ibid. is very similar in shape to the Stovall jug, as is another Black-on-Red II(IV) oinochoe illustrated in fig. 10 of V. Karageorghis's article, "Chronique des Fouilles à Chypre en 1973," *BCH* 98 (1974). In addition, no. 920 in the Walters catalogue has not only a similar shape but also a comparable rectilinear design on the front of the shoulder. H. B. Walters, *Catalogue of the Greek and Etruscan Vases in the British Museum*, vol. 1, pt. 2, *Cypriote, Italian, and Etruscan Pottery* (London, 1912), p. 185.

In the classification and dating system arranged by the Swedish Cyprus Expedition, Black-on-Red II(IV) is incorporated under Type IV, which appears very infrequently at the end of the Cypro-Geometric IIIB period but predominates in the Cypro-Archaic I and the Cypro-Archaic IIA periods and finally disappears in the Cypro-Archaic IIB. *SCE IV (2)*, pp. 202–203, 427. The Stovall example, therefore, belongs in the Cypro-Archaic I or the Cypro-Archaic IIA periods, ca. 700–550 B.C. The alternative system would place it in the late Middle Iron Age I or the early Middle Iron Age II periods, ca. 800–700 B.C. Birmingham, *Chronology*, pp. 40–42.

temporary with the fourth class of other Iron Age wares such as White Painted and Bichrome. Gjerstad, *CP*, p. 1. The vessel displays the characteristics of one type of Black-on-Red II(IV) oinochoai, namely, a spherical body, a long, straight, cylindrical neck, and a rim bent slightly inward. The decoration here is called the circle style, which began on Cypriote pottery in the White Painted and Bichrome III wares and reached its climax in Type IV vases, especially Black-on-Red II(IV). Furthermore, rectilinear ornamentation is used much more frequently on Black-on-Red II(IV) than on White Painted and Bichrome III wares. By the time of this distinctive pottery, the latticed lozenge ornaments, which decorated earlier vases, "have developed into a group of intersecting straight lines." *SCE IV (2)*, pp. 69–71. Also, on Black-on-Red II(IV) ware groups of circles frequently border the circular intersecting lines; both these distinguishing traits appear on this vase and determine its proper classification. The intersecting concentric

Plain White Ware

Plain White ware was an extremely long-lived and common type of Cypriote pottery. It is represented from the beginning of Cypro-Geometric I (ca. 950 B.C.) until the Roman III period (ca. A.D. 250 and later). The forms in this type of pottery are quite persistent, and consequently it is difficult to distinguish categories for vases without a very specific Cypriote provenance. For this reason, the categories suggested for these objects are necessarily only tentative. The fabric of Plain White ware in the Cypro-Geometric through the Cypro-Classic periods is generally that of the contemporary White Painted ware. The clay of Plain White ware in the Hellenistic and Roman I periods is generally of variable texture, with a buff, greenish, yellow, or pink texture. In the Roman II and III periods, the clay may vary from rough, hard, and thin to finely silted and smooth. *SCE IV (2)*, pp. 85–91; also *SCE IV (3)*, pp. 57, 63, 66, 69. In the Cypro-Geometric IA period Plain White ware comprised only 12 percent of all Cypriote pottery, but by the Cypro-Classic IIB it constituted 73 percent. Ibid., p. 205. Inasmuch as jugs are the most common type of vase during the Hellenistic period in Cyprus, and fusiform unguentaria are characteristic of the Hellenistic Mediterranean in general, it is appropriate that the Stovall Museum's collection of Plain White ware consists of four jugs and a fusiform unguentarium.

67 Cypriote Plain White V–VII sack-shaped jug

Cypro-Archaic through Cypro-Classic Periods (ca. 700–325 B.C.)
Height to lip, 15 cm; diameter, 7.1 cm (C53–54/23)

This small jug, composed of brownish-buff, soft, coarse clay with much foreign matter, has a flat base, a slim cylindrical body, a handle attached at the rim and midbody, and a neck widening without articulation to a flaring rim with rounded lip. This shape is commonly labeled "sack-shaped," and has been compared to that of a milk bottle. J. L. Benson, *AJA* 60 (1956): 43–50. The handle seems to be unusual, since the handles of most sack-shaped jugs are placed higher on the body.

Cypriote plain white ware. *Left*: No. 71; *right*: No. 67.

The sack-shaped jug apparently developed during the period of Plain White III ware and was common thereafter; its shape was originally Syrian. *SCE IV (3)*, p. 73. Brownish clay is common in many Cypro-Archaic and Cypro-Classic periods, and the form of the sack-shaped jugs appears to have been fairly stable in those periods. *SCE IV (2)*, pp. 48–59, 87. For these reasons, the Stovall example is very difficult to date. The usual sack-shaped jugs of Plain White IV ware, which are derived from those of Plain White III ware, have an angular shoulder. Ibid., p. 87. The Hellenistic version of the sack-shaped jug, on the other hand, is much slimmer than this jug. These factors suggest that this vessel should be placed somewhere in the Plain White V–VII wares. Also, a jug similar to ours is illustrated in no. 12 by Benson (*AJA*, p. 44) and assigned to Plain White V or VI ware. It appears, therefore, that this Stovall jug should be assigned to Plain White ware types V–VII, which are common in both the Cypro-Archaic and Cypro-Classic periods. However, it may be noted that it is only from the Cypro-Archaic II onward that Plain White ware constitutes appreciably more than 10 percent of the total amount of Cypriote pottery. *SCE IV (2)*, pp. 204, 427.

68 Cypriote Plain White VI–VII ovoid jug

Cypro-Classic Periods (ca. 475–325 B.C.)
Height to lip, 15 cm; diameter, 12 cm (C53–54/26)

Made of soft, rather coarse, brownish-buff clay with much foreign matter, this vessel has a small ring base, an ovoid body, concave neck articulated above the shoulder, a flaring rim with round lip, and a handle attached at the rim and shoulder. This ovoid jug is also difficult to categorize and date. As with the preceding specimen, the brown clay is one possible indication of a pre-Hellenistic date. According to Vessberg and Westholm in *SCE IV (3)*, p. 60, the wide-necked jug with oval, depressed body is a common and relatively unchanging type in Cypriote pottery, and the type also often has a concave neck widening toward the rim. The Hellenistic version of this type of jug is squatter than the Stovall example, another feature that may suggest an earlier date for it. Cf. fig. 23.20 in ibid. One variety of the ovoid jug in Plain White VI ware is described as being "with wide mouth, and with or without distinct neckline, flat base or base ring, concave, splayed neck, and a handle from neck to shoulder," a description that seems to fit a jug much

Cypriote plain white ware. *Left*: No. 69. *Right*: No. 70.

70   Cypriote Plain White lagynos

Hellenistic I period (ca. 325–150 B.C.), probably ca. 325–
   200 B.C.
Height, 15.1 cm; diameter, 13.2 cm (C53–54/24)

With a ring foot, broad biconical body, slender, almost cylindrical neck, collared mouth, and handle extending from below the rim to the shoulder, this vase is composed of soft, pinkish-white clay. It is decorated with a single groove underneath the mouth and a very shallow groove on the shoulder. Lagynos is the name given to many jugs whose only common features are a long narrow neck and a single handle. G. McFadden, *AJA* 50 (1946): 449–89. These jugs were common in the Hellenistic world east of the Adriatic. R. M. Cook, *Greek Painted Pottery*, 2d ed. (London, 1972), p. 207. Many places have been proposed for the origin and development of this shape, including Cyrenaica, East Greece, Cyprus, Asia Minor, and Egypt. McFadden, *AJA* 50 (1946): 473; O. Broneer, *Hesperia* 16 (1947): 240. At any rate, local centers of production seem to have thrived, and the lagynoi of Cyprus are especially distinctive according to H. Thompson, *Hesperia* 3 (1934): 450. Although the lagynos was at first a unit of measure of a little less than three quarts, it came to be the name for this type of wine decanter. In the Hellenistic I period on Cyprus two types of lagynoi appear. One type has an almost horizontal shoulder, a fairly well-marked shoulder line, and lower sides gently curved toward the base. Those specimens illustrated in fig. 22.20–24 in *SCE IV (3)* and the Stovall jug are all of this type. The second type

like this one. *SCE IV (2)*, pp. 89–90. Especially noteworthy is the reference to a distinct neckline, which is a feature of this jug not mentioned in other accounts of the ovoid, widemouthed jug. This example, then, is tentatively assigned to Plain White VI or VII ware, which are types almost exclusively from the Cypro-Classic periods, ca. 475–325 B.C. Ibid., pp. 203, 427.

69   Cypriote Plain White jug

Cypriote Hellenistic I period (ca. 325–150 B.C.), probably
   early Hellenistic I
Height to lip, 17.2 cm; diameter, 12.7 cm (C53–54/25)

This is a globular jug made of soft, rather coarse, pinkish-buff clay, with a ring foot, a very round body, small cylindrical neck, trefoil rim, and handle from rim to shoulder rising above the rim. A group of three small ridges encircles the neck below the lip. Narrow-necked jugs of this kind also have a long history on Cyprus. Although one obvious analogy in shape is with the concentric circle jugs of Red-on-Black II(IV) ware, nevertheless this specimen seems to be an early Hellenistic vase. The pinkish-buff clay is one indication of that date, and a second is the close similarity to an early Hellenistic jug illustrated in fig. 22.16 in *SCE IV (3)*. The Hellenistic I period on Cyprus spans the years between 325 and 150 B.C.

of Cypriote lagynoi has slanting shoulders and a more carinated shoulder. Both types can be linked not only with contemporary Cypriote narrow-necked jugs but also with jugs of Types VI and VII from the Cypro-Classic periods. Lagynoi like those seen in fig. 22.20–24, one of which is very similar to ours, have been placed at the beginning of the first type, and furthermore have been found in third-century tombs at Kountoura Trachonia. *SCE IV (3)*, pp. 59, 75. In addition, McFadden (*AJA* 50 [1946]: 473) mentions a lagynos of similar shape, except for a twisted handle, from the Athenian agora that was found with late fourth- or early third-century lamps. These observations combine to suggest a date in the late fourth or third century B.C. for the Stovall lagynos.

71 Cypriote Plain White fusiform unguentarium

Late Hellenistic I or early Hellenistic II periods (ca. 150–50 B.C.)
Height, 21.2 cm; diameter, 6.1 cm (C53–54/27)

This Hellenistic unguent pot is made from coarse, soft, pinkish-buff clay. The lower part of the body spreads out to form a small foot, the middle of the vase widens out to form a slight shoulder, and the mouth is collared. The fusi-form unguentarium is one of the characteristic shapes of the Hellenistic periods and was distributed widely over the Mediterranean. It is the successor of the lekythos in both time and purpose, since it was used as a container for perfumes and oils. H. Thompson, *Hesperia* 3 (1934): 472; Hetty Goldman, *Excavations at Gözlü Kule, Tarsus*, vol. 1, *The Hellenistic and Roman Periods* (Princeton, N.J., 1950), p. 171. Although Thompson in his article argued in favor of a single place of production for unguentaria, it has since become clear that there were many local centers of production. Egypt has been proposed for the place of development and initial diffusion of this form, but this theory also has been disputed in *SCE IV (3)*, p. 74; Goldman, *Excavations*, p. 171 n. 65. The shape of this pot is very similar to one illustrated in fig. 24.32 in *SCE IV (3)*, which is of a type from rather late in the Hellenistic I period that also continues into the Hellenistic II period. This date for our example is further confirmed by comparison with another unguentarium illustrated in fig. 211:188.49 in "Tombes d'Argos," a pot dated to the late second or early first century B.C. P. Bruneau, *BCH* 94 (1970): 437–531, esp. p. 517. Therefore, the Stovall unguentarium is probably from the second half of the second century or the first half of the first century B.C.

Geometric and Archaic

(BARBARA L. GUNN)

The following abbreviations are used in this section:

Coldstream, *GGP* J. N. Coldstream, *Greek Geometric Pottery* (London, 1968).

Cook, *GPP* R. M. Cook, *Greek Painted Pottery*, 2d ed. (London, 1972).

CVA *Corpus Vasorum Antiquorum*

Payne, *Necrocorinthia* H. G. G. Payne, *Necrocorinthia: A Study of Corinthian Art in the Archaic Period* (Oxford, 1931).

Young, *Hesperia*, Suppl. 2 R. S. Young, *Late Geometric Graves and a Seventh-century Well in the Agora. Hesperia*, Supplement 2 (Princeton, N.J., 1939).

72 Late Geometric tankard

LG IIa (ca. 735–720 B.C.)
Height with handle, 24.7 cm, without handle, 18.5 cm; diameter at lip, 12.7 cm (C45–46/4)

This vessel, made of hard, coarse, orange-buff clay and covered with an orang-buff slip, is variously called a jug, mug, mug-olpe, or tankard but will here be labeled a tankard because Coldstream (*GGP*, pp. 23, 47, 86), who uses this name, gives the best account of the development of this shape. The Stovall example has a rounded squat base, a broad flaring neck that joins the base at a slight angle, a plain rim, and a high strut handle that is attached at the rim and base.

It is decorated in black paint with a solid-colored base, three encircling lines, a triglyph-metope panel with dotted St. Andrew's crosses as metopes and vertical lines as triglyphs. Above this are three narrow bands, an encircling band of triangles, three more lines, a broad panel with a

44

conventionalized dotted snake, three lines, a second band of triangles, and three bands. Horizontal lines and large dots are used as fillers in the area decorated with the snake. Provenance is unknown.

Several features in this tankard's shape, decoration, and fabric suggest the date to which it should be assigned. Coldstream (*GGP*) has traced the development of our tankard's shape through several periods. In the Attic Middle Geometric II period (ca. 800–760 B.C.) one variation developed with a vertical, everted lip that is clearly taller than the body, and a handle that swings up above the rim; this shape is an early form of the tankard. An exaggerated, angular form of the tankard was produced in the Dipylon workshop, while a form similar to ours but still too angular, was made in the Hirschfeld workshop. Ibid., pls. 8g and 8f. During the Late Geometric Ia period (ca. 760–750 B.C.), the shape of the tankard becomes progressively taller, the junction between the lip and body losing some of its clear definition; also, the handle becomes more vertically placed and is joined to the vase by a strut. Tankards become, in general, more attenuated and "the articulation between neck and body loses its sharpness." Ibid., p. 86. The LG Ib (ca. 750 – 735 B.C.) type with a rounded body, which is the closest parallel to this tankard, lasts throughout the LG IIa period (ca. 735–720 B.C.). Cf. ibid., pl. 9e. In the LG IIb period (ca. 720–700 B.C.) the rim overhangs the body of the tankard. The shape of ours dates it to the LG Ib and LG IIa periods, that is, ca. 750–720 B.C. This shape is common in Late Geometric and reaches the climax of its popularity in the LG IIa period. Ibid., p. 47.

The decoration on this item is another indicator of its probable date in LG IIa. Triangles at the top and bottom of the neck are fairly common in the Late Geometric periods. Nos. 46 (fig. 16), 55 (fig. 19), and 66 (fig. 21) in D. Burr, "A Geometric House and Proto-Attic Votive Deposit," *Hesperia* 2 (1933): 561–62, are sherds that all have such triangles and are all attributed to the Simple, Developed, or Ripe styles, the latter two of which are of the same period as Coldstream's Late Geometric. Thus, this decorative motif is found in Late Geometric wares. The conventionalized snake is another common Late Geometric motif, and probably has cult significance. Young, *Hesperia*, Suppl. 2, p. 217. According to Eva Brann (*Late Geometric and Protoattic Pottery: Athenian Agora*, vol. 8 [Princeton, N.J., 1962], p. 13), snakes were guardians of the underworld. The religious significance of snakes and the common use of tankards for funerary purposes (Coldstream, *GGP*, p. 86) strongly suggest that our tankard was a grave offering. Finally, there is the triglyph-metope frieze around the body, the most important index for the dating of this tankard. The triglyph-metope system, which B. Schweitzer (*Greek Geometric Art* [London, 1971], p. 34) claims was a product of eastern, especially Cypriote, influences, begins to appear as early as the Middle Geometric I period (ca. 850–800 B.C.) and reaches its highest point in LG I. However, it underwent a rapid decline beginning near the end of LG Ib when triglyphs and metopes began spreading, and finally in LG II, triglyphs surpassed metopes in size. Since the triglyph-metope frieze on the Stovall tankard has a very wide metope, it is likely that the vessel should not be placed earlier than the LG IIa period.

A final question concerns place of origin. The shape of the Stovall tankard parallels that of specimens from Attica, yet the orange-buff clay is different from the buff to pink-buff clay characteristic of Attic Geometric wares. Young, *Hesperia*, Suppl. 2, p. 195. But Boeotian clay in the Geometric periods varies from brown to orange-brown, and is in general a shade deeper than Attic clay. Coldstream's warning (*GGP*, p. 196) about the ease of mistaking provincial Attic clay for Boeotian must be remembered. It is likely, then, that this tankard is provincial Attic or Boeotian.

73 Late Geometric high-rimmed bowl

LG IIa (ca. 735–720 B.C.)
Height, 7.7 cm; diameter at lip, 13.9 cm (C56–57/11/1)

This high-rimmed bowl, made of buff or pinkish-buff clay and slipped with a clay of similar color, has a shallow body, a high slightly flaring rim, and handles that are attached horizontally and flare out at the ends. It is decorated with a brown glaze paint on the outside, red glaze on the inside. The outside decoration is composed of narrow bands, a triglyph-metope frieze with a checkerboard as the metope and stacked M's at the center of the triglyph, and a star-burst pattern on the edges of the triglyph-metope pattern. The rim is decorated with narrow bands that horizontally frame the primary rim decoration of a chain of dotted lozenges. The handles are decorated with a pattern of connected thick-and-thin slanting segments. Provenance is unknown, but the clay and parallel specimens suggest an Attic origin.

This shape is almost exclusively a Late Geometric one, created by the Dipylon master or his workshop. Coldstream, *GGP*, p. 34. The creation probably came about as the result of the fusion of two Middle Geometric II by-forms of the skyphos, an elongated variant of the skyphos with a shallow body and reflex handles, and the lakaina, which had a very high rim. The bowls probably did not begin until the Late Geometric Ib period (ca. 750–735 B.C.) and went through a brief experimental stage before settling down to a standard form in which the body is very shallow and the rim straight and considerably taller than the body. Ibid., p. 48. At the time of the transition to LG IIb, the common LG Ib and LG IIa type changes: the bowl contracts and the rim slants outward, and furthermore most LG IIb high-rimmed bowls have stands. The Stovall bowl does not follow the described orthodox shape of either the LG Ib and LG IIa type or the LG IIb type. It has a slightly flaring rim, but the bowl is deeper than usual for either of those periods. This shape of bowl was very popular during the Late Geometric periods; probably such vessels were used primarily for funerary purposes. Often these bowls were employed to stop the mouths of other, much larger vases, such as those placed outside Geometric graves. L. Shear, *AJA* 34 (1930): 411; and fig. 5 in M. S. F. Hood, *Archaeological Reports for 1959–60*. Although the so-called ribbon handle is purely decorative on high-rimmed bowls, it may reflect a metallic origin, since it could have been used to hang plates on a wall. Young, *Hesperia*, Suppl. 2, p. 205.

The shape of our bowl seems to indicate that it was made near the transition from the straight-rimmed, very shallow LG Ib and LG IIa bowls to the slant-rimmed bowls with stands of LG IIb.

With respect to the decorative elements, one prominent feature is the use of red glaze on the interior; this does not seem to be especially common, although other examples are known, including no. XI.4, fig. 32, in ibid. and no. 319, p. 67 with pl. 18 in Eva Brann, *Late Geometric and Proattic Pottery: Athenian Agora*, vol. 8 (Princeton, N.J., 1962). The dotted lozenge chain appeared in the Middle Geometric II period (ca. 800–760 B.C.) and continued through the Late Geometric periods (ca. 760–700 B.C.). Coldstream, *GGP*, p. 24. The checkerboard is also a common Late Geometric motif in continuous friezes as well as in the triglyph-metope system. Variations in the checkerboard occur almost exclusively in its execution. Jean Davison in *Attic Geometric Workshops* (Rome, 1968), p. 20, has detected three methods of creating a checkerboard: painting both horizontal and vertical lines and filling in the squares carefully, painting both horizontal and vertical lines and filling in the squares with dots and thereby leaving the corners unpainted, and painting horizontal lines and obtaining the checkered effect by using upright strokes of paint more or less evenly spaced. The checkerboard metope on this bowl seems to have been executed with the first method. In the LG Ib period checked areas began to be used as the central part of triglyphs, in some cases the checked areas becoming virtual metopes in their own right. Coldstream, *GGP*, p. 50. At a later point the checkerboard did become a metope in its own right, as our Stovall example illustrates: here the check has been used as the metope, but the metope is wider than was usual in the earlier, more orthodox form of triglyph-metope frieze. S. McNally (*AJA* 73 [1969]: 459–61) has arranged what she calls steep-rimmed bowls into four classes, based on their decoration. The Stovall bowl does not seem to fit well into any one of these classes, but probably is related to Class 3, which has a triglyph-metope pattern on the handle zone and a wolf's tooth frieze on the rim. According to B. Schweitzer (*Greek Geometric Art* [London, 1971], p. 25), the slanted thick-and-thin segment pattern is a Geometric version of the Mycenaean false spiral, and patterns such as the checkerboard and the lozenge chain are possibly derivatives from weaving patterns. Both the wide-checked metope and the shape of our bowl probably indicate a date in the LG IIa period for it. Perhaps the closest parallel in shape is no. 275 in A. Fairbanks, *Catalogue of Greek and Etruscan Vases in the Museum of Fine Arts, Boston* (Cambridge, Mass., 1928), pp. 82–83 with pl. 24.

74   Sherd from an Attic Geometric vase

9 × 8 cm (C85/8/1)

A thick fragment of buff clay with vertical and horizontal lines and an aquatic bird (head missing) painted in black; from the Athenian agora excavations. The original vase must have possessed a wide neck and a bulbous body and thus was perhaps a tankard or an oinochoe; this sherd comes from the lower portion of the neck at the shoulder. The aquatic bird, which is a common creature on Attic vases often termed "Dipylon" (Cook, *GPP*, p. 20), is similar to birds pictured on Dipylon vases in *Collection de feu M. Jean P. Lambros d'Athènes et de M. Giovanni Dattari du Caire* (Paris, 1912), pl. III, nos. 4, 6, 19 and pl. V, nos. 9, 11, 15–18. Compare also the bird figures set off by vertical and horizontal lines on Attic Geometric vases illustrated in P. V. C. Baur, *Catalogue of the Rebecca Darlington Stoddard Collection* (New Haven, Conn., 1922), fig. 11, no. 55, p. 49; Young, *Hesperia*, Suppl. 2, fig. 60, XVIII.1, p. 89; and Coldstream, *GGP*, pl. 10j. On the basis of these examples our fragment should likely be assigned to the Late Geometric period, ca. 750–700 B.C.

Attic fragments. *Left*: No. 93, skyphos fragment. *Center: above*, no. 87, black-figured sherd; *below*, no. 92, fragment of red-figured kylix. *Right*: no. 74, sherd from geometric vase.

75   Subprotogeometric sherd (Euboean?)

Likely eighth century B.C.
9.1 × 9.7 cm (C57–58/10/3)

This is a thick (1 cm) fragment composed of pinkish-buff, fine clay and covered with a buff slip. The decoration is executed in red-orange paint and consists of intersecting semicircles suspended from two lines. The sherd may have come from a type of cup called Shessalo-Cycladic or Pendent-Semicircle, which generally had a low foot, inturning rim, and two sets of intersecting pendent semicircles. These cups were likely produced in more than one center, but Euboea seems to have been the most important source, and they were also apparently made from the beginning of the ninth to the middle of the eighth century B.C., perhaps even later. Cook, *GPP*, p. 10. The style of Pendent-Semicircle cups is essentially Protogeometric but when found in later contexts they are labeled Subprotogeometric. These cups were widely exported and have been found at Delphi, Delos, Euboea, Rhodes, Cyprus, Al Mina, and other sites. Ibid.; M. Robertson, *JHS* 60 (1940): 2–21. Pendent-Semicircle cups were surprisingly not discovered in the West for a long time, but not many years ago a specimen was found at a cemetery in Veii, its date of manufacture being placed in the eighth century B.C. D. Ridgway and O. T. P. K. Dickinson, *BSA* 68 (1973): 191–92. Our sherd is interesting because it and the following three pieces were picked up on the surface at Elche, Spain.

76   Subprotogeometric sherd (Euboean?)

Likely eighth century B.C.
6.7 × 5.3 cm (C57–58/10/2)

This fragment is similar to the preceding number (75) with the same red-orange paint and semicircles with linear decoration, but it is not as thick and the clay is slightly pinker. Presumably the same comments apply to it.

77   Subprotogeometric sherd (Euboean?)

Likely eighth century B.C.
7.5 × 6.6 cm (C57–58/10/4)

The description of this fragment is the same as that given to the preceding (no. 76) sherd.

78   Subprotogeometric sherd (Euboean?)

Likely eighth century B.C.
8.7 × 5.5 cm (C57–58/10/1)

This fragment is of a buff clay fired gray and has linear and zigzag patterns painted also in red-orange; its thickness is about the same as the two preceding sherds (nos. 76 and 77). Nothing too specific can be said about it, but since it also was picked up on the surface at Elche, probably the same comments apply to it as were given for the first of these fragments.

79   Corinthian pointed aryballos

Late Protocorinthian through Early Corinthian (ca. 650–600 B.C.)
Height, 6.9 cm; maximum diameter, 3.9 cm (C53–54/37)

This small pointed aryballos, composed of fine, rather soft, pinkish-buff clay and decorated in a black glaze that is predominantly misfired red, has a small ring foot, elongated and pointed shape, short neck, disk lip, and strap handle attached at lip and shoulder. The decoration consists of two concentric bands on the lip, encircling bands on the body, interrupted in the middle by a silhouette "running dog" frieze, and dot rosettes on the shoulder. The shape is known as pointed aryballos, a distinctively Late Protocorinthian form. Provenance is unknown.

According to Payne (*Necrocorinthia*, p. 5), the appearance of the rounded aryballos in the Early Protocorinthian period (ca. 720–690 B.C.) was the result of Cretan influence, but a good

case may be made for its invention at Corinth. T. J. Dunbabin, ed., *Perachora. The Sanctuaries of Hera Akraia and Limenia: Excavations of the British School of Archaeology at Athens, 1930–1933*, vol. 2, *Pottery, Ivories, Scarabs, and Other Objects from the Votive Deposits of Hera Limenia* (Oxford, 1962), p. 11. At any rate, the change in form of the aryballos from the ovoid to the pointed shape is an important sign of the beginning of the Late Protocorinthian period (ca. 650–625 B.C.). In addition to the change in body shape, the mouth of the aryballos becomes wider and heavier at this time. Payne, *Necrocorinthia*, p. 17. One common form of decoration on pointed aryballoi consists mainly of bands and rays, with a frieze of "running dogs" on the shoulder or near the middle of the body. The "running dog" style appears on ovoid aryballoi in the Protocorinthian period and does not continue, for the most part, much beyond the Early Corinthian period (ca. 625–600 B.C.), although there are a few examples of its use on Middle Corinthian vases. Pointed aryballoi with this decoration do not, in general, appear after the first part of the Early Corinthian period. R. J. Hopper, *BSA* 44 (1949): 185–86. The band decoration on the lower portion of our specimen, where rays were often placed, is a survival of an earlier system from the eighth and early seventh centuries, but the bands do appear later on some of the poorer aryballoi. Dunbabin, ed., *Perachora*, p. 18. Although the style and shape are Late Protocorinthian, pointed aryballoi with linear and silhouette decoration were produced early in the Corinthian period. Additionally, the production of this type seems to have ceased sometime in the Early Corinthian period because there is practically no evidence of the pointed aryballos shape in the sixth century. Payne, *Necrocorinthia*, p. 286. Concentric bands on the mouth do not seem to be a necessarily late feature on pointed aryballoi, since an ovoid aryballos illustrated in Dunbabin, ed., *Perachora*, no. 18, pl. 2, has thin concentric circles on its disk. (A specimen precisely similar to the Stovall aryballos in respect to dimensions, concentric circles, and a "running dog" frieze can be found in Chr. Blinkenberg, *Lindos: Fouilles de l'Acropole 1902–14, vol. 1, Les Petits Objets* [Berlin, 1931], no. 1078 with pl. 49.) On the evidence of both its shape and decoration, our example should be placed in the Late Protocorinthian through the Early Corinthian periods (ca. 650–600 B.C.).

80 Early Corinthian aryballos

Early Corinthian period (ca. 625–600 B.C.)
Height, 6 cm; diameter, 5 cm (C45–46/3)

This is a small round aryballos composed of hard, fine, buff clay that is covered with a buff slip. The decoration, which has been incised, is painted in black but traces of red remain. The vessel has a tiny depression at the bottom, a round body, small neck, strap handle attached at lip and shoulder, and everted disk lip. The decoration consists of tongues on the base, shoulder, and lip and a lion and swan to the left on the body. The filling ornament consists of normal incised rosettes and incised "plus" rosettes. The incision is generally careful, but not very realistic, especially on the lion. The provenance is unknown.

The round aryballos appeared rarely in the Late Protocorinthian and Transitional periods but became very common in the Early Corinthian period, eventually displacing the alabastron as the favorite shape for unguent vases. Payne (*Necrocorinthia*, pp. 281, 287–89) divided the round aryballos into three major shapes, A, B, and C, then subdivided Shape B into two classes. This example is to be classified as Shape B1, which is rounder with a longer neck and a slimmer disk than either Shapes A or B2. Shape B1 appeared in the Early Corinthian period and continued into the sixth century B.C.

The style of decoration is an important factor in dating Corinthian vases. The general scheme on this vase belongs to Payne's Group E, aryballoi without bounding lines above and below the main subject; this type of decoration, painted on aryballoi of Shape B1, was common in the seventh century B.C. and lasted into the sixth century B.C. The swan is a common motif on Corinthian vases, but the lion decreases in popularity throughout the Corinthian period and is almost completely replaced by the panther in the Late Corinthian period (ca. 575–550 B.C.). The style of the Corinthian lion, as well as the

rosette, seems to be Assyrian in origin. Ibid., pp. 30, 67, 76, 287–90. According to C. Boulter (*AJA* 41 [1937]: 228), the absence of bounding lines and the presence of small tongues on the base, shoulder, and mouth are elements that point to an Early Corinthian date. The style of decoration and shape, then, suggest that the Stovall specimen is from the Early Corinthian period, possibly even the early Middle Corinthian period (ca. 600–575 B.C.)

Several features of our lion are unusual, e.g., the peculiar shoulder muscle complex, and the scarcity of incision in the midsection, legs, and flanks. Other features, however, may indicate the general influences on the painter of this aryballos. The lion is reminiscent of the type often painted by the early Middle Corinthian Chimaera Painter and his group, especially the mane with its double lines and the tail rising from behind the front flank. But the similarity is only general, since the characteristic shoulder and body markings of the Chimaera Painter and his close associate, the Painter of the Louvre E574, are very different from the few incisions on the body of this lion. Nevertheless, the lion type depicted by these two painters was the result of "a natural, continuous development from the type introduced by the Painter of Palermo 489," and the lion on our vessel is quite likely the product of a painter somewhere in the stream of this process. P. Lawrence, *AJA* 63 (1959): 362. The tail rising from behind the front flank, while not very common, appears on the vases of the Dodwell Painter and elsewhere, as well as on those from the Chimaera group. R. J. Hopper, *BSA* 44 (1949): 167 n. 19. In general, the tongues at base and neck, the quality of the rosettes, the absence of bounding lines, and the scarcity of incision on the lion combined with the style of the lion, all indicate that our round aryballos should be placed in the Early Corinthian period, although an early Middle Corinthian date should not be ruled out.

81 Corinthian flat-bottomed aryballos

Late Middle Corinthian or Late Corinthian (ca. 580–550 B.C.)
Height, 11 cm; diameter, 10.1 cm (C46–47/2)

Composed of hard, fine, buff clay and covered with a buff slip, this flat-bottomed aryballos has a decoration in dark brown paint that has been fired red over a large part of the surface. There

are traces of reddish-purple paint on the necks of the two birds. It is a rather large, round vessel with a fairly wide, shallow ring foot, short neck, strap handle, and everted disk lip. The decoration consists of four concentric circles on the mouth, tongues on the neck, two encircling rings, and an animal frieze with a bird to the right, a siren with head to the left and body to the right, and a bird to the left. Three bands decorate the lower body and exterior of the base, while three concentric circles decorate the underside of the base. The filling ornament consists of incised rosettes with a double inner circle and small blobs. Provenance is unknown.

This aryballos corresponds to the flat-bottomed variant of Payne's Shape C. This shape, rare before the sixth century B.C., is a revival of a Protocorinthian type. The sixth-century flat-bottomed aryballos is relatively tall (usually 12 to 15 cm), is higher in proportion, and with a foot wider than earlier versions. Flat-bottomed aryballoi usually have tongues on the mouth and shoulder in the Middle Corinthian period (ca. 600–575 B.C.), while Late Corinthian (ca. 575–550 B.C.) versions regularly display concentric circles on the mouth, tongues on the shoulder, and bounding lines above and below the frieze. Payne, *Necrocorinthia*, pp. 287, 291, 304, 321. The general scheme of decoration on the Stovall specimen is like that on Late Corinthian flat-bottomed aryballoi. Also, the form of double-centered rosettes seems to have become common in the late Middle Corinthian period. Ibid., p. 157. Concentric circles, however, do appear on Middle Corinthian examples. Ibid., p. 305. The siren is a popular subject on Corinthian vases, as is also the swan, which is probably the bird depicted on our specimen. The face of the siren, with its relatively small nose and prominent chin, seems to be late, much like the faces on the Late Corinthian subjects seen on pl. 37 in ibid., even though their features are still very ar-

chaic. The scheme of decoration, the careless incision, and the face of the siren all suggest a late date for our flat-bottomed aryballos, probably in the Late Corinthian and no earlier than the late Middle Corinthian. A rather close parallel will be found in Chr. Blinkenberg and K. F. Johansen, *CVA, Denmark, Copenhague: Musée National*, fasc. 2 (Paris, 1925), p. 67 with pl. 87.3 (undated).

82   Late Corinthian kotyle

Late Corinthian period (ca. 575–550 B.C.)
Height, 10.8 cm; diameter at rim, 16.3 cm (C56–57/12)

This is an animal-figured kotyle made of brownish-buff, fine, hard clay and covered with a similar slip. The ring foot, which flares outward and is slightly beveled, is fairly small in comparison with the body. The sides are slightly incurving and somewhat steep; loop handles are attached near the rim. It is decorated in red and black paint with encircling lines, a handle frieze of vertical wavy lines, thick-and-thin encircling lines, an animal frieze, thick-and-thin encircling lines, attenuated rays, and a partially glazed foot. The abundantly incised animal frieze consists of a panther to the left, a goat to the right, a panther to the right, a goat to the right, and a panther to the right. The filling ornament consists of small blobs and horizontally incised rosettes. The slightly convex underside of the foot is decorated with a thin black line on the resting surface, a thick line on the ring, another thick black line farther in, a thin black line, and two thin black lines around a central dot. Provenance is unknown.

The kotyle seems to have been invented at Corinth, its form said to have been influenced by metallic prototypes. Payne, *Necrocorinthia*, p. 294. In the late eighth century B.C. two distinct types of kotylai existed. The tall and thin shape continued into the seventh century, one of the primary shapes of Corinthian ceramics for centuries. S. Weinberg, *The Geometric and Orientalizing Pottery: Corinth*, vol. 7, pt. 1 (Princeton, N.J., 1943), p. 52. In general, the body was tall and flaring with a small ring foot in the Early Corinthian period (ca. 625–600 B.C.). In the Middle Corinthian period (ca. 600–575 B.C.) the body was more squat and the foot wider, but by the Late Corinthian period (ca. 575–550 B.C.) the sides of the kotyle had regained much of their earlier flare and the foot was narrower than in the Middle Corinthian period. Ibid., pp. 86–87. But since the development of the kotyle was uneven, this evolutionary scheme provides only a general

guideline. The section of the foot ring and the curvature of the bottom are more helpful in dating the shape of Corinthian kotylai. The foot-ring profile of this kotyle, which is flaring and slightly beveled, fits best into Type VII of the typology arranged by D. A. Amyx and P. Lawrence, *Archaic Corinthian Pottery and the Anaploga Well: Corinth*, vol. 7, pt. 2 (Princeton, N.J., 1975), pp. 74–78. In addition, the Stovall example has a slightly convex bottom, typical of Type VII kotylai, even though the shape of the sides of the drawing of Type VII seems different from those of ours. Finally, Type VII is also characterized by a Late Corinthian foot-ring profile (ibid.), and this last element confirms the impression that our vessel, with its rather narrow, flaring foot and high, flaring sides, is indeed a Late Corinthian kotyle.

Elements in its decoration urge the same conclusion. For example, the filling ornaments indicate that this is a late, though not necessarily Late Corinthian, kotyle. The elongated proportions and careless incision of the animals are further indices of a late date. Payne, *Necrocorinthia*, p. 59. The foot decoration is more definitive: the thin line on the underside of the foot rest, the broad band near the foot ring, and the fine line rings at the center all characterize late Corinthian kotylai. Amyx and Lawrence, *Corinthian Pottery*, p. 75. There is a very close parallel in decoration on another Corinthian specimen in

Chr. Blinkenberg and K. F. Johansen, *CVA, Denmark, Copenhague: Musée National*, fasc. 2 (Paris, 1925), p. 71 with pl. 91.3 (undated).

The animals on our kotyle are carelessly and lavishly incised; red paint, whether in broad areas or dots, is also abundant. Panthers are relatively rare on Protocorinthian vases, but they become very popular on Corinthian ones, almost entirely displacing lions by the Late Corinthian period. Payne, *Necrocorinthia*, p. 30. Goats, too, are fairly common on Corinthian vases, but are of two types that are often confused; the goats on the Stovall vase seem to be of the form native to Greece. Ibid., p. 70 n. 6; D. A. Amyx, *Corinthian Vases in the Hearst Collection: University of California Publications in Classical Archaeology*, vol. 1, no. 9 (Berkeley, Calif., 1943), p. 209. The features of our animals show some similarities to those painted by the Geledakis Painter, who appears to have been active in the late Middle Corinthian and early Late Corinthian periods. D. A. Amyx, *Hesperia* 25 (1956): 73–77. Admittedly, our animals do not have the two curved parallel lines enclosed by the shoulder, which extend downward into the near foreleg or the fringe along the animals' hindquarters, that are characteristic of much of the Geledakis Painter's work. But they do have other elements similar to his manner. On the Reading pyxis, one of this Painter's vases, there is only one line in the shoulder that extends into the leg, and on the Munich pyxis both single and double lines are present. One of the panthers on our kotyle exhibits this single line extending into the near foreleg, while all our animals share the kidney-bean–shaped shoulder muscle characteristic of the Geledakis Painter. In addition, our panthers have broad faces and circular markings for facial features, as do those on the Munich and Reading pyxides by the Geledakis Painter. Other strong parallels include the low, sloping lines on the flank, the straight lines marking the midsection (although on this kotyle some of these lines were hurriedly executed and have hooks), the horns and faces of the goats, and the red dots on the shoulders. The practice of placing red dots on the shoulder is shared also by the Ampersand Painter, although the originator of the practice is unknown. J. L. Benson, *AJA* 64 (1960): 281–83. The Stovall kotyle is not quite sufficiently similar to be labeled the work of the Geledakis Painter, but since it displays several of his mannerisms, it probably should be classified as a work of one of his followers.

83 Corinthian "Conventionalizing" skyphos

Second half of the sixth century through the first half of the
fifth century B.C.

Height, 5.4 cm; diameter at rim, 7.8 cm (C53–54/36)

Made from hard, fine, brownish-buff clay and
covered with a buff slip, this skyphos has a
painted decoration executed in red, brown, and
orange paint. It possesses a small ring foot, sides
that widen upward from bottom to top, and two
horizontal loop handles, one of which slants
downward slightly. The decoration of the body
consists of a series of encircling bands, with a
handle frieze of unconnected lotus buds on
one side and an empty panel on the other side.
Traces of orange and black paint decorate the
handle, and there are traces of two orange bands
inside the cup. The decoration on the bottom of
the foot consists of a black band on the foot rest,
next a wide red band, and then four orange
bands, two of which are near the center. Provenance is unknown.

Payne (*Necrocorinthia*, p. 331) was among the
first to recognize that a group of vases with linear and floral patterns was of Corinthian origin;
he labeled this class Late Corinthian II, assigning
it the years from about 550 to 450 B.C. This style,
later called "Conventionalizing" because of the
conventional nature of its decoration, is characterized by small skyphoi covered almost entirely
with bands except for a section near the rim that
is filled with conventional patterns, including the
lotus-bud motif. A. Stillwell, *AJA* 35 (1931): 17.
The Late Corinthian II or "Conventionalizing"
style was thought at first to end in the midfifth
century, but excavations in and around Corinth
have shown that it continued into the fourth century B.C. T. J. Dunbabin, ed., *Perachora: The Sanctuaries of Hera Akraia and Limenia: Excavations*
*of the British School of Archaeology at Athens, 1930–
1933*, vol. 2, *Pottery, Ivories, Scarabs, and Other Objects from the Votive Deposits of Hera Limenia* (Oxford, 1962), p. 272. In Late Corinthian II, and
perhaps at the end of Late Corinthian I, there
was a large class of kotylai with lotus buds just
below the handle frieze and rays just above the
base. Payne, *Necrocorinthia*, p. 334. It is quite possible that the Stovall example represents a sim-
plification of this type.

Although "Conventionalizing" vases appear
extremely degenerate when compared with earlier Corinthian products, a great demand for
them existed both at home and abroad. In the
graves from the North Cemetery at Corinth, a
cup, either skyphos or kylix, was an essential
part of the grave furnishings from the sixth
through fourth centuries B.C. Quite often the
cup was in the form of a "Conventionalizing"
skyphos like this one. The skyphos, indeed, is
the most common shape among the grave groups
at the North Cemetery, but it is even more
frequent in domestic deposits. Usually pattern-
skyphoi (as they are sometimes called) have tapering walls and a small ring foot; most are decorated with bands on the body and vertical
zigzags in the handle zone, but several have lotus
buds in the handle section. C. Blegen, H. Palmer, and R. Young, *The North Cemetery: Corinth*,
vol. 13 (Princeton, N.J., 1964), pp. 80, 101, 105,
123. A vase such as ours is difficult to date closely
because it was a common and long-lived form;
further, the "Conventionalizing" style itself lasts
from the midsixth through the fourth centuries.
The pattern-skyphos was widely exported, even
after the midfifth century when they ceased to be
used as grave furniture at Corinth. Ibid., p. 123.
At the North Cemetery, the two pattern-skyphoi
with unattached lotus buds are late, probably
from the first half of the fifth century. Ibid.
However, the pattern on the underside of the
foot of the Stovall skyphos is similar to certain
Late Corinthian kotylai, a circumstance that perhaps suggests that an earlier date is more appropriate. D. A. Amyx and P. Lawrence, *Archaic Corinthian Pottery and the Anaploga Well: Corinth*, vol.
7, pt. 2 (Princeton, N.J., 1975), p. 75. In the face
of such contradictory and uncertain evidence, a
tentative date in the second half of the sixth century B.C. through the first half of the fifth century seems the most plausible suggestion.

Classical and Hellenistic Pottery

(BARBARA L. GUNN AND A. J. HEISSERER)

The following abbreviations are used in this section:

ABV	J. D. Beazley, *Attic Black-figure Vase-painters* (Oxford, 1956).
ARV²	J. D. Beazley, *Attic Red figure Vase painters*, 2d ed. (Oxford, 1963).
Paralipomena	J. D. Beazley, *Paralipomena: Additions to Attic Black-figure Vase-painters and to Attic Red-figure Vase-painters* (Oxford, 1971).
CVA	*Corpus Vasorum Antiquorum.*
LCS	A. D. Trendall, *The Red-figured Vases of Lucania, Campania, and Sicily*, 2 vols. (Oxford, 1967).
RVA	A. D. Trendall and A. Cambitoglou, *The Red-Figured Vases of Apulia*, vol. 1 (Oxford, 1978).

Attic Black-figure and Red-figure (A. J. Heisserer)

84 Attic Black-figured eye cup (Group of Courting Cups)

Last quarter of the sixth century B.C.
Height, 11.6 cm; diameter at lip, 22 cm, at foot, 9.8 cm (C47–48/1)

Interior of the kylix is black, with narrow red band at rim and red space at center containing small concentric circles. Side A of the exterior has a pair of apotropaic eyes flanking figures of a standing warrior and a horse, both facing left, and above a small bird flying to left. The outermost ring of the eye is painted red, the next is painted white, the next black, then a thin white ring followed by a black heart and a red dot at center. Side B of the exterior has a similar design with a standing warrior and horse facing left but a different symbol in place of the bird. Under each handle is a dog. The cup is complete, although mended. See color plate.

This kylix is an unpublished example that belongs to a large group of vases organized under the rubric, "Group of Courting Cups," by Beazley (*Paralipomena*, pp. 82–83), because the subject on so many is nearly always a courting scene. But on a few the scene is a horseman, as here, and the Stovall kylix is similar to that seen in no. 290, p. 104, with pl. XXX in D. M. Robinson and C. G. Harcum, *A Catalogue of the Greek Vases in the Royal Ontario Museum* (Toronto, 1930), republished by John W. Hayes, *CVA, Attic Black Figure and Related Wares: Royal Ontario Museum*, Canada, fasc. 1 (Oxford, 1981), 920.68.74. Beazley, *Paralipomena*, cites others as being located in the Thorvaldsen Museum at Copenhagen, at Hamburg, and the Museo Civico at Orvieto. A new example of one with a courting scene, instead of the horseman, has recently been published by H. A. Shapiro, *Art, Myth, and Culture: Greek Vases from Southern Collections* (New Orleans, 1981), no. 64, pp. 162–63. The shape of the Stovall cup corresponds to that given by Shapiro for these courting cups, "a shallow bowl, plain lip, short, splaying foot with a moulding separating it from the bowl." Ibid., p. 162. Our shape is also very similar to München 2033 (which, however, is of a different typology), illustrated as an example of *Schallen* A1 in J. Bloesch, *Formen Attischer Schalen* (Bern, 1940), pl. 2.3a.

85   Attic Black-figured neck amphora (by the Diosphos Painter)

Early fifth century B.C.
Height, 21.2 cm; diameter at lip, 9.5 cm, at base, 7 cm (C45–46/5)

Foot and one handle broken and mended; handles double ribbed. Reserved panel on neck with palmette pattern. Thin double lines in a red color different from the pinkish-buff of the vase at base of scene panels. See color plates.

This elegant small neck amphora is to be attributed to the Diosphos Painter, as Stovall Museum accession records precisely indicate. J. D. Beazley in his *Greek Vases in Poland* (Oxford, 1928), Addenda, p. 79, first attributed this vase to the Diosphos Painter, describing it as "one which was formerly in Dr. Hirsch's possession (A, chariot and fallen warrior; B, chariot wheeling around)." C. H. E. Haspels in her *Attic Black-Figured Lekythoi* (Paris, 1936), p. 240, assigned 161 vases to the Diosphos Painter; under no. 151 she gives the same description, citing Beazley's work, and adds that the vase was in the "Paris market (Hirsch)." Finally, Beazley (*ABV*, p. 509) correctly noted that Haspels's no. 151 was at the University of Oklahoma. Indeed, the accession records show that our vase was purchased from Dr. Hirsch in 1946; and a former curator at the Stovall Museum had already suggested before the publication of *ABV* that our vase might be identified with no. 151 in Haspels.

Vases by Diosphos are very well known. His name is taken from the inscription on the famous amphora (no. 219) in the Cabinet des Médailles, illustrated in J. Boardman, *Athenian Black Figure Vases* (New York, 1974), pl. 272. S. B. Luce, Jr., in *AJA* 20 (1916): 439–59, has pointed out (p. 450) a predominant characteristic of vases by the Diosphos Painter, namely, the fact that the central palmette on the neck panel points upward. For illustrations of amphorae by this Painter, see ibid., pl. 271; G. M. A. Richter and M. J. Milne, *Shapes and Names of Athenian Vases* (New York, 1935), fig. 17, republished by M. B. Moore and D. von Bothmer, *CVA, Metropolitan Museum of Art*, fasc. 4 (New York, 1976), pl. 50.1–2; H. A. Shapiro, *Art, Myth, and Culture: Greek Vases from Southern Collections* (New Orleans Museum of Art, 1981), nos. 16 and 24; *ABV*, pp. 507–17; *Paralipomena*, pp. 248–53. On the techniques of the Diosphos Painter, see especially Haspels, *Attic Lekythoi*, pp. 94–130, 232–41.

86   Attic Black-figured lekythos (Class of Athens 581)

Early fifth century B.C.
Height, 19.8 cm; diameter at shoulder, 8.3 cm; diameter at base, 5.3 cm (C45–46/2)

Foot partially restored in plaster; otherwise intact. The shape is Richter's Type II, with the shoulder set off from the body. G. M. A. Richter and M. J. Milne, *Shapes and Names of Athenian Vases* (New York, 1935), p. 15 with fig. 95; cf. R. S. Folsom, *Attic Black-Figured Pottery* (Park Ridge, N.J., 1975), p. 33, fig. 19. The scene depicts Heracles and the Cretan Bull, not Theseus and the Bull of Marathon, because one can see the archer's bow and quiver on the wall of the vase; this distinction is discussed by Jane Henle, *Greek Myths: A Vase Painter's Handbook* (Bloomington, Ind., and London, 1973), p. 63. A standing warrior flanks each side of the scene. The labor of Heracles was extremely popular among ancient vase painters, and the arrangement of the scene on our vase is similar to that on an Attic Black-figured neck amphora, attributed to the Antimenes Painter. H. A. Shapiro, *Art, Myth, and Culture: Greek Vases from Southern Collections* (New Orleans Museum of Art, 1981), no. 23. The type of lotus chain on the Stovall lekythos is illustrated in Donna Kurtz, *Athenian White Lekythoi* (Oxford, 1975), fig. 2c (the Leagros group). The treatment of the warrior on the right side of this vase is reminiscent of a warrior on a large amphora published by Cedric G. Boulter and Kurt

T. Luckner, *CVA, The Toledo Museum of Art*, fasc. 1 (Toledo Museum of Art, 1976), pl. 3, a vase which, however, is dated to ca. 540 B.C. and has been attributed to the Swing Painter.

Despite the monumental work of Haspels and Beazley, the history and identity of this lekythos cannot be traced. Its shape and style are most similar to those illustrated by C. H. E. Haspels, *Attic Black-Figured Lekythoi* (Paris, 1936), pl. 31, 1–3 and 5 (all encompassed by Beazley, *ABV*, p. 487, under the heading, The Class of Athens 581); also her pl. 40, 2, which she labeled, The Group of Athens 496, near both the Sappho and Diosphos Painters. Haspels, *Lekythoi*, p. 231. The Class of Athens 581 comprises an exceptionally large group, and there can be little doubt that the Stovall vase should be added to it. For general description of this Class, see J. Boardman, *Athenian Black Figure Vases* (New York, 1974), p. 148 with figs. 258–59.

87 Black-figured sherd

Maximum height. 5.9 cm (C39–40/5)

Composition is fine, hard, orange-buff clay; this rim sherd perhaps was from an eye kylix. To the left are the head and shoulders of a satyr, with his left hand extended forward; on the right are vine tendrils and traces of what appears to be a large eye. Interior is glazed black, the exterior ground reserved. Date uncertain. (Before 1940 this piece was accessioned as no. 39.280 in the Fogg Museum, Harvard University.)

88 Attic head vase (Group N, the Cook Class)

Early fifth century B.C.
Height with handle, 22.1 cm, without handle, 18 cm; width at base, 7 × 6.6 cm (C49–50/3)

An exquisite oinochoe in the form of a woman's head; except for a chipped base, it is intact. Made of hard, fine, light orange clay; decoration in black glaze, red miltos on flesh areas; some lime incrustation on the handle. The rolled handle originates from a trefoil lip. Traces of a wreath in added white, barely visible, around head. No incision for ears.

The Stovall head vase very likely should be attributed to Beazley's Group N, the Cook group. *JHS* 49 (1929): 61–65 and especially his fig. 15 of the Berlin 2192. This group of head vases is by far the most numerous. Beazley updated his listings for the Cook group in *ARV²*, pp. 1539–

44, Addenda I, p. 1698, Addenda II, p. 1704; and in *Paralipomena*, pp. 503–504. The Stovall vase likely should be numbered among those marked as having been in the market; it cannot be located in Beazley's works but was purchased in 1949 from Morley (ex coll. I. N. Phelps Stokes).

Among the numerous head vases in the *Antikensammlungen* of Munich, this vase compares most favorably with Munich 2743 (assigned by Beazley to Class O, the Sabouroff Class), but also with Munich 2744 and 2745 (Class N). Munich 2744 and 2745 as well as Berlin 2192 all have a painted wreath, as does another head vase similar to this one. C. G. Boulter, *CVA, The Cleveland Museum of Art*, fasc. 1 (Princeton, 1971), pl. 39.7–8 (also Class N). Munich 2743 lacks the wreath. In addition, the line of the eyebrow and the type of archaic smile on this vase have analogies with those of Class N. On this basis, therefore, we attribute the Stovall head vase to this group.

89 Attic Red-figured lekythos (the Seireniske Painter or his followers)

Middle of the fifth century B.C.
Height, 17 cm; width at shoulder, 5.8 cm, width at base, 4.3 cm (C48–49/1)

Made of fine, hard clay with a pinkish-buff finish, this small lekythos stands on a small discoidal base; broken and mended at the neck, a running maenad on the body. The identifying attributes of maenads are an animal skin and thyrsus. Only

the former is present on this small lekythos, but the animal skin often covers a fully clothed maenad. Cf. J. Boardman, *Athenian Black Figure Vases* (New York, 1974), pp. 232–33; H. A. Shapiro, *Art, Myth, and Culture: Greek Vases from Southern Collections* (New Orleans, 1981), p. 46.

This Stovall vase shows a striking similarity to a lekythos in the *Antikensammlungen* at Munich, no. 7522 (= Beazley, *ARV²*, p. 707, under the heading, "The Following of the Seireniske Painter"). The measurements for the two vases are virtually identical; so also the style of the meander band at the shoulder, the decoration on the flair of the neck, the single white base line for the figure (Munich 7522 shows a siren with thyrsus), the arrangement of the hair, and the cap. The Stovall lekythos, therefore, may be securely attributed to the Seireniske Painter or one of his imitators. None of the lekythoi with maenads listed in Beazley under the Icarus Painter, the Seireniske Painter, or their followers can be identified with this vase. *ARV²*, pp. 696–708,

Addenda I, pp. 1666–67, Addenda II, p. 1702; *Paralipomena*, pp. 407–408.

The simple lines and graceful symmetry of the Stovall lekythos suggest a mid-fifth–century B.C. date, which is also the *floruit* of the Icarus and Aeschines Painters. Cf. Gisela M. A. Richter, *Attic Red-Figured Vases* (New Haven, Conn., 1946), p. 114.

90   Attic Red-figured pelike (by the Hasselmann Painter)

Ca. 430 B.C.
Height, 15.3 cm; maximum width, 12.7 cm (C55–56/7/1)

Fine, hard, pinkish-buff clay; black glaze. On side A two youths, dressed in himatia and wearing headbands, are apparently playing with a ball. On side B a youth, also dressed in a himation, holds a staff in his right hand and faces to the left. The ball might represent a phiale, but game scenes are fairly frequent on pottery from all localities. For example, a similar scene showing a woman bouncing a ball appears on a Lucanian bell crater from about 370 B.C. *LCS*, pl. 46.1. Another game scene, rather similar, can be found in *RVA*, pl. 15.1–2. The style of the drapery on the youths (who perhaps are ephebes) corresponds to the "Classical Free Style, ca. 450–420," described in R. S. Folsom, *Attic Red-Figured Pottery* (Park Ridge, N.J., 1976), p. 185.

A close parallel in shape and decoration is an Attic red-figured small pelike in Copenhagen. Chr. Blinkenberg and K. F. Johansen, *CVA, Denmark, Copenhague: Musée National*, fasc. 4 (Paris, 1931), p. 118 with pl. 152.3; a vase attributed to the Hasselmann Painter by Beazley, *ARV²*, p. 1135. An even more striking resemblance in shape, size, and depiction is found in another pelike also attributed to the Hasselmann Painter. K. Herbert and S. Symeonoglou, *Ancient Col-*

lections in Washington University (St. Louis, Mo., 1973), p. 23 and figs. 29–30. On the St. Louis vase we see on one side two youths facing each other, and on the other a walking youth; when compared to the Stovall pelike, one observes that the folds of the garments on all these youths are quite similar, and further that the band at the neck of the vases carries precisely the same decoration. On these grounds we attribute the Stovall pelike to the Hasselmann Painter, who is generally placed at the end of the fifth century B.C. As far as can be determined, the Stovall pelike is not catalogued in Beazley's *ARV*² nor in his *Paralipomena*.

91   Fragment of Attic Red-figured pelike

Maximum height, 10.5 cm; minimum diameter at neck, 6.1 cm (C53–54/60)

Since this piece was found in the excavations of the Athenian agora, its provenance is presumably Athenian. The front panel shows a veiled female with head to right; in front of her is the head of a griffon to right. The back panel depicts two cloaked figures facing one another. Traces of both handles are preserved and suggest that this fragment was from a pelike with ovoid body on a low base ring, flaring neck, and everted undercut lip. The clay is typically Attic, fine, hard, with a pinkish buff; the black glaze, of a slightly metallic luster, also bears added white paint on the face of the obverse, with thin brown glaze for the details of the eyes. This piece may be compared with specimens found in *Hesperia* 3

(1934): 333–34, nos. B1–B2, and also pp. 332 and 427–29; since these are dated ca. 325 B.C., the same date applies to this fragment.

92   Fragment of an Attic Red-figured kylix

Maximum height, 6.5 cm (C57–58/8)

This piece is from the center of the floor with part of the stem remaining. On the interior (i.e., the center) is a warrior running to the right with shield and spear, but the head, the lower part of the legs, and much of the shield are missing. The style, even on such a small fragment, is exquisite and suggests therefore a fifth-century B.C. date.

93   Skyphos fragment

Maximum height, 11 cm (C56–57/2/1)

Portion of an Attic Red-figured skyphos, part of the wall to the lip being preserved. On the right a nude youth, quite muscular, faces to the left; at the lower right appears part of an unidentified rectangular object. Date uncertain.

94   Fragment of an Attic Red-figured kylix

Maximum height (axis of the flute player), 16.2 cm; maximum width, 14 cm (C56–57/1/1)

The center of the floor and part of the stem are preserved. On the interior a boy, facing to the right, plays double flutes. On the exterior are one palmette and traces of the lower legs of two persons, both participating in some activity (likely musical or athletic). Date uncertain.

South Italian Ware
(A. J. Heisserer)

95   Apulian bell crater (the Tarporley Circle)

Ca. 400 B.C.
Height, 34.5 cm; diameter at lip, 37 cm (C54–55/8)

This large crater is complete but was broken and irregularly repaired; the surface and painting have suffered much wear, but additionally the glaze appears to have fired unevenly on the orange-red clay. Despite its condition, the bell crater is a noteworthy member of the Stovall Museum's collection. The bell rises in a gentle curve from a solid base; the looped handles turn inward but do not project beyond the edge of the lip, the result of careful workmanship. The meander belt, which serves as a floor for the figures on both sides, contains no alternating figures such as saltire crosses. Below the rim runs a laurel-wreath border within a red band.

Side A suggests a banquet scene, one that is peaceful and serene, graced by the presence of a female flute player. Another very similar scene is found on a Red-figured Boeotian bell crater in P. V. C. Baur, *Catalogue of the Rebecca Darlington Stoddard Collection* (New Haven, Conn., 1922), no. 324, fig. 45. Side B, whose surface has suffered much more severely than its opposite, presents three young men engaged in a discussion; the central figure has his himation drawn up around his right shoulder. Such scenes are typical of many South Italian vases. It is true that similar scenes and vase shapes are commonly found outside South Italy (*RVA*, pp. xlviii, 4), and also that a shape very similar to the Stovall vase appears among the early Lucanians, such as the Pisticci and Amykos Painters (*LCS*, pls. 3–5 and 9–15, but in these the meander belt runs in the opposite direction). Nevertheless, we feel that stylistic criteria strongly suggest that this bell crater is Apulian.

It is generally recognized that there existed a series of early South Italian Red-figured vases that preceded "the developed local styles—Apulian, Lucanian, Paestan, Campanian—of the fourth century" (A. Bromberg, *HSCP* 64 [1959]: 238), and that are characterized by uniform style, simple shapes with only a few figures, and an absence of the ornate tendencies of later painters. Trendall (*RVA*, pp. 28–43) associates the plain style with the Tarporley Painter and his followers, the ornate style with individuals such as the various "Dionysiac" painters and the Gravina Painter. The Stovall bell crater should be attributed to a painter of the Tarporley Circle. The plain style was greatly influenced by Attic models of the second half of the fifth century B.C. Trendall, in ibid., p. 5 with pl. 1.2, in discussing the earliest of the Apulian Red-figured vase painters, the painter of the Berlin Dancing Girl, cites one example of an Attic influence: the pose in which a youth, with one shoulder bare, leans upon a stick held in one hand while the other hand rests on the hip, as illustrated in Benevento 348 III by the Kleophon Painter. Our bell crater shows this identical stance; and it also shares with the pioneer Apulians the penchant for extremely straight, vertical lines in female clothing. One may also compare the three figures on our side B with the three figures shown on a vase by the Tarporley Painter. *RVA*, pl. 14.1–2. On the basis of these observations we urge an attribution to the Tarporley Circle and a date of about 400 B.C. for our bell crater.

96 Fragment of an Apulian crater (the Darius Painter)

Middle of the fourth century B.C.
Height, 23.5 cm; width, 25.6 cm (C53–54/55)

This is a fragment of a wall from either a volute or a calyx crater, more likely a volute crater. Cf. *RVA*, pls. 149.1–2 and 150.1–2. The design is exceptionally ornate, added white and red

being prominent. Two figures are shown with their names inscribed, to the left Peleus and to the right Phoenix. One interesting feature is that Phoenix is clearly depicted as blind. According to the Greek legend, Phoenix instructed Achilles in the arts of war and was a good friend of Peleus, the father of Achilles, but he had undergone a traumatic experience: after his own father blinded him, he sought his way to the kingdom of Peleus at Phthia in Thessaly and was received by Peleus, who prevailed upon Chiron the Centaur to heal the blind man. Our fragment "is of particular interest since it is the only scene in vase painting which seems definitely to be associated with the lost *Phoinix* of Euripides. It clearly depicts the arrival of Peleus to take Phoinix to Cheiron for healing." A. D. Trendall and T. B. L. Webster, *Illustrations of Greek Drama* (London, 1971), III.3, 42, p. 100.

Sources: K. Schauenburg, *BonnJbb* 161 (1961), p. 217 n. 7; T. B. L. Webster, *Monuments Illustrating Tragedy and Satyr-play*, 2d ed. (*BICS* Suppl. 20, 1967), p. 129, TV 52; A. D. Trendall and T. B. L. Webster, *Greek Drama*; F. Brommer, *Vasenlisten zur griechischen Heldensage*, 3d ed. (Marburg, 1973), p. 543; Margaret E. Mayo, ed., *The Art of South Italy: Vases from Magna Graecia* (Virginia Museum of Fine Arts, Richmond, 1982), no. 49, p. 127; A. D. Trendall and Alexander Cambitoglou, *The Red-Figured Vases of Apulia*, vol. 2 (Oxford, 1982), no. 78, p. 503 (attributed to the Darius Painter).

97 South Italian Red-figured hydria

About 350 B.C.
Height, 18 cm; width at shoulder with handle, 12.5 cm, without handle, 10.5 cm; width at base, 5.4 cm (C55–56/1/1)

A small vase with three loop handles, decorated with two female figures, painted in red. Foot and lip broken and mended. The object that the woman on the left holds does not appear to be a thyrsus, so commonly seen on South Italian vases, but a combination of fan with some type of scarf or sash. Scarves are frequently seen on Greek vases, but the one on the Stovall vase is arranged in a rather unusual manner. For similarly painted scarves, compare the scarf on an Apulian hydria in *RVA*, pl. 63.1, and those on several Campanian vases in *LCS*, pls. 216.2, 218.3, and 218.5.

Reported as having come from Apulia, this hydria may indeed have been made in that area.

The dull ornamentation, the swarthy appearance of the figures, and the heaviness of the chitons all are representative of a stage in Apulian vase painting. These features generally are found in painters of the Lecce group, most of whom date to the second quarter of the fourth century B.C., some a bit later. A. Cambitoglou and A. R. Trendall, *Apulian Red-Figured Vase-Painters of the Plain Style* (Archaeological Institute of America, 1961), p. 62. The painting of the women and their drapery on this vase has some parallels, albeit not strict ones, with scenes depicted on nos. 184 (pl. 37), 200 (pl. 40), and especially 207 (pl. 41) in ibid.; these all fall within the Lecce group and are by the Truro Painter, the Thyrsus Painter, and the Lampas Painter, respectively. Without further parallels we suggest tentatively that our hydria was made in Apulia sometime near the middle of the fourth century B.C.

98   Apulian Gnathia epichysis

Ca. 300 B.C.
Height with handle, 17 cm; diameter at base, 9.3 cm
(C53–54/33)

Made of fine, hard, pinkish-buff clay, this epichysis is decorated in white, dark red, and yellow paint on a black glaze. It rests on a flat, projecting base and has a concave body with projecting shoulder; tall, narrow neck with lip molded as spout. The handle, flat in section, is attached at shoulder and at lip, rising above the lip; human faces are modeled at the points where the handle is attached to lip. The vessel is covered with a black glaze except for the lower surface of the base, where the glaze has been fired red; the base carries grooved circles. On the concave body there is a small crater in yellow, with yellow dots underneath and white rosettes (with a yellow dot

at center) on either side. A white egg-and-dot pattern occupies the outer edge of the shoulder. Above this is a laurel wreath composed of dots and leaves, the latter alternating in red and white; in the front center of this wreath is a ball, very similar to one shown on an Apulian Gnathia Askos illustrated as no. 126 in Margaret E. Mayo, ed., *The Art of South Italy: Vases from Magna Graecia* (Virginia Museum of Fine Arts, Richmond, 1982). A series of vertical, white ribs appear at the base of the neck. There is no pattern on the foot nor any on the base of the handle.

The Stovall epichysis is representative of a large number of similar Apulian specimens to which the term "Gnathian" has been applied, even though it is evident that not all 'Gnathian ware' was manufactured in the ancient town of Gnathia on the coast of Apulia. See ibid., pp. 252–58. The decoration on this vessel has close parallels with three other epichyses: no. 131, p. 272 (dated to ca. 325 B.C.) in ibid.; no. 524, p. 246, illustrated on pl. LXXXIX in D. M. Robinson and C. G. Harcum, *A Catalogue of the Greek Vases in the Royal Ontario Museum* (Toronto, 1930), a vessel dated to the third century B.C.; and no. 3 (undated) on pl. 52 in M. Bernardini, *Vasi dello Stile di Gnathia, Vasi a Vernice Nera* (Bari, n.d.). Mayo, *Vases*, also illustrates a number of others that bear some similarity to ours, e.g., no. 65, p. 159 (dated to 330 B.C.), no. 127, p. 268 (dated to 320–300 B.C.), and nos. 132–33, p. 273 (dated to ca. 320 B.C.). On the basis of these parallels we may assign the Stovall Museum's epichysis to ca. 300 B.C.

99   Apulian pot with lid

Ca. 300 B.C.
Height with lid, 12.2 cm; maximum diameter, 9.4 cm (C55–56/1/2)

Fine, hard, buff clay; red, white, and black paint added to form geometrical designs. In the center is an encircling band of red paint with added white dots, and two thin red bands surround this central one. Above this is a pattern of partial rosettes, in black, intersected by black vertical lines; each rosette is composed of tongues surrounding a single dot, but the lower third of each rosette is severed by the uppermost encircling red band. On the shoulder are tongues in added black, on the lid a wavy black pattern surrounded by two bands in black with white dots; knobbed handle in black.

A pyxis exceptionally similar to this one in size, shape, and decoration comes from Cam-

pania. Chr. Blinkenberg and K. F. Johansen, *CVA, Denmark, Copenhague: Musée National*, fasc. 5 (Paris, 1931), p. 180 with pl. 231.9 (undated). But pots with lids of this general shape and decoration more frequently have an Apulian or Messapian provenance. Cf. M. Bernardini, *Vasi dello Stile di Gnathia, Vasi a Vernice Nera* (Bari, n.d.), pl. 23.6 (from Gnathia) and pl. 24.2–4 (from Rudiae), all of which are undated. Other South Italian examples that show some parallel in shape, but not decoration, are illustrated in D. M. Robinson and C. G. Harcum, *A Catalogue of the Greek Vases in the Royal Ontario Museum* (Toronto, 1930), no. 441, p. 221, pl. LXXXII (dated to the late fourth century B.C.), and the individual bowls with their knobbed-handled lids on no. 455, p. 225, pl. LXXXIII (dated simply to the fourth century B.C.). Since our specimen is less ornate and developed than those seen in the Toronto catalogue, we tentatively suggest a date of ca. 300 B.C. for it.

100   Messapian volute crater

Ca. 300 B.C., perhaps later
Height to rim, 36 cm, with handles, 41.5 cm; diameter at rim, 20 cm, with handles, 24.8 cm (C53–54/54)

Made of fine, rather soft, buff clay, this tall crater has a large, discoidal foot, a flaring lip, and volute handles, each volute containing a human face (likely Gorgoneia) at both the front and back, but only the front two are painted white and yellow. Flanking each handle are two lugs, modeled and painted as swan's heads. The vessel is covered with a black paint, the decoration being added white and yellow. The reserved areas are on the rim of the foot, at the base of the body, the band below the lip, and the upper surface of the lip. On the front of the crater is a figure of a child, striding, carrying a whip in one hand and pulling a wheeled toy behind, and flanked by two stems of foliage. On the neck in front is a lion flanked by two tendril patterns. No decoration appears on the back of the vessel. One lug is missing, and a portion of the foot is mended; otherwise it is intact.

A vase virtually identical to this in shape and decoration is found in Lidia Forti, *La Ceramica di Gnathia* (Naples, 1965), pl. XXX(d). The vase there, described as an "amphora with volutes," has on the neck exactly the same lion, even to the swirl of the tail, the same tendril patterns, and the same reserved areas. The Gorgoneia are quite close in parallel, while on the front appear

remarkably similar stalks with foliage arising from a dotted base line. While our figure is a child to left pulling a toy, the vase in Forti has a youth walking to left, garment over left arm and some object in the right hand. This extraordinary likeness strongly suggests that the same vase painter decorated both these craters.

The gaudy rococo style of decoration on the Stovall crater corresponds to that found in South Italian centers in the period ca. 350–250 B.C., and in particular the use of applied color on a dark background is a well-known Gnathian technique. Cook, *GPP*, pp. 194–95, 200–201. T. B. L. Webster has asserted that volute craters appear only in miniature at Gnathia (*BICS* 15 [1968], p. 2), and it is true that the vase in Forti is from Bari. The provenance of ours is reported as being Messapian, and it seems best to employ that term of description for our vessel since "there is no good evidence that the pottery we

call Gnathia was ever manufactured there." Margaret E. Mayo, ed., *The Art of South Italy: Vases from Magna Graecia* (Virginia Museum of Fine Arts, Richmond, 1982), p. 252. Volute craters are very common from almost all parts of South Italy. The vase in Forti is cited twice as an illustration of decoration (pp. 61 and 63), but no date is offered for it. Since the Stovall crater bears the characteristics of South Italian pottery that Cook dates to ca. 350–250 B.C., but lacks the fine detail that is seen on so many fourth-century Apulian and Messapian vases, we suggest that it be placed near the end of the fourth or early part of the third century B.C.

101   Squat lekythos (Gnathian?)

Probably third century B.C.
Height with handle, 8.4 cm; diameter, 3.8 cm (C39–40/15)

Made of hard, fine, orange-buff clay, this is a miniature lekythos with rounded base and ring foot, a barrel-shaped body, and a tall neck rising from a flat shoulder; the handle, round in section, is attached below the shoulder and at the neck. The painted decoration consists of two horizontal bands below the shoulder, one at the base, and one on the foot. The surface of the body is filled with a wide, diagonal latticed pattern, white dots appearing at some of the inter-

sections. The upper part of the neck is painted solid, and vertical stripes extend down to the base of the neck. The upper part of the handle is painted solid also; a solid band encircles the lower attachment of the handle. The top of the neck is missing, and the foot is chipped. Provenance is unknown.

Net vases of this type had a very wide distribution throughout the Greek world, as J. D. Beazley demonstrates in *BSA* 41 (1940–45): 17–21 with figs. 16 and 17. Our example appears to be closest in size and decoration to those of the late Apulian type known as Gnathian ware, at least to judge from the illustrations in D. M. Robinson and C. G. Harcum, *A Catalogue of the Greek Vases in the Royal Ontario Museum* (Toronto, 1930), nos. 511–515, pp. 243–44, pl. LXXXVIII (cf. especially the wide lattice pattern on no. 515). Most of these date to the third century B.C. See also, M. Bernardini, *Vasi dello Stile di Gnathia, Vasi a Vernice Nera* (Bari, n.d.), pl. 50.1–5 (especially the "piccola lekythos" which is no. 5 of that pl.); and Chr. Blinkenberg and K. F. Johansen, *CVA, Denmark, Copenhague: Musée National*, fasc. 5 (Paris, 1931), p. 180 with pl. 232.5–8. All of these are undated, but three are pronounced as coming from Bari. Our specimen has less decoration than is usual for its class, and given the great numbers and wide distribution of lekythoi of this type, we assign this as Gnathian ware only tentatively. Its date is probably the third century B.C., but certitude is impossible.

Miscellaneous Vases
(Barbara L. Gunn and A. J. Heisserer)

102 Small Attic banded olpe

Ca. 500 B.C.
Height, 8.4 cm; maximum diameter, 5.9 cm, diameter at rim, 4.2 cm (C55–56/3)

This small olpe is made of fine, hard, pinkish-red clay and covered with a thin red glaze except for the base, which is left unglazed. It has a flat base, swelling body, short and wide neck, flaring lip, and strap handle. A line in black paint encircles the body at the point where the handle joins the body. A second band decorates the exterior and interior edges of the lip, while a third appears on the outer portion of the handle. It was acquired in the Athens market, but provenance is uncertain.

Small olpai are classed in three categories—banded, black and footless, and black and

footed—but are very uniform and consistent in size, shape, and history. The presence of certain black glaze inscriptions on the shoulder of banded olpai shows that this class served as measures; one small olpe has been shown to hold one kotyle, and other examples probably held fractional amounts. Black-glazed olpai may also have been used as measures. E. Vanderpool, *Hesperia* 15 (1946): 276; B. Sparkes and L. Salcott, *Black and Plain Pottery of the 6th, 5th, and 4th Centuries B.C.: Athenian Agora*, vol. 12 (Princeton, N.J., 1970), p. 78 with n. 9. This example is similar in shape to no. 258, pl. 17, in ibid., but its dimensions correspond almost exactly to those of their no. 257, pl. 12. All the Athenian agora banded olpai are dated to ca. 500 B.C. Ibid., p. 254.

103 Attic black-glazed stemmed dish

Late sixth through mid-fifth century B.C.
Height, 8.6 cm; diameter at lip, 19.7 cm (C53–54/6)

Composed of hard, fine, pinkish-buff clay and covered with a black glaze, which has partially worn away, this vessel is called both a stemmed dish and a handleless kylix. It has a rather shallow bowl on a short stem and a discoid foot with an almost straight edge. The grooved lip curves

inward sharply and is slightly offset on the exterior. The edge of the stem where it ends on the top of the foot is reserved; the edge and hollow interior of the underside of the foot are also reserved. There is a groove on the upper surface of the foot as well as on the vessel wall below the lip. The dish is of Cypriote provenance (ex Kolokasides coll.).

Although the stemmed dish is not very common in Attic black-glazed ware (J. Boardman, *BSA* 53–54 [1958–59]: 179; L. Salcott, *Hesperia* 5 [1936]: 341), it has appeared in the Athenian agora material from the late sixth century to the second quarter of the fifth century B.C. The large version of the stemmed cup was probably used as a fruit and nut dish or, less likely, as a pyxis. Our specimen does not have a reserved rim, as is usual on pyxides, but does have a groove on the lip. B. Sparkes and L. Salcott, *Black and Plain Pottery of the 6th, 5th, and 4th Centuries B.C.: Athenian Agora*, vol. 12 (Princeton, N.J., 1970), p. 138. The Stovall dish clearly belongs to the class of convex and large stemmed dishes. Usually specimens of this class have a wide shallow bowl with thickened lip and rest on a broad stem with a broad, flat foot. The outer edge of the foot is reserved, as is the resting surface and the center of the underside of the stem. An early version from ca. 550 B.C. has a bulging lip that is sharply undercut and a broad, flat foot. As the series develops, the sharply undercut lip is replaced by a slight, lightly undercut thickening and eventually by an incised groove at the bottom of the lip. The bowl becomes deeper and the foot gradually begins to slope downward from the stem to the outer edge. Ibid., pp. 138–39; E. Vanderpool, *Hesperia* 15 (1946): 276. Our example is significantly different from both early and late examples in the Athenian agora series.

It has the broad, shallow bowl, flat foot, and rather slender stem of the early type, but the rim is only very slightly offset and also has a groove below. Furthermore, it varies from the entire Athenian agora series in that it has an incurving lip, a stem that terminates at the top of the base, and an unreserved foot edge. It may be, however, a later version of the black-glazed stemmed dish. Fig. 198 in Boardman, *BSA* 53–54 (1958–59): 179, shows a rim section from a mid-fifth-century dish that has an incurving lip and an exterior groove like ours; but since the foot of this dish illustrated in Boardman has not been reconstructed, it is uncertain whether it shares further similarities with ours. In general, it may be said that our stemmed dish dates at least from the mid-fifth century B.C., and it may even be earlier.

104 Attic black-glazed stamped amphoriskos

Late fifth century B.C.
Height, 16.4 cm; diameter, 7.7 cm (C55–56/2)

This amphoriskos, acquired in the Athens market, is made from fine, hard, pink clay and covered with a good black glaze. Its shape is characterized by a collared, cup-shaped mouth, a slender neck, two handles from the shoulder to the neck, an egg-shaped body, and a foot in several degrees. Ridges are present where the neck joins the body and the mouth. Two thin reserved lines decorate the foot and the bottom edge of the collar of the mouth. The primary decoration, stamped and lightly ribbed, consists of a band of ovules and a meander band around the base of the neck on the shoulder, ribbed arches with three palmettes inside each arch, and what seems to be another palmette at the side of the base of each arch. This vertical scheme of decoration is then broken with a meander band, from which ten pairs of ribbed lines reach to the base.

Small curls are placed at the upper edges of the arches in the upper portion of the decoration.

This shape is classified by Gisela N. A. Richter and M. Milne (*Shapes and Names of Athenian Vases* [New York, 1935], p. 4) as a Type IId amphora, "Type II" because the neck is set off from the body, "d" because of the pointed base. The small amphora with a pointed base, which is an imitation of large pointed oil and wine jars, appeared in Attica in the sixth century B.C. However, the shape of this jar is a late fifth-century type, associated with sixth-century types only in that both imitate larger pointed amphoras. This shape spans the period from 430 B.C. into the beginning of the fourth century, and probably began in Red-figure. The vase was used as a container for perfumed oil and was supported by a small ring. Brian Sparkes and Lucy Salcott, *Black and Plain Pottery of the 6th, 5th, and 4th Centuries B.C.: Athenian Agora*, vol. 12 (Princeton, N.J., 1970), pp. 155–56, 180; J. D. Beazley, *BSA* 41 (1940–45): 10, 13. Containers for perfumed oil like lekythoi and amphoriskoi have a characteristic shape of mouth: the cup mouth, its top jutting inward slightly, serves as a basin in which the perfumed oil collects and from which the oil is taken by dipping a finger. Sparkes and Salcott, *Black and Plain Pottery*, pp. 150–51.

The decoration of this amphoriskos, in addition to its shape, indicates that it is a late fifth-century product. Vertical ribbing began in black by 480 B.C. and was fairly popular in the fifth and fourth centuries. In earlier works the arcs are separate from the ribbing, as in this specimen, and may have been executed with a stick after the grooving was completed. On later works the arc was joined to the ribs. Stamped decorations began to be used by Attic potters just before the middle of the fifth century. At first it was subsidiary to other decoration, whether Red-figure or ribbing, but by 430 B.C. stamping was usually the most important element of the pattern on a stamped vase. The stamps seem to have been convex and made from a mold. The impression was obtained by applying the stamp at an angle and then rotating the stamp. When applied carefully this would result in a perfect stamp, but even on the most carefully executed examples there are frequently some faulty strikes. Ibid., pp. 17–18, 21–23, 28; P. Corbett, *Hesperia* 24 (1955): 172–73. In the early years of the Attic stamping technique, many different motifs and

schemes of composition were tried, but "by the last quarter of the fifth century impressed decoration had become largely a matter of stereotyped formulae." P. Corbett, *Hesperia* 18 (1949): 304. This was certainly true of amphoriskoi, whose closed shape limited the possible schemes of decoration. A meander band was often placed just below the middle of the vase, as on this one and on three in Copenhagen. Chr. Blinkenberg and K. F. Johansen, *CVA, Denmark, Copenhague: Musée National*, fasc. 4 (Paris, 1931), p. 140 with pl. 179.8, 9, 11). On later examples this feature is replaced by three grooves. The shoulders invariably were decorated with ovules; the remainder of the decoration varied somewhat but almost always consisted of some sort of palmette design.

Several elements of its decoration suggest that the Stovall example may be early in the series of stamped amphoriskoi. The generally good execution of the stamping is one sign, although in itself is by no means definitive. The meander band is a relatively early feature, while the neat palmettes, broadly curved from the top to the base, are also probably no later than the end of the fifth century (Sparkes and Salcott, *Black and Plain Pottery*, p. 25; L. Salcott, *Hesperia* 4 (1935): 490–91. This amphoriskos may be placed in the late fifth century or early fourth century on the basis of its shape, and, to judge from the stamped and ribbed decoration, should be placed early in that period, ca. 430–410 B.C.

105 Hellenistic kantharos

Early Hellenistic period, ca. 325–250 B.C.
Height, 7.5 cm; diameter at lip, 7 cm (C56–57/3)

A red-glazed cup with two vertical handles and low ring foot; lime deposit on top of one handle and on large portion of one side. There are two incised horizontal lines at level of upper handle attachment, one at level of lower handle attachment.

Because cups of this type were such common ware during Hellenistic times, and because the provenance of this one is unknown, it is impossible to suggest any specific period with certitude. The shape of the Stovall kantharos, however, is virtually identical with a cup illustrated in fig. 21.20 in Olog Vessberg and Alfred Westholm, *The Swedish Cyprus Expedition*, vol. 4, pt. 3, *The Hellenistic and Roman Periods* (Lund, 1956), which is dated to the Hellenistic I Period, ca. 325–150 B.C. (pp. 55–57, 73). Similar incised

lines are found on two Corinthian Hellenistic cups, nos. 378 and 380, dated respectively to 300 and 325 B.C., in G. Roger Edwards, *Corinthian Hellenistic Pottery: Corinth*, vol. 7, pt. 3 (Princeton, N.J., 1975), p. 76 with pl. 52; and on another similar cup, but which is black-glazed, dated to the middle of the third century B.C., in P. V. C. Baur, *Catalogue of the Rebecca Darlington Stoddard Collection* (New Haven, Conn., 1922), no. 495, fig. 47. Without further comparative examples, we suggest that our kantharos dates from the early Hellenistic period.

106   Rim lug from a Hellenistic brazier

Preserved height, 14.5 cm; preserved diameter, 14.2 cm
  (C57–58/11/7)

This fragment, found in the excavations of the Athenian agora, is made from coarse, red, micaceous clay. It constituted one of three rim lugs with which its Hellenistic brazier held a cooking pot. A satyr's face decorates the lug; his projecting beard held the pot. This lug is from a brazier of the commonest type in Hellenistic times. According to one description, these braziers had a rather large stand with a bowl-shaped container for coals; the rim of the brazier had protuberances, called rim lugs, to support the cooking pot, and the stand had vents in the bottom to provide the draft. B. A. Sparkes, *JHS* 82 (1962): 131. A slightly different description of the Hellenistic brazier provides it with a higher, hollow stand surrounded by a channel. H. A. Thompson, *Hesperia* 3 (1934): 421. This same author suggests that these braziers provided "a small but significant indication of the community of ways and manners that developed in Hellenistic times." Ibid., p. 468. It seems likely that these common braziers were not made in Athens, to

judge from the nature of the clay, the comparatively small number of specimens in Athens, and the failure to discover molds for the masks in Athens. D. Burr, *Hesperia* 2 (1933): 190; Thompson, *Hesperia* 3 (1934): 467. Burr suggests that these Hellenistic braziers originated from a large manufacturing center in Asia Minor, and Thompson proposes a source in the Aegean islands, perhaps at Delos, where such objects are especially frequent finds. Fig. 108 in Thompson shows one reconstruction of a Hellenistic brazier, while pl. VI.6 in Sparkes (*JHS* 82) gives a slightly different version. The rim lugs on D76 in Thompson's fig. 109 in *Hesperia* 3 (1934): 468 are quite similar to ours, and his specimen comes from groups of braziers dated to the second and early first century B.C.

107   Oinochoe (Rhodian?)

Hellenistic
Height with handle, 29.7 cm, without handle, 26.8 cm;
  maximum diameter, 18 cm, diameter at base, 10 cm
  (C57–58/5)

Soft, buff clay; reddish glaze; plump body, flaring foot; broad neck with a slight ridge near the trefoil mouth. Double-rolled handle rising above the lip. Decoration in white paint: bands of white around the body; rosettes on shoulder; dots at the base of the neck and on the slight ridge. Handle broken and mended. Reported as being probably Rhodian.

It is difficult to determine even an approximate date for this jug because its shape was extremely long-lived. For example, the shape was rather common among the East Greeks in the archaic period. Cf. two cases with very similar shape in D. M. Robinson and C. G. Harcum, *A Catalogue of the Greek Vases in the Royal Ontario Museum* (Toronto, 1930), pp. 66–68, nos. 205 and 206, pl. XVIII. The absence of prominent painted decorative motifs, however, likely suggests that this vessel is neither Archaic nor Classical (unless classified as ordinary household ware from those periods), while its slightly shiny red surface immediately prompts assigning it a Hellenistic date. Cook, GPP, p. 211. Pottery of this kind during the Hellenistic era has often been called "Pergamene," a term that has been attacked as being too general and misleading. O. Vessberg and A. Westholm, *The Swedish Cyprus Expedition*, vol. 4, pt. 3, *The Hellenistic and Roman Periods* (Lund, 1956), pp. 53–54. These same authors illustrate two jugs with trefoil mouth (fig. 23.7–8) that are quite close in shape to ours (al-

though theirs are covered with lotus flowers and other elements) and are dated to the Hellenistic I period (ca. 325–150 B.C.). The shape lasted into the Roman era, as one sees from two examples in Henry S. Robinson, *Pottery of the Roman Period: Athenian Agora*, vol. 5 (Princeton, N.J., 1959), M 42, pl. 20 (late first and second half of the second century A.D.) and K 83, pl. 14 (middle of the third century A.D.). In the face of these examples, no one of which truly parallels the Stovall oinochoe, it is reasonable to suggest merely a general Hellenistic date and to venture nothing about its possible place of origin.

Small Bowls and Saltcellars
(Barbara L. Gunn)

Small bowls and saltcellars were common household items during the classical period. They were used primarily to place salt and other condiments on the table, but were also convenient for other functions such as paintpots, funnels or door knockers, strainers, and possibly targets in the after-dinner game of Kottabos. A popular game in classical Greece, Kottabos in one variant consisted of a player throwing wine lees from a spinning cup in an attempt to sink small bowls floating on water in a lekane. B. Sparkes and L. Salcott, *Black and Plain Pottery of the 6th, 5th, and 4th Centuries B.C.: Athenian Agora*, vol. 12 (Princeton, N.J., 1970), p. 132; B. Sparkes, *Archaeology* 13 (1960): 202–207. The shapes of the small bowls vary considerably, but the contents remain about the same throughout the classical period, and it is quite possible that the small bowl was a measure as well as a shape. Both small bowls and saltcellars were uncommon in the Hellenistic and Roman eras, perhaps because the greater use of seasonings reduced the need for separate sauce dishes at the table. Sparkes and Salcott, *Black and Plain Pottery*.

Several different shapes are represented among the examples at the Stovall Museum. They are catalogued in roughly chronological order, but consistency and certainty in identification are not always possible with such common and long-lived shapes.

108   Small bowl

Middle of the fifth century B.C.
Height, 3.4 cm; diameter at rim, 8.4 cm (C85/1/1)

Fine, hard, pink clay; black glaze, partially misfired; heavy bowl; upper sides and the rim incurv-

Classical and Hellenistic bowls and saltcellars. *Above, left to right*: nos. 111, 110, 113, 108. *Below, left to right*: nos. 109, 112, 114.

ing slightly; rather high ring foot; rim chipped; from the Athenian agora excavations.

The underside is decorated like no. 876, pl. 33, in B. Sparkes and L. Salcott, *Black and Plain Pottery of the 6th, 5th, and 4th Centuries B.C.: Athenian Agora*, vol. 12 (Princeton, N.J., 1970), p. 132, and this example probably is a member of the early and heavy class of small bowls. Even though this class is not a homogeneous category, it is generally characterized by a heavy bowl, thick rim, and solid foot. The Stovall small bowl resembles the later examples of this type, as it has a slightly incurving rim and a less marked incurve of the wall toward the foot. The class dates in general from the second and third quarters of the fifth century B.C., and this specimen probably should be assigned to the third quarter of that century. Ibid., p. 134.

109   Saltcellar

Ca. 425 B.C.
Height, 2.3 cm; diameter at base, 6.3 cm (C53–54/35)

Hard, fine, pink clay; black glaze, partially misfired; flat, reserved base; convex wall with lip curving inward; deep bowl with a slight point at the center bottom; provenance unknown.

This example belongs to the class of convex-walled saltcellars. The earlier variety of this class has a recessed underside, while the later version has a flat underside like ours. The shape of this one seems to occur late in the series of convex-walled saltcellars with flat bases, and therefore it

probably should be dated to the second half of the fifth century, perhaps ca. 425 B.C. It resembles nos. 897 and 898, pl. 34, in ibid. (with pp. 135–36, 299–300).

110   Fragmentary saltcellar

Latter half of the fifth century B.C.
Height, 2.8 cm; diameter at base, 6.2 cm (C85/2/1)

Similar to no. 109 but the base is heavier and the bowl is flatter inside; glazed base; reserved groove near the edge and two reserved circles around the center; unreserved groove near the center; section of rim and base missing; from the Athenian agora excavations.

This convex-walled saltcellar is unusual because the base is glazed, whereas Sparkes and Salcott assert that all the agora examples of this type are reserved on the base. Nevertheless, this sherd is Attic, as indicated by its provenance and clay. The profile is similar to no. 896, pl. 34, in ibid. The grooves on the underside may be simply decorative, or may indicate relatively close connections with the earlier variant of convex-walled saltcellars, which have recessed undersides. The Stovall piece probably dates from the mid to late fifth century B.C. Ibid., pp. 135–36.

111   Fragment of a small bowl

Ca. 400 B.C.
Height, 2.2 cm; diameter unobtainable (C85/3/1)

Hard, fine, pink clay; black glaze; low bowl with rounded lip; ring base projecting outward; reserved areas just above the foot, on the bottom edge of the foot, and in the center of the foot; from the Athenian agora excavations.

This sherd belongs to a class of later and light small bowls, which developed from the earlier heavy versions. It is characterized by a plain rim, rounded above, about the same thickness as the wall; the bowl is usually low and broad, as here, and the resting surface and underside are reserved. The area at the junction of the wall and foot is also sometimes reserved, again as on this one, because it was difficult to glaze with a brush as the wheel turned, although when executed carefully the technique produced a most effective decoration. In the late fifth and fourth centuries B.C., when the practice of dipping came into use, this area was scraped to provide decoration, even though the practical purpose of this unglazed area was outlived. The shape began in the late fifth century, probably ca. 430 B.C., and lasted into the very early years of the fourth century. Our sherd exhibits a profile similar to that of no. 868, pl. 33, in ibid. (with pp. 17–18, 134).

112 Saltcellar

Second half of the fourth century B.C.
Height, 2.8 cm; diameter at rim, 7.2 cm (C39–40/20)

Hard, fine, pink clay; poor black glaze, misfired in spots; small reserved ring foot with a point in the center; rather steep sides, which curve inward at lip; provenance unknown.

This object may be a small bowl, but it seems to resemble the late series of footed saltcellars more than any other category. A few footed saltcellars appear late in the fifth century with a disc foot and low bowl, and an even later series has a ring foot. Within this later series the broad resting surface of the foot becomes less broad, the resting surface itself being grooved. In addition, the walls become higher and thinner and, in the later examples, the rim is more incurving. The Stovall piece resembles these late examples from the second series of footed saltcellars. Since specimens with a ring foot belong predominantly to the second and third quarters of the fourth century, the later examples of this series, such as this one, probably date to the second half of the fourth century B.C. Ibid., pp. 137–38.

113 Saltcellar

Latter part of the fourth century B.C.
Height, 2.9 cm; diameter at base, 6.6 cm (C85/4/1)

Hard, fine, pink clay; reddish glaze fired black in places; ring foot with slightly convex base; concave sides; edge of rim chipped; from the Athenian agora excavations.

This object is an almost intact concave-sided saltcellar. (It can also be labeled a pyxis.) The recessed underside places this example in the later series of concave-sided saltcellars. Although there are a few slightly earlier examples, the series begins in the late fifth century but becomes common only during the fourth century, being most popular in the second and third quarters of that period. This piece, which is very similar to no. 937, fig. 9, in ibid. (with pp. 136–37, 302), probably dates to the latter part of the fourth century B.C.

114 Small bowl

Hellenistic
Height, 2.4 cm; diameter at rim, 8.2 cm (C39–40/25)

Hard, fine, pink clay; poor black glaze; ring foot, partially glazed; sharply incurving rim that comes to a point just below the top and then angles up and inward; thin walls; obvious wheel marks; provenance unknown.

The lip of this small bowl is shaped in a manner similar to nos. 854 and 855, pl. 33, in ibid., but it has high, sharply angled sides and a smaller foot. Since it does not seem to fit into any of the categories arranged by Sparkes and Salcott, it may be an early Hellenistic version of the small bowl with incurving rim. H. Thompson (*Hesperia* 3 [1934]: 432–34) notes that in the Hellenistic period there was a tendency in black-glaze pottery toward light, angular shapes in imitation of metallic forms; he also points out the careless execution common in Hellenistic Attic black-glaze wares, a feature that led to visible wheel marks inside and out. The light construction, angular shape, and visible wheel marks of ours suggest that it is probably an early Hellenistic example, although this is by no means certain.

Unguentaria
(Barbara L. Gunn)

For a general discussion of the unguentarium, see no. 71 above under Cypriote Plain White ware ("Cypriote Iron Age"). All the dates given below are tentative because of the difficulty of dating unguentaria outside a series.

115 Small fusiform unguentarium

Late Hellenistic, probably second or first centuries B.C.
Height, 9.1 cm; diameter, 2.9 cm (C39–40/3)

Hellenistic unguentaria. *Left to right*: nos. 119, 115, 118 (*below, center*), 116, 117.

This small vessel, of unknown provenance, is made of yellowish-brown clay and covered with a white slip. It has the typical fusiform unguentarium shape, but the body is comparatively slender and the mouth is relatively wide. These features indicate a relatively late date, probably the second or first century B.C. H. Thompson, *Hesperia* 3 (1934): 472–73.

116   Small fusiform unguentarium

Second century or early first century B.C.
Height, 9.8 cm; diameter, 3.2 cm (C39–40/24)

This vessel, again of unknown provenance, is made of fine, hard, reddish-brown clay and is covered with a red slip that is painted or misfired black in places. The mouth is small in comparison to the foot. The shape of this unguentarium is like those of the second and the beginning of the first century B.C. illustrated in figs. 210–11 of Ph. Bruneau's article in *BCH* 94 (1970): 516–17. However, the mouth is smaller on this specimen than on any of those illustrated. This unguentarium may be assigned a tentative date in the second or early first century B.C.

117   Unguentarium

Second half of the second century or first half of the first
     century B.C.
Preserved height, 13.8 cm; diameter, 3.9 cm (C85/5/1)

Found during the excavations of the Athenian agora, this vessel is made of coarse clay containing much foreign matter and is fired gray throughout; it is broken at the neck. It is deco-

rated with two thin bands of white paint, and its shape is similar to that in ibid., fig. 210:58.8, an example from Argos dated in the second half of the second century B.C. The slender shape and ash-gray clay are indications of a late date in Athens. Thompson, *Hesperia* 3 (1934): 472–73. Thus, our unguentarium is assigned a date in the second half of the second century or the first half of the first century B.C.

118   Small unguentarium

Second–first centuries B.C.
Preserved height, 5.6 cm; diameter, 2.6 cm (C85/6/1)

The clay and decoration here are like those of the previous unguentarium (no. 117), except that this small example has a third encircling band of paint, the usual number on such unguentaria from Athens. It too comes from the excavations of the Athenian agora and is broken at the neck. The clay indicates a late date, but the plumper shape may indicate a slightly earlier date than the previous piece. Ibid.

119   Unguentarium

Probably third or second century B.C.
Preserved height, 16.9 cm; diameter, 6.2 cm (C85/7/1)

This fragment of a large unguentarium is composed of fine, red clay and is covered with a brown slip; again, from the excavations of the Athenian agora and broken at the neck. The relatively plump shape of the body and the type of clay indicate that this vessel is relatively early, probably third or second centuries B.C. Ibid.

ETRUSCAN OBJECTS

The Stovall Museum's collection of artifacts from the Etruscan civilization is quite small, but its possession of three most interesting bronze figures has insured their inclusion in this catalogue. Two of these pieces were borrowed by Mario A. Del Chiaro for an exhibition in Santa Barbara during 1981, and we are pleased now to bring them to the attention of a wider public.

The culture that became predominant in central Italy, roughly between the Arno and Tiber rivers and called today Tuscany, is unique in the annals of man. The name Etruscan is given to the people in this area, called Etruria by the ancient Romans. Their culture, which held greatest sway in the period from ca. 800 to 500 B.C. but continued for many centuries after this until finally absorbed by the Roman civilization to its south, has fascinated historians and archaeologists for many centuries. With its unusual art, religion, and language, it is unlike anything else in the history of Italy. Furthermore, even though the Etruscan language was written in a Greek script, and thus Etruscan names can be pronounced with some accuracy, the language has not yet been fully deciphered; even the discovery of Etruscan inscriptions in the last quarter century has not provided the key to unlock completely the mysteries of this language. For these reasons the study of the artistic changes in various Etruscan artifacts has come to occupy a foremost place in our understanding of this remarkable ancient civilization.

Bronzes

(MARIO A. DEL CHIARO)

120 Reclining satyr

Mid-fifth century B.C.
Length, 5.2 cm; height, 3.6 cm (C48–49/4)

This charming reclining banqueter who must be a satyr to judge by the large and crudely executed ears (best seen at the right side of the head) rests on his left side with weight supported by the left elbow, the left forearm extended, with hand (summarily indicated or damaged) upraised as if originally intended to hold a patera or drinking cup. The right arm rests along his right side, the hand placed gently near the right knee. He is dressed solely in a heavy mantle which is draped over the lower part of the body, thereby presenting a bare torso and exposed feet. The satyr is not young (i.e., clean-shaven) but old/mature (i.e., bearded) with the short beard and hair rendered in neat, vertical striations that yet disclose a bead or plait texture. The hair is worn short at the nape of the neck and, above the forehead, is styled in bangs which at first glance resemble a diadem. The satyr's eyes are large and clearly defined by raised ridges which show an almond-shaped configuration retained from the Archaic period. His mouth is large, the lips full.

Reclining satyrs—and more normal banqueters in general—are not uncommon as decorative elements to be placed along the rim of large bronze vessels (cauldrons and the like) or on rings often found near the base of bronze tripods. See *Studi Etruschi* 10 (1936): pl. 3. The satyr is rather squat and compact with its awkward proportioning of heavy torso and stunted

legs, a feature which recalls the reclining figures found on the lids of countless Etruscan cinerary urns as well as stone sarcophagi. M. Del Chiaro, *Etruscan Art from West Coast Collections* (Santa Barbara, Calif., 1967), nos. 14, 18, 20 and 23; G. Giglioli, *L'Arte etrusca* (Milano, 1935), pls. CCCXCIX–CCCCI. The Stovall satyr unquestionably descends from the earlier, clearly Archaic counterparts of more elegant proportions. M. Del Chiaro, *Etruscan Art*, no. 44; G. Richter, *Handbook of the Etruscan Collection: Metropolitan Museum of Art* (New York, 1940), figs. 76–77; A. Boethius et al., *Etruscan Culture, Land, and People* (Malmö, 1962), fig. 422. An intermediary or link with the latter more graceful type may be offered by an example in Verona, who also reclines on his left elbow but who extends his right arm, with patera (or phiale) in hand. L. Franzoni, *Bronzetti etruschi e italici del Museo Archeologico di Verona* (Verona, 1980), no. 188.

121 Patera (pan) handle

Early fourth century B.C.
Maximum length, 15 cm (C57–58/13/23)

Although it may be argued that this human-shaped handle served a bronze mirror, as is commonly encountered for Greek and South Italian mirrors, it proves a relatively rare occurrence among the Etruscans, who favored handles of a totally different character for their mirrors. One rare example in Paris (Cabinet des Médailles, inv. no. 1326) represents a winged female. D. Rebuffat-Emmanuel, *Le miroir étrusque d'après la collection du Cabinet des Médailles* (Paris, 1973), pl. 44 bis. They did, however, share with the Greeks a special fondness for anthropomorphic handles on paterae (sometimes phialae). See

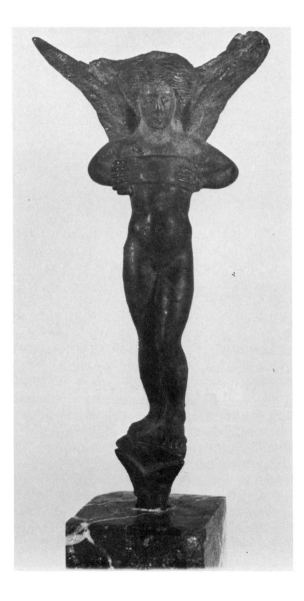

M. Gjødsen, *Acta Archeologica* 15 (1944): 170–74; P. Amandry, *Monuments et Mémoires: Fondation Piot* 47 (1953): 47–70; U. Jantzen, *Berlinwinckel-mansprogram* 114 (1958): 5–29. This handle in the form of a nude and winged female is, in essence, a standing figure who holds a broad scroll-like band across her breasts. The "scroll" is blank, i.e., does not bear an inscription as known from an Etruscan mirror in the British Museum engraved with a scene in which a winged, but draped, female figure holds an open scroll showing the word "Lasa" within the inscription. See A. Rallo, *Lasa: iconografia e esegesi* (Florence, 1974), pl. 1; for the symbolism of the Etruscan scroll—an irrevocable decision of Fate—see F. De Ruyt, *Charon, démon étrusque de la mort* (Brussels, 1934), pp. 158–62; J. Heurgon, *La vie quotidienne chez les étrusques* (Paris, 1961), p. 274. In such a case, some clue would have been present to aid identification of the winged maiden as a *Lasa* or *Vanth*, each a unique Etruscan minor deity or demon. Rallo, *Lasa*, in which the author discusses and illustrates various aspects of both *Lasa* and *Vanth*; see also R. Enking, *Mitteilungen des deutschen archäologischen Instituts. Römische Abteilungen* 58 (1943): 48–64. It may very well be, however, that the winged female is simply putting on her bra (*strophion*) which, much in the manner of our 1920s era, was a broad sashlike cloth band wrapped around the upper body at the breasts.

The wings spring upward and outward from the back in a solid mass close to the neck and solidly serve to cradle the curve of the pan (patera) proper at a point where the handle was attached. Unfortunately, the bronze is not sharp and clear in its modeling and detailing, especially in the rendering of the hair, feathers of the wings, and facial features. The feet, with their heels close together and the toes pointed outward, stand on a long tapering base which is three-sided in cross section and, significantly, pierced by a hole intended to take a metal ring, thong, or the like for hanging. See G. Giglioli, *L'arte etrusca* (Milan, 1935), pl. CCLXIII, 1; D. Mitten and S. Doeringer, *Master Bronzes of the Classical World* (Mainz, 1968), no. 223. A number of Etruscan patera handles are known, and among those representing women (wingless or winged) some may hold a mirror, but none a scroll, or a cloth bra (for wingless women). See A. Hus, *Les bronzes étrusques* (Brussels, 1975), pl. 71; *Greek, Etruscan, and Roman Art: Boston*

Museum of Fine Arts (Boston, 1963), fig. 193; for winged women see Giglioli, *L'arte etrusca*, pl. CCCXIII, 3 and 4 (draped); R. Teitz, *Masterpieces of Etruscan Art* (Worcester, Mass., 1967), no. 84 (nude); E. Fiumi, *Volterra, Il Museo Etrusco* (Pisa, 1969), fig. 124 (nude) and fig. 167 (draped); *Studi Etruschi* 40 (1972): pl. LXXXIV (nude); an especially handsome example in *Bulletin of the Cleveland Museum of Art* 34 (1947): cover and pp. 164–66 (nude); D. K. Hill, *Greek and Roman Metalware in the Walters Art Gallery* (Baltimore, Md., 1976, pl. 40 (nude). Of the winged specimens, the closest parallel to the Stovall Museum's figure may be the patera handle in the Walters Art Gallery, Baltimore, Md., which reveals similar short, narrow, and strongly upswept wings, as well as a tight and slender aspect to the body of the nude maiden. Hill, *Metalware*; likewise, a handle in the British Museum, on which see Rallo, *Lasa*, pl. 36, fig. 1.

Identification of the female figure who comprises the handle presents a difficult task. Is she a *Lasa* or a *Vanth*? The former, once exclusively associated with the Etruscan goddess of Love, *Turan* (Aphrodite or Venus) is her attendant who often bears cosmetic paraphernalia (alabastron, or vase containing perfumed oil, its dipstick, mirror, and the like). Investigation of the *Lasa* by A. Rallo, however, has disclosed a multifaceted being who, in some of her aspects, can be linked with the underworld. *Vanth* figures, on the other hand, are always depicted as partially or fully clothed and, from their context, seem to be exclusively tied to the underworld and the cult of the dead. Hence, the popularity of *Vanth* in the reliefs which decorated Etruscan sarcophagi and cinerary urns on which one or more *Vanth* figures carry a torch, e.g., Giglioli, *Metalware*, pl. 410, 1–3. In view of the nudity of the woman on this patera handle and the uninscribed scroll she holds across her breasts, it may be best to identify the figure as a *Lasa*.

Source: Mario Del Chiaro, *Re-Exhumed Etruscan Bronzes* (Santa Barbara, Calif., 1981), pp. 27–29, no. 25, with revisions made by Del Chiaro *per ep.*

122   Aplu (Apollo) with lyre

Fourth century B.C.
Height, 8.5 cm (C57–58/13/25)

This statuette is one of the most interesting specimens of Etruscan bronzes because of the rarity of Etruscan divinities in bronze sculpture other

than *Menrva* and *Hercle*. Rather than "youth" with lyre, the identification *Aplu* is more apt for a small bronze of such fine workmanship. Although the god is encountered in Etruscan vase painting and bronze engraving with or without his lyre or *kythera*, in this instance he holds the lyre with his left hand which is slipped under a strap at the wrist, while his right holds the *plectrum* or picklike object. Only three other Etruscan bronze statuettes are known to us which may portray *Aplu*, and one of these may be a Muse. All are markedly different in style. See *Memoirs of the American Academy in Rome*, vol. 21 (1953), p. 92, fig. 6; *Archeologia Classica* 20 (1968): pl. LXX, fig. 1, perhaps "Muse" rather than Apollo, as suggested by Mario Torelli; *Studi Etruschi* 42 (1974): pl. IX, figs. d and e. On the evidence of style—the shape and detailing of face, hair, and the general solid and stocky character of the body—the statuette may be a product of an Etruscan center renowned for its bronzes, namely, Vulci. K. Neuegebauer, *Archäologisches Anzeiger* 38–39 (1923–24): 302ff.; M. Guarducci, *Studi Etruschi*

10 (1936): 15ff.; V. Ferraguti, *Studi Etruschi* 11 (1937): 107–20; P. J. Riis, *Tyrrenika* (Copenhagen, 1941), Chapter 8; G. Fischetti, *Studi Etruschi* 18 (1944): 9–27; J. Jannot, *Revue Archéologique* (1977): 3–22. A fully clothed reclining figure with lyre in the British Museum (inv. no. 1916.3–28.17) cannot be regarded as *Aplu* but, as Sybille Haynes rightly judged, must be a musician-banqueter of a type which may have decorated the rim of a bronze vessel used for *symposia*. See *The British Museum Quarterly* 32 (1966): pl. XXXV. In all probability, this *bronzetto* served as a decorative finial to a candelabrum.

Source: Mario Del Chiaro, *Re-Exhumed Etruscan Bronzes* (Santa Barbara, Calif., 1981), pp. 15–16, no. 7, from which the foregoing description has been taken with the author's permission.

Attic black-figured eye cup (no. 84), last quarter of
sixth century B.C. Above: side A; below: side B. (Stovall
Museum acc. no. C47-48/1.)

Attic black-figured neck amphora (no. 85), side A. (Stovall Museum acc. no. C45-46/5.)

Attic black-figured neck amphora (no. 85), side B. (Stovall Museum acc. no. C45-46/5.)

Left: Syro-Palestinian toilet bottle (no. 167). (Stovall Museum acc. no. C48-49/9.) Center: Roman Palestine jug (no. 179). (Stovall Museum acc. no. C49-50/2.)

Right: Syro-Palestinian flaring rim jar (no. 172). (Stovall Museum acc. no. C45-46/16.)

Pottery

(BARBARA L. GUNN)

Etruscan Bucchero Vases

Etruscan bucchero ware is a type of pottery in which the clay is black or gray throughout. This distinctive fabric was produced by firing the vases in a low, smoking fire in order to reduce the iron oxides and carbon in the clay. See O. Brendel, *Etruscan Art* (New York, 1978), p. 77; Th. Rasmussen, *Bucchero Pottery from Southern Etruria* (Cambridge, 1979), p. 2. This technique seems to have developed by improving the earlier indigenous impasto technique. Etruscan bucchero appeared before the middle of the seventh century B.C., probably as early as ca. 675–665 B.C. Cerveteri seems to have been the pioneer in this technique, but several regional styles developed, although only the South Etruscan style has been identified. Rasmussen, *Bucchero Pottery*, pp. 1–5. As with many types of Etruscan art, the finest vases, with their high metallic sheen and thin walls, were produced in the early years of the technique. The degeneration of the bucchero technique was fairly rapid, the walls becoming thicker and the sheen becoming dulled. Ibid., p. 3. Early decoration consisted predominantly of incision, but from ca. 730–700 B.C. the decoration of bucchero vases changed to low relief. Indeed, relief decoration was characteristic of sixth-century Etruscan bucchero. The early thin-walled ware is sometimes called *bucchero sottile* while the later, heavier type is labeled *bucchero pesante*. Brendel, *Etruscan Art*, pp. 66 and 77. The goblet or chalice was a very popular shape in bucchero, and the kyathos was a particularly varied and long-lived shape. Both the chalice and the kyathos are now believed to be derived from impasto shapes. Ibid., p. 79; R. M. Cook, *Greek Painted Pottery*, 2d ed. (London, 1972), pp. 152–53; Rasmussen, *Bucchero Pottery*, p. 76. Etruscan bucchero disappeared for the most part after the end of the sixth century B.C.

123 Chalice

Last quarter of the seventh century B.C.
Height, 11 cm; diameter at rim, 12.6 cm (C48–49/3)

This chalice is made from hard, fine, black clay; decorated with incision, it has a wide, hollow foot, a medium length, rather broad stem, a low bowl, and high, slightly convex rim. There is a ridge where the stem and bowl meet, as well as where the bowl and rim are carinated. The decoration is in the form of a vertical pattern of tongues, called arcading, circling the middle of the rim. The shape of this chalice seems close to those of Rasmussen's Type 2d, which was a common and long-lived type. The single ridge on the stem is the most important indication that the chalice should be assigned to Type 2d, but other signs include the similar placement of the ridge on Rasmussen's no. 142, pl. 28, and the comparatively short stem on no. 140, pl. 28. According to Th. Rasmussen in *Bucchero Pottery from South Etruria* (Cambridge, 1979), pp. 98–99 and pl. 28, this type dates to the last quarter of the seventh century and the first half of the sixth century B.C. The incision on our vase indicates that it is early in this series, probably from the last quarter of the seventh century. No. H109 in Walters's catalogue has a similarly incised pattern, which is labeled arcading. P. 230, pl. XIII in H. B. Walters, *Catalogue of the Greek and Etruscan*

Etruscan ware. *Left*: no. 123, chalice. *Right*: no. 125, miniature kyathos.

Vases in the British Museum, vol. 1, pt. 2, *Cypriote, Italian, and Etruscan Pottery* (London, 1912).

124   Chalice

Late seventh century or early sixth century B.C.
Height, 11.4 cm; diameter at rim, 14 cm (C48–49/2)

Composed of hard, fine, black clay, this chalice is decorated with three broad grooves near the top of the bowl, three ridges on the stem, and a ridge at the carination of the bowl and rim. It has a wide foot, relatively short stem, low bowl, and high rim; the point where the bowl and rim meet is carinated and has a glossier finish than the previous one (no. 123). With its three ridges on the stem, this chalice does not seem to fit into any

of the types listed by Rasmussen (see previous commentary on no. 123). However, R. M. Cook and C. B. R. Butchart (*PBSR* 17 (1949): 1–4) mention that chalices with three rather broad grooves around the outside of a lip with a diameter of ca. 14 cm are common and generally have a low foot; such chalices have been found in tomb groups containing Italo-Corinthian pottery from ca. 600 B.C. This seems to indicate that the Stovall chalice is probably from the late seventh or early sixth century B.C.

125   Miniature kyathos

Probably sixth or fifth century B.C.
Height with handle, 5.2 cm, without handle, 2.5 cm; diameter at rim, 5.1 cm (C53–54/41)

Made of hard, fine, black clay, this tiny kyathos is possibly handmade. It has a concave disk foot, carination at the point where the handle attaches to the body, a wide rim, and a high, strutted handle. Carinated cups with an elevated handle are common in impasto, and bucchero kyathoi derive ultimately from this source. However, kyathoi changed near the middle of the seventh century B.C., probably as a result of the influence of ivory chalices. These changes produced a sharper carination and a taller, straighter lip. This cup should be assigned to Rasmussen's kyathos Type 1e, which comprises miniature kyathoi. The vases of this type vary greatly with respect to their profile, in the handle as well as the body; they usually have a concave disk foot or base and are undecorated. Type 1e is common throughout the sixth and probably the fifth centuries B.C. Rasmussen, *Bucchero Pottery*, pp. 112–13.

126   Sherd

Late seventh or early sixth century B.C.
9.6 × 6.3 cm (C39–40/21)

Composed of the usual bucchero clay, this sherd appears to have impurities. It comes from a bucchero vessel that was curved both horizontally and vertically. A pair of narrow horizontal incised lines form the decoration, which lines may be an indication of an early date, perhaps in the late seventh century B.C. Groups of incised lines were ordinary features on the bowls of cups and on the cuplike kantharoi of Rasmussen's Type 2; they also occur on amphoras, oinochoai, and on some open shapes just below the rim. Ibid., p. 132.

Italo-Corinthian Vases

Italo-Corinthian ware is the name given to Etruscan imitations of Corinthian ware. Many Italo-Corinthian vases can be distinguished from Corinthian only by the character of the clay, while others are not very similar at all. Italo-Corinthian began around 700 B.C. with simple decorations on a few shapes, then expanded near the end of the century to a much wider scope of decoration and shape; it seems to have ended around the middle of the sixth century B.C. Technique and style vary widely, for example, the clay from a fine texture, which fires from a light cream to a medium brown, to a coarse, pink texture with a cream slip, which is used especially for the larger vases. Linear decoration on the round aryballos and the alabastron is common but performed with varying skill. R. M. Cook, *Greek Painted Pottery*, 2d ed. (London, 1972), pp. 148–51. The alabastron appeared in Protocorinthian ware a little earlier than the middle of the seventh century; its shape has an oriental origin, and it may have come to Corinth directly from the East. The pierced earlike handles, such as that on our no. 127, are one sign of this close relationship since they resemble the handles of Egyptian and oriental alabastra. The alabastron is the most common unguent vase of the late seventh century. The Early Corinthian shape is slim and piriform, with a pronounced inward curve at neck and a mouth rectangular in section. H. G. G. Payne, *Necrocorinthia* (Oxford, 1931), pp. 268–69, 281. The Italo-Corinthian version of the Early Corinthian alabastron in general retains this Early Corinthian shape, except that it is often flatter at the base. Cook, *Greek Painted Pottery*, p. 149. Later alabastra are generally much larger than the majority of late seventh-century examples. Near the end of the century alabastra begin to be displaced as the favorite unguent vase by the round aryballos; thus, Middle and Late Corinthian alabastra are relatively uncommon. The round aryballos began to appear in large numbers in the Early Corinthian period, and became the most popular unguent pot in the Middle and Late Corinthian periods. Corinthian aryballoi were produced in three main types, Payne's Shape A, Shape B, and Shape C (flat-bottomed). Linear aryballoi are usually of Shape B, which itself has two varieties—Shape B1 has a longer, slimmer neck and rounder body than Shape B2. Payne, *Necrocorinthia*, pp. 281 and

287. One common form of Italo-Corinthian aryballos is very close to Shape B1. Cook, *Greek Painted Pottery*, p. 149. All the Italo-Corinthian vases in the Stovall Museum have linear decorations.

127 Alabastron

Early Corinthian, ca. 625–600 B.C.
Height, 9.2 cm; diameter, 4.7 cm (C53–54/40)

Made of hard, fine, yellowish-buff clay and covered with a light slip, this alabastron carries a decoration painted in two shades of reddish-brown. It is shaped much like Early Corinthian alabastra, except that it has a flatter bottom: a piriform shape with an extremely short neck, an everted, almost discoid lip and vertical pierced lug attached from rim to shoulder. The decoration consists of two groups of parallel bands encircling the shoulder and above the base; two rows of dots and three narrow bands are between the thick bands. Vertical tongues decorate the neck, and horizontal dashes highlight the lug. Circular bands decorate the surface of the lip. In *Necrocorinthia* (Oxford, 1931), p. 284, fig. 121 bis), H. G. G. Payne distinguishes two types of linear Early Corinthian alabastra, one deriving from the Protocorinthian in its decorative scheme, the second with a decoration that is never found on Protocorinthian alabastra. This second type may have continued into the early sixth century B.C. Our small alabastron has a decoration that follows the scheme of this second type in some respects. Furthermore, R. M. Cook and C. B. R. Butchart, (*PBSR* 17 [1949]: 1–4 with pl. 1), in describing an alabastron with decoration and shape similar to ours and which they date to the late seventh century, state that the flat shape and the decoration "have an un-Corinthian

Italo-Corinthian vases. *Left to right*: no. 129, aryballos; no. 128, alabastron; no. 127, alabastron.

flavor." Because of the shape and decoration of the Stovall alabastron, it is to be assigned to the late seventh century, corresponding to the Early Corinthian period ca. 625–600 B.C. Ours is also remarkably similar in decoration to an Italo-Corinthian alabastron (undated) in Chr. Blinkenberg and K. F. Johansen, *CVA, Copenhague: Musée National*, fasc. 2 (Paris, 1927), p. 73 with pl. 94.12.

128 Alabastron

Late seventh century or perhaps early sixth century B.C.
Height, 5.7 cm; diameter, 3.8 cm (C53–54/39)

This tiny alabastron is composed of hard, fine, yellowish-buff clay, and carries a light slip as well as painted decoration in two shades of reddish-brown. Compared with no. 127 the shape is plump and the base much flatter. The lip is everted into a disk and a small strap handle (similar to those on aryballoi) is attached at the lip and shoulder; there is also a slight ridge on the neck. The vase is decorated with two groups of parallel bands around the body; between these bands run two rows of dots separated by two thin bands. There are horizontal bands on the handle, tongues on the neck, and concentric circles on the flat surface of the lip. It seems to be an unusual shape, but the band and dot on the body are similar to that on a similar vase illustrated in Cook and Butchart, *PBSR* 17 (1949): pl. 1a. The small size and the decoration on our alabastron indicate that it is probably a late seventh-century

example, but it may date from early in the sixth century B.C.

129 Aryballos

First half of the sixth century B.C.
Height, 6.4 cm; diameter, 5.7 cm (C53–54/38)

This round aryballos, made of pinkish-buff clay and covered with a light slip, possibly is an example of the coarser Italo-Corinthian fabric described by R. M. Cook (*Greek Painted Pottery*, 2d ed. [London, 1972], p. 150). With a round body, relatively long neck, and a strap handle, its shape seems to be closer to Payne's Shape B1, although the bottom is flatter. The decoration, in brownish-black and a mat purplish-red paint, consists of three thick bands and one thin band on the body, tongues on the shoulder radiating from a circle at the base of the neck, horizontal bands on the handle, and concentric circles on the mouth. The decoration is essentially in black except for the center line on the body and the ring on the top. According to Payne (*Necrocorinthia*, p. 291), aryballoi with linear decoration last well into the sixth century B.C., as indicated by the mouths, which are often decorated with broad concentric rings. The concentric circles on the mouth of this aryballos indicate that it should very likely be assigned a date in the first half of the sixth century B.C. It also has a very close parallel with an Italo-Corinthian aryballos (undated) in Blinkenberg and Johansen, *CVA*, p. 75 with pl. 95.2.

TERRA-COTTAS

Figurines

(A. J. HEISSERER)

Terra-cotta is a term used variously for statuettes, figurines, and reliefs made of clay, and is also used for sizes ranging from the very small to the monumental. The term is usually applied in a primary sense to small statues and figurines. Terra-cottas may be made by modeling, a method employed almost exclusively until ca. 700 B.C., by thowing on the wheel, and by using a mold. Most early terra-cottas were made not far from where they have been found, often being associated with funerary or votive offerings. The great variety of shapes they were given and the fact that they are invariably found in abundance at archaeological sites attest to their popularity during all ancient history. The following abbreviations arc uscd:

Bell	Malcolm Bell, III, *Morgantina Studies*, vol. 1, *The Terrracottas* (Princeton, N.J., 1981).
BMT	R. A. Higgins, *Catalogue of the Terracottas in the Dept. of Greek and Roman Antiquities, British Museum*, 2 vols., 2d ed. (London, 1968).
Higgins, *GT*	R. A. Higgins, *Greek Terracottas* (London, 1967).

130   Miniature standing woman

Likely seventh century B.C.
Preserved height, 6 cm (C41–42/7/1)

Brownish-buff clay; solid; handmade; head and one arm stub missing; chipping at the base. Provenance and origin are unknown.

Small Greek figurines of this kind are usually assigned to the Archaic period, and the large

Terra-cotta figurines. *Left to right*: no. 133, votive egg; no. 130, standing woman; no. 140, small mask; no. 139, Aphrodite.

majority of them are clearly female. Our standing woman shares some features with similar figurines from Argos (*BMT*, pl. 138 no. 979, of the seventh or sixth century B.C.) and with two dated examples from Attica (Higgins, *GT*, pls. 7E and 17C, from the eighth and seventh centuries, respectively), but the most remarkable analogy is with a primitive figurine found in the excavations of the Athenian agora. G. R. Davidson and D. B. Thompson, *Small Objects from the Pnyx*, vol. 1, *Hesperia*, Suppl. 7 (Princeton, N.J., 1943), p. 135, fig. 52.1. Despite this association with archaic Attica, one cannot help but be impressed by a comparison with the numerous primitive terra-cottas of Laconia that have the same general shape and dimensions as ours, in particular nos. 1004–1008 on pl. 141 in *BMT*, all of which date to about the seventh century B.C. The origin for this miniature standing woman, therefore, remains obscure, but its date of about the seventh century cannot be far from the mark.

131   Horse and rider

Likely Boeotian, sixth century B.C.
Height, 8.1 cm; length, 10.1 cm (C45–46/6)

This small horse and rider is modeled from brownish-buff clay and painted in black. The intact figurine consists of a narrow-waisted, short-necked, dish-faced horse with a short but high tail, and tapering, unjointed sawhorse legs that have no hooves. The rider has a pointed head, and carries a shield on his left side; he sits high on the horse's neck and has no legs or arms. The decoration in black consists of vertical stripes on the horse's body, tail, and neck, including the rider and shield, and horizontal stripes on the neck and legs, again including the rider and shield. The horse and rider, therefore, are decorated as a unit.

The horse is, after human figures, the favorite subject in Greek art. The terra-cotta and bronze horses of Geometric art are considered one indication of the change from the "pre-Hellenic matriarchal religion to the new patriarchal religion." Jean Charbonneaux, *Treasures of the Louvre* (New York, 1966), p. 126. Geometric horses do not have natural proportions, but they do follow a characteristic system of anatomy and proportion. Sidney Markman, *The Horse in Greek Art* (Baltimore, 1943), p. 19. Markman has categorized Geometric terra-cotta horses into four groups. The first and earliest group is Class A, which is characterized by short, stumpy body and limbs. The second group, Class B, also often has short and stumpy features but is less marked by these traits than Class A. Markman dates Class

A to ca. 850–800 B.C., Class B to ca. 850–825 B.C. Class C consists primarily of plastic horses on the covers of pyxides, and of horses with elephantlike members and short, thin tails. In addition, these horses usually have features marked on their faces in paint. The horses from this class date ca. 800–750 B.C. Class D terra-cottas have members that are tapered at the ends, like a sawhorse, with eyes and other facial features painted in. These horses are assigned to the period ca. 725–700 B.C., perhaps lasting until 675 B.C. Ibid., pp. 26–40. The Stovall horse and rider has the tapering sawhorse legs of his Class D (compare our terra-cotta with one illustrated in ibid., fig. 16, and p. 31) but otherwise does not especially resemble any of the other horse figurines illustrated or described. This specimen, therefore, is not likely Geometric, but it does resemble sixth-century Boeotian terra-cotta horses in a number of respects. For instance, these figurines are made from drab or brown clay and painted in black; sometimes they are striped all over with parallel bands, even where the eye should be located. The Boeotian terra-cotta horses also seem often to have short, stumpy tails. P. N. Ure, *Aryballoi and Figurines from Rhitsonia in Boeotia* (Cambridge, 1934), pp. 53, 61–64, with pls. xv–xvi. The Stovall figurine shares all these attributes and furthermore is quite similar to the mid-sixth–century horse and rider figurines illustrated in *BMT*, pl. 105, nos. 782–83 and 785–86. The date for our terra-cotta, therefore, is likely the sixth century B.C.

132   Seated woman

Likely Rhodian, end of the sixth century B.C.
Height, 12.4 cm (C57–58/12/5)

The woman, who perhaps is to be identified with the goddess Persephone, is seated on a throne, with hands at knees. Brownish clay, washed with white slip; traces of red paint near the legs. Small hole underneath; base raised with modern plastic wood. A few cracks to the clay.

This piece, with its severe style and graceful lines, belongs to an early date. The plainness and anonymity of its features suggest the late Archaic period. It is a fine specimen, almost identical in shape and dimensions with one excavated in Sicily. Pl. 5, no. 10 in Bell (two views given). Bell (p. 125) recognized this as an Ionian import, and dated it "by context of third quarter of sixth century." Two other examples, similar with respect to size and composition and date, can be found illustrated in Chr. Blinkenberg, *Lindos, Fouilles de l'Acropole 1902–1914*, pt. 1, *Les Petits Objets* (Berlin, 1931), nos. 2133 and 2192. We suggest a likely Rhodian origin for our figurine by comparison with additional Rhodian specimens. *BMT*, pl. 15, no. 65 (end of the sixth century B.C.), and pl. 22, nos. 122–23 (early fifth century); Higgins, *GT*, pl. 13B (late sixth century), and pl. 24B (early fifth century).

133   Votive egg

Perhaps Boeotian, sixth–fourth centuries B.C.
Length, 6.9 cm; diameter, 5.3 cm (C55–56/4)

This terra-cotta egg is made from fine, pinkish-buff clay and is unslipped. It is slightly flattened on the base of the large end and has three holes, one in the top and one on each side approximately 2.5 cm below and in line with the top hole. This egg has a patterned decoration in faded red and black paint consisting of thick and thin lines framing a frieze of black oval blobs that are within a similarly shaped red-orange outline. This pattern may be a degenerate form of linked lotus buds. Near the base there is a thick wavy line between encircling straight lines. It has been broken and mended. According to the accession sheet it is a Boeotian votive egg from the sixth century B.C., and no evidence has been found to either confirm or disprove this information.

Eggs—real, terra-cotta, and even stone— were a common component of late Archaic and Classical Greek grave offerings. B. Sparkes and L. Salcott, *Black and Plain Pottery of the 6th, 5th, and 4th Centuries B.C.: Athenian Agora*, vol. 12, pts. 1 and 2 (Princeton, N.J., 1970), p. 181. Eggs appear on sepulchral vases and monuments, including many fourth-century Red-figured Apulian vases. A. D. Trendall and A. Cambitoglou, *The Red-Figured Vases of Apulia*, vol. 1 (Oxford, 1978), pp. 186–88. One interesting Attic sepulchral vase shows two women placing offerings at a grave that has on it, in addition to a stele, a large egg-shaped object. The commentator speculates that this was indeed meant to represent a huge egg. L. Shear, *Hesperia* 6 (1937): 361–62 with fig. 25. Real eggs were fairly common in the graves of the North Cemetery in Corinth, as well as in many other burials, and one has been found in the pot burial of a chicken at Corinth. C. Blegen, H. Palmer, and R. Young, *The North*

Cemetery: Corinth, vol. 13 (Princeton, N.J., 1964), p. 84; cf. O. Broneer, *AJA* 37 (1933): 569. A plain terra-cotta egg has been found in the Athenian agora, and Black-figured, Red-figured, and patterned eggs are also extant. The majority of these terra-cotta eggs have a hole through the top, and some have an additional hole in the bottom. Such eggs may have been meant to be hung. Sparkes and Salcott, *Black and Plain Pottery*, p. 181 with pl. 44.

Several theories concerning the purpose of eggs offered as funerary gifts have been advanced. One early theory was that the eggs were dedicated to the dead simply as food, but this seems unlikely in light of the stone and terra-cotta eggs. A more common view is that eggs as funerary offerings are symbolic of resurrection or eternal life. Shear, *Hesperia* 6 (1937): 362. However, in Blegen, Palmer, and Young, *North Cemetery*, p. 84, Palmer rejects this theory because eggs are almost totally lacking in men's graves in the North Cemetery. Instead, he theorizes that eggs were symbols of fertility and growth, and that this is the reason they are absent from men's graves but present in those of women and children. Our terra-cotta egg, then, is probably a funerary offering from the period of the sixth through the fourth centuries B.C., and may indeed be from sixth-century Boeotia. The style of painting on this egg is also reminiscent of that which appears on late sixth-century aryballoi, such as those illustrated on pl. 5.5–8 in P. N. and A. D. Ure, *University of Reading, CVA* (Great Britain, fasc. 12: Oxford, 1954).

134   Standing woman

Likely Boeotian, mid-fifth century B.C.
Height, 12.8 cm (C39–40/6)

This terra-cotta, a hollow figure with large rectangular opening in back, is made of brownish clay, rather coarse and soft. It is a standing female in Doric chiton; arms hanging at sides; crown on head. White paint overall; traces of red paint on the right side of the drapery. Broken and mended; lower part of legs and feet missing.

The classical severity of this piece is immediately evident. It compares most favorably with an intact Boeotian figurine of the mid-fifth century B.C. illustrated in *BMT*, pl. 112, no. 813, a bit less so with no. 814 on the same plate; this figurine, if intact, would have about the same measurements as the two from Boeotia. The hair and

down across the neck it falls behind the left shoulder to the knees. Leaf-shaped fan is held in the left hand; remains of pinkish paint on protruding surfaces; rectangular vent pierced in middle of back.

Evidence for the popularity of these graceful statuettes is the fact that they commonly appear as forgeries on the modern market. A comparison of the Stovall Tanagra with others suggests strongly that it is authentic. There is exquisite detail to the face, hood, and the pleats. The closest comparison that we have been able to find is pl. 92b in Gisela M. A. Richter, *The Metropolitan Museum of Art: Handbook of the Greek Collection* (Cambridge, Mass., 1953). Examples similar to ours can be found in Higgins, *GT*, pls. 34C, 42A–B, 57E (Priene), 60B and 61C (both South Italy). These specimens date from the middle fourth century or later, and suggest a similar period for this example; those from Boeotia date from the middle or late fourth century B.C. Cf. also *BMT*, pl. 127, no. 876; and M. B. Huish, *Greek Terracotta Statuettes* (London, 1900), pl. V, a Tanagra statuette whose hooded head, drapery, and fan bear analogy to the one in the Stovall Museum.

136   Aphrodite and Eros

Ca. fourth century B.C.
Height, 12 cm (C56–57/4)

This intact figurine is made of yellow-brownish clay; traces of white and bits of blue paint are preserved. The right arm of the woman crosses over her waist, a goose is held in the crook of this arm; the left arm holds Eros and a basket of fruit. It has prominent earrings and headdress, a circular hole in the back, and it is hollow. Provenance is unknown.

A precise parallel is no. 85, fig. 26, pp. 23–24, in Alda Levi, *Le Terrecotte Figurate del Museo Nazionale di Napoli* (Florence, 1926). Of the same shape and size, this terra-cotta from Locri has the same headdress and same type of decoration on the clothing as ours; the only differences are that the Locri example has a more prominent Eros (but held in the left arm) and Aphrodite's right arm holds, not an animal, but a rosette. The Locri example is not given a date, but two terra-cottas from Tarentum of the mid-fourth century that show some similarity to ours suggest the date given at the heading. Pl. 186, no. 1338

crown of our figurine is also similar to that on a small figurine of Artemis, of unknown provenance, from the early fifth century B.C. (Higgins, *GT*, pl. 35D with pp. 81–82), believed to originate from Corinth. The Stovall statuette, however, has the greatest affinities with those from Boeotia of the mid-fifth century B.C.

135   Tanagra statuette

Boeotian, mid-fourth century B.C.
Height, 16.2 cm (C45–46/1)

This figurine is a specimen of a type so-called from a cemetery in Boeotia, at Tanagra, the place where such graceful terra-cottas were found. This hollow figurine, on a flat base, is a draped, standing female; the mantle is pulled up to make a hood over the head, and crossing

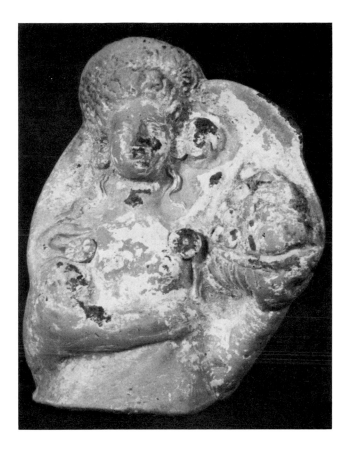

and pl. 189, no. 1354 bis in *BMT*. Levi cites another example in the museum at Reggio.

137 Standing woman

South Italian (Tarentine?), ca. first century B.C.
Height, 52.2 cm (C84/4/11)

Soft, coarse, buff clay; slight remains of brown paint. A standing female in Doric chiton and himation; head covered by a caplike headpiece with elevated headband; disk earrings with pendants on each ear; the right arm is held in at the waist, the left reaches up to the clasp for the chiton; the pleats of the drapery are very deep, especially on the back. Circular hole in the back. Considerable traces of lime incrustation over the surface. Intact, except for a portion of the right and left earrings; neck broken off and mended; hole at the rear of the head.

138 Standing woman

South Italian (Tarentine?), ca. first century B.C.
Height, 49.4 cm (C84/4/12)

Same description as above, except for the following: this figure has a less pronounced headband, lacks a base, and is missing only a part of the right earring.

The absence of a *polos* (a kind of diadem worn by certain goddesses) shows that these figures are not divinities. And even though it has been suggested that many statuettes from South

Italy are votive figures of mortals (E. Langlotz, *Ancient Greek Sculpture of South Italy and Sicily* [New York, n.d.], p. 30), the type of cap on our two statuettes may mean that these two women represent priestesses.

This pair of terra-cotta statuettes is reported to have come from "near Taranto." Despite the fact that there is no publication of all the terra-cottas from the area in or near Taranto, and nothing precisely similar appears in Helga Herdejürgen's *Die tarentinischen Terrakotten des 6. bis 4. Jahrhunderts v. Chr. im Antikenmuseum Basel* (Mainz, 1971), there are sufficiently general par-

allels from the south of Italy to suggest that Tarentum or any one of several Greek cities was the place of origin. Indeed, the clothing on the women is of the standard classical Tarentine type, as illustrated by fig. 26 in Higgins, *GT*, p. 90. Taranto has also yielded a staggering number of terra-cottas, one votive deposit alone containing some 30,000 figurines. Ibid. The clay from which these two figures were made might urge a Locrian attribution, but Tarentum is still quite possible. Ibid., pp. 88–90.

A famous terra-cotta mold, found at Taranto and now in the British Museum, shows a woman with rather similar drapery, headdress, facial features, and earrings. M. B. Huish, *Greek Terracotta Statuettes* (London, 1900), pl. LXXV with pp. 191 and 227. Another Tarentine figure in the British Museum, undated like the preceding one, has a left arm holding the garment at the left shoulder, although in this instance the woman is clearly a secular person. Ibid., pl. LXIV with p. 191. A Tarentine figurine with right arm crossed at the waist and holding Eros on her left shoulder with her left arm dates from the first half of the fourth century B.C., but the author observes that similar examples derive from Locri and Medma. Herdejürgen, *Terrakotten*, no. 45, pp. 57–58 with pl. 17. No. 29 (sixth century B.C.) in Langlotz, *Greek Sculpture*, presents a terra-cotta head from a cult image or a votive statue that has the typically Tarentine ringlets falling over the forehead, as is the case with our no. 137. So too the headdress on a fifth-century Tarentine marble statue of an enthroned goddess (no. 50 in ibid.) is virtually identical to that on our no. 137, and the author proposes that this feature and others exercised an influence on the figurines of Tarentum and may have been copied in clay (p. 266). But the drapery on the two Stovall statuettes may point to a later, Hellenistic period. Cf. the two girls seen in pl. 143 of ibid., dated to the third and mid-second century B.C., respectively; and it is recognized that terra-cottas could be, and likely were, copied repeatedly in later centuries, with alterations made for the sake of style (ibid., p. 295). But in a recent personal communication to the editor of this catalogue, Dr. Helga Herdejürgen, of the German Archaeological Institute, Bonne, Federal Republic of Germany, points out that the style of the Stovall Museum's two terra-cotta priestesses is not really classical but rather classicizing, that is, a later affectation of the classic form. Thus the date for these two terra-cottas is likely ca. the first century B.C.; cf. for general parallels, with additional bibliographical citations, E. Berger, ed., *Antike Kunstwerke aus der Sammlung Ludwig II* (Basel, 1982), pp. 107ff., No. 155, and pp. 167ff., No. 209. (We express our gratitude to Dr. Herdejürgen for this information, which arrived as this work was in press.)

139 Aphrodite figurine

South Italian, third century B.C.
Maximum height, 8.2 cm (C53–54/56)

Made of fine, fairly hard, orange-buff clay, this is a hollow, draped figurine of Aphrodite, with Eros clinging to the right shoulder, a dove perched on the left shoulder. The face is turned toward the right, seen in three-quarter view from front; right arm lies along side, and is bent at elbow; left arm is entirely missing. The head of the dove is also missing.

Reported as being "South Italian, third century B.C.," this figurine does indeed show similarities to other South Italian statuettes of the Hellenistic period—perhaps not so surprising in light of the enormous number of terra-cotta finds from that region. Ours has facial features quite similar to two in Bell, nos. 199–200, pl. 51, p. 154, both of which are described as being the head of a goddess and dating to the second half of the third century B.C. The hairstyle to some extent parallels that on two terra-cotta standing women, neither of whom is Aphrodite but both from the Hellenistic era, illustrated in L. von Matt and U. Zanotti-Bianco, *Magna Graecia* (New York, 1967), pl. 212. An interesting terra-cotta that shows Aphrodite nursing Eros is seen on fig. 5, p. 20, in M. B. Huish, *Greek Terracotta Statuettes* (London, 1900). But actually we find no parallels to our terra cotta Aphrodite with both Eros and a dove on her shoulders.

140 Small mask

Hellenistic
Height, 4.4 cm (C57–58/13/27)

Buff clay; slight traces of red paint. Two drilled holes in the top of the head. Intact; the base is formed by an oblique angle running from the neck to the back of the head.

This male head represents a comic actor, and is an extremely common type in Hellenistic times. Rather similar, of the many illustrations available, are nos. 726 and 729 on pl. 116 in Bell.

141 Grotesque old woman

Hellenistic
Height, 8.3 cm (C57–58/7)

Naked old woman seated on a stool; large pendant breasts and extended abdomen. Light buff clay; lime incrustation; no apparent traces of paint. Drilled holes at sides of the head (ears?). Broken and mended, the figurine lacks the right arm, the left hand and wrist, lower portion of the right leg, and much of the front part of the stool.

This piece, a common type during the Hellenistic era, is similar to a statuette of a grotesque fat woman in Higgins, *GT*, pl. 44D (from Boeotia, 330–200 B.C.), except that the Boeotian terra-cotta is standing. Our figurine does not appear to represent a comic actor.

142 Tarentine terra-cotta revetment

Likely third century B.C.
Height, 20 cm; width, 20.7 cm (C48–49/12)

This small piece is composed of brownish-buff, coarse clay. On the front, in relief, there is an acanthus flanked by palmettes and tendrils. Complete, but with some weathering; a small fragment, broken away from the right edge, has been glued in place, but a chip from the lower right corner is missing. Source: E. Jastrow, *Opuscula Archaeologica*, vol. 2, pt. 1 (1938), p. 19 with fig. 7.

Lamps

(BARBARA L. GUNN AND A. J. HEISSERER)

Ancient lamps were made from many materials, but clay was undoubtedly the most common raw material. The basic form of the terra-cotta lamp was a bowl of oil and a wick. Artificial light was needed for many different purposes. Lamps were important for lighting in domestic and commercial buildings and were used at many religious festivals; they were also commonly offered as votive gifts and tomb furniture. The most common fuel in the ancient Mediterranean was olive oil, but plant oils (sesame, castor, and others) were also used. Wicks were made from materials that were able to draw the fuel to the wick hole by capillary action. Examples of such substances included linen, papyrus, mullein, oakum, fibers of the castor plant, and perhaps asbestos. Bailey, *GRPL*, pp. 10–12. In broad terms, the ancient Mediterranean lamp developed gradually from open handmade or wheelmade bowls to the closed moldmade shapes of the Roman Empire. The unbridged nozzle of the early lamps was gradually bridged, and the filling hole became smaller and smaller during the process of development. Lamps, relatively early in the process of development, began to be glazed, slipped, or coated with egg white inside to prevent the oil from permeating the lamp. In this catalogue the lamps are divided into two broad categories, wheelmade and moldmade, and the production technique of each category is discussed. Then each lamp is described and assigned a date or type. The lamps are listed in roughly chronological order within their categories, but it is not always possible to distinguish a specific time period for a particular lamp. It is important to note that the early moldmade lamps are contemporary with or earlier than the late wheelmade varieties. The following abbreviations are used throughout the lamp descriptions:

Athenian Agora IV	Richard Howland, *Greek Lamps and Their Survivals: Athenian Agora IV* (Princeton, N.J., 1958).
Athenian Agora VII	Judith Perlzweig, *Lamps of the Roman Period*, vol. 7, *Athenian Agora VII* (Princeton, N.J., 1961).
Bailey, *GRPL*	Donald M. Bailey, *Greek and Roman Pottery Lamps*, rev. ed. (London, 1972).
BML	Donald M. Bailey, *A Catalogue of the Lamps in the British Museum*, vol. 1, *Greek, Hellenistic, and Early Roman Pottery Lamps* (London, 1975); vol. 2, *Roman Lamps Made in Italy* (London, 1980).
SCE IV (3)	Olof Vessberg and Alfred Westholm, *The Swedish Cyprus Expedition*, vol. IV, pt. 3, *The Hellenistic and Roman Periods* (Lund, 1956).
Szentléleky, *AL*	Tihamér Szentléleky, *Ancient Lamps* (Budapest, 1969).

Wheelmade Lamps

Wheelmade lamps were manufactured by throwing on the wheel. "Cocked hat" or shell-shaped lamps such as no. 143 were formed by fashioning a low open saucer by hand or on the wheel and then pinching in the nozzle. Later wheel-made lamps with a filling hole, bridged nozzle, and perhaps a handle were made by throwing the lamp as a bowl and then adding a nozzle, handle, and lug when the bowl was leather hard.

143 Greek lamp

Length, 10.2 cm; width, 10 cm (C53–54/29)

Pinkish-buff clay, unglazed; shallow open lamp in the form of a small round dish with a broad lip; approximately half of the circumference pinched in to form a nozzle.

This type of lamp is usually called either a "cocked hat" or a shell lamp. This specimen is from Cyprus, where the "cocked hat" lamp lasted from the Cypro-Geometric II period (ca. 950–850 B.C.) until at least the third century B.C.; such a type of lamp was developed in Palestine in the second millennium B.C. and probably came to Cyprus through the Phoenicians. *SCE IV (3)*, pp. 121, 184, and fig. 37; Bailey, *GRPL*, p. 17; F. W. Robins, *The Story of the Lamp* (Bath, 1970), p. 42. The Greek form of this type has a handle and is dated to the seventh century B.C. *Athenian Agora IV*, pp. 7–8. Such lamps are very difficult to date because they had a very long-lived and relatively unchanged form. In Palestine the type gradually acquired a flatter base and a more definite wick nozzle, and this process probably also took place in Cyprus to some extent. Robins, *Story of the Lamp*, p. 42. Our

specimen greatly resembles a "cocked hat" lamp dated to the fourth and third centuries B.C., as well as classical "cocked hat" lamps found at Bamboula and an early Hellenistic type. John Myres and M. Ohnefalsch-Richter, *A Catalogue of the Cyprus Museum* (Oxford, 1899), p. 80; J. L. Benson, *AJA* 60 (1956): 44–45, pl. 36; *SCE IV (3)*, p. 184 and fig. 37.1–4. Compare also the Cypriote specimens in *BML*, vol. 1, pl. 96, nos. Q491–93, which are dated to the fourth or third century B.C.

144 Greek lamp

Preserved length, 7.5 cm; width, 6 cm (C57–58/11/26)

Fine, hard, pinkish-red clay; black glaze with metallic sheen; unglazed, slightly concave, heavy disk base that forms a point inside; globular body; reserved groove around filling hole; slightly concave lip sloping down and inward; flat, heavy nozzle, partially missing; remnants of a pierced lug on the left; from the Athenian agora excavations.

Typologically this Attic lamp, with its relatively small filling hole, bridged nozzle, and black glaze, is far more developed than no. 143, although they may be very close in time. Athens during the sixth through the fourth centuries was apparently the major producer of new types of lamps, which were widely exported. Bailey, *GRPL*, p. 17. The shape of the Stovall lamp places it in Howland's Type 25 and Broneer's Type VII. Additionally, the kind of pierced lug

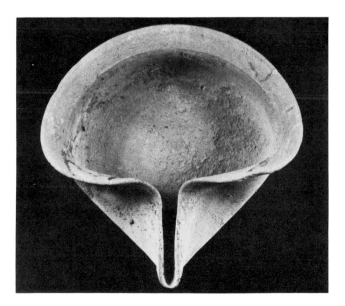

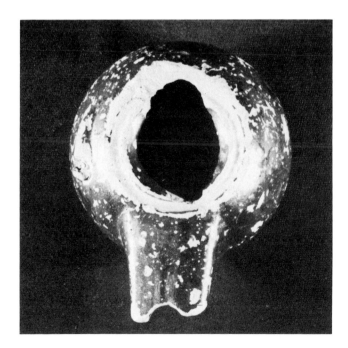

on the left side indicates that it belongs to Howland's Type 25B, which dates to the second half
of the fourth century into the last quarter of the
third. Lamp no. 301, pl. 10 in *Athenian Agora IV*
has a very similar section to ours, except that its
nozzle is much wider. The lugs on such lamps
were probably added in order that the lamp
could be suspended when on sale or not in
use. Finally, the slightly concave lip of this lamp
places it early in the Type 25B series, probably in
the third quarter or second half of the fourth
century B.C. Ibid., pp. 67–74, pls. 10 and 38.
Compare also *BML*, vol. 1, pl. 16, no. Q88 and
pl. 18, nos. Q92–94.

145   Greek lamp

Preserved length, 8.8 cm; preserved width, 6.1 cm (C57–
58/11/27)

Fine, pink clay, heavily incrusted; black glaze
with metallic sheen; similar to the preceding lamp
(no. 144), except that the base does not seem to be
as heavy and the lip is convex rather than concave; from the Athenian agora excavations.

This lamp belongs to Howland's Type 25A
or B (*Athenian Agora IV*, pp. 67–74, pls. 10 and
38), but to which of these two cannot be determined because most of the body, and therefore
any lug or handle, is missing. It is probably later
than the preceding lamp (no. 144), to judge by
the top, and is likely to be dated to the second
half of the fourth century or the first quarter of
the third century B.C.

146   Greek lamp

Length, 9.4 cm; width, 6.6 cm (C53–54/30)

Pinkish-buff, hard, fine clay; blackish-brown
glaze on the upper portion applied by dipping;
slightly concave disk foot; long, deep nozzle with
the bottom side extending outward and then
tapering sharply up to the lip; shoulder slopes
upward from a fairly angular edge to a ridge
surrounding the filling hole; small, unpierced
lug on the left side.

This lamp from Cyprus greatly resembles
Type 3 in the *SCE IV (3)* typology of lamps, except that the nozzle termination on ours is not
quite so angular; Type 3 is close to Broneer's
Type IV in form, and lasted throughout the
Hellenistic period on Cyprus. Ibid., pp. 121,
184, and fig. 37. For other comparable Cypriote
examples see *BML*, vol. 1, pl. 96, no. Q499, and
pl. 99, no. Q500.

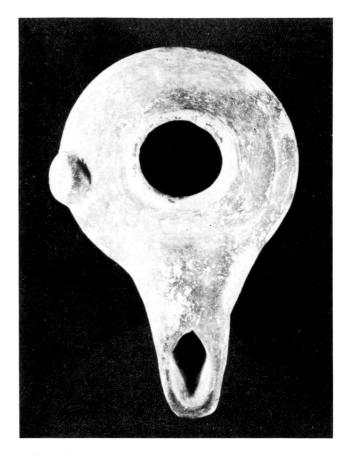

147   Greek lamp

Length, 7.6 cm; width, 6.9 cm (C39–40/10)

Soft, fine, buff clay; raised disk base with wheel
marks showing; small circular body; angular
shoulder, large filling hole; small pointed nozzle,
with wick hole slightly away from the nozzle
point; strap of clay rectangular on section across
the back to serve as handle.

The date for this lamp is undetermined,
neither provenance nor origin being known.
The light fabric may indicate that it is Corinthian. In general, angularity of shape and obvious wheel marks are characteristic of Hellenistic
work, but the relatively large filling hole and the
strap handle may be early. Homer A. Thompson, *Hesperia* 3 (1934): 432–34. The shape, however, corresponds to a Hellenistic type very common at Halicarnassus. *BML*, vol. 1, pl. 40, nos.
Q225–31 and pl. 42, nos. Q232–35. Nothing
definite can be said about this lamp.

Moldmade Lamps

Moldmade lamps began to be made in the Greek
world in the early third century B.C. This process

allowed the decoration of lamps to become much more elaborate. In the Hellenistic period mold-made lamps were manufactured primarily in the eastern Mediterranean, but around the first century A.D. new Italian shapes with voluted nozzles flooded the market. Lamps were usually molded in two halves and then joined in the mold. In the Hellenistic period clay molds were taken from the archetype, but plaster molds were used by Roman times. The lamps were formed by pressing wet clay into each half of the mold; the halves were joined while still on the mold by matching registration bosses or grooves. Bailey, *GRPL*, pp. 13–14; Donald M. Bailey in *Roman Crafts*, eds. Donald Strong and David Brown (New York, 1976), pp. 96–99. The X-shaped mark on the back of our no. 166 below is probably the result of registration grooves in the mold. After the lamp dried it was removed from the mold and the junction of the two halves was trimmed, as well as any other needed repairs being executed.

148 Greek lamp

Preserved length, 7.4 cm; width, 6.3 cm (C53–54/61/2)

Pinkish-buff clay; red glaze; slightly concave disk base; ring around filling hole; remnants of a wide strap handle; nozzle missing; ray pattern on upper side; from the Athenian agora excavations.

Although it is difficult to be certain since the nozzle of this lamp is missing, it probably should be assigned to Howland's Type 48A. *Athenian Agora IV*, pp. 158–60. This type is characterized by a concave base, broad and spreading body,

and an oval nozzle with two lines down the top; normally it also has a lug, is decorated on top with rays, and is covered with a black glaze that is usually worn or fired red. The Stovall example lacks a lug, a condition that adds to the uncertain classification caused by the missing nozzle. Type 48A dates from the late third quarter of the third century into the last quarter of the second century B.C. A Hellenistic lamp in Szentléleky, *AL*, no. 39, of unknown provenance, is virtually identical to ours.

149 Greek lamp, "Ephesus Type"

Preserved length, 8 cm; width, 5.7 cm (C53–54/61/1)

Fine gray clay; dark gray glaze; low flat base, mostly missing; angular shoulder; high collar; very slight ridge around filling hole; remnants of strap handle; nozzle mostly missing; two rows of chevrons in relief on the upper side; from the Athenian agora excavations.

This type of lamp is known as the "Ephesus Type" because many such lamps, including molds, were found at that site. These lamps were certainly made in Asia Minor and were widely exported. Bailey, *GRPL*, p. 18. "Ephesus Type" lamps began to appear in Athens after 125 B.C., but were produced beginning in the early second century. The bases on this type of lamp are typically oval, the sides double convex, the strap handle broad, the top flat with a filling hole surrounded by a ridge and a high collar, which was made separately and added by hand when the

clay was leather hard. The "Ephesus Type" was made in imitation of metal forms, as the oval base and the broad strap handle illustrate. The normal nozzle is triangular with sharp flukes, but some later versions have oval nozzles. The top of the nozzle and the upper sides are usually decorated in relief. Our lamp has no drain holes and a very low ridge around the filling hole, and therefore may be a late example of the "Ephesus Type," which lasted into the first quarter of the first century A.D. at Athens. *Athenian Agora IV*, pp. 166–69. For many specimens of this "Ephesus Type" see *BML*, vol. 1, pls. 30–38, nos. Q159–202.

150   Greek lamp, "Ephesus Type"

Preserved length, 8.1 cm; width, 6 cm (C39–40/14)

Hard, fine, gray clay; dark gray glaze; low, flat base, mostly missing; angular shoulder; remnants of strap handle; collar and slight ridge around filling hole; rosette pattern on upper side.

This "Ephesus Type" lamp dates within the last two centuries B.C. and the first century A.D., but the very low ridge around the filling hole and the lack of drain holes may indicate a date late in that period. *Athenian Agora IV*, pp. 166–69. The Stovall example carries a rosette pattern distinctive to specimens from Ephesus during this very period. *BML*, vol. 1, pl. 33, nos. Q168 and 177, pl. 37, nos. Q185 and 191. There seems

no doubt that this lamp is definitely Ephesian, despite the fact that there were local imitations at other cities. Ibid., pp. 90–91.

151   Greek lamp, "Ephesus Type"

Length, 11 cm; width, 6.6 cm (C39–40/26)

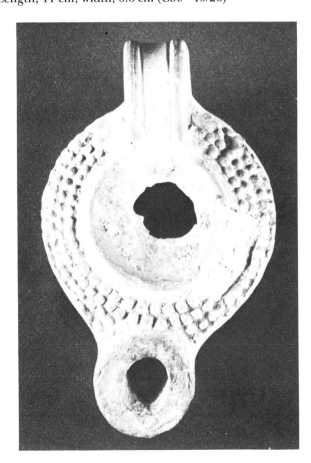

Pinkish-orange clay; red glaze; flat base; looped strap handle; low sloping upper side; plain discus; very large nozzle that is especially thick around the wick hole; upper side decorated with four rows of globules.

This lamp too is of a well-known Ephesian type and dates from the same general period as the preceding one (no. 150). This type is distin-guished by the use of globules (or very similar decoration) on the ridge, the three-ring handle, and rounded, swollen wick hole. For comparable examples see *BML*, vol. 1, pl. 34, no. Q184, and pl. 36, nos. Q190–96.

152   Greek lamp

Length, 9.1 cm; width, 6.6 cm (C53–54/31)

Soft, fine, buff clay; flat base; round, voluted nozzle; concave discus decorated with short rays and circles that form a point near the nozzle.

This lamp from Cyprus belongs to the class of lamps with voluted nozzles, which was introduced during the late first century B.C. and lasted throughout the first century A.D. (Bailey, *GRPL*, p. 18); it corresponds to *SCE IV (3)* Type 10. The Stovall specimen probably was made from a mold taken from an original Italian lamp, since Cyprus in the first century A.D. was almost entirely dependent for its lamp archetypes on imported Italian models. *SCE IV (3)*, pp. 126, 188, and fig. 123; Bailey, *Roman Crafts*, p. 101. According to G. McFadden, the narrow rim seen

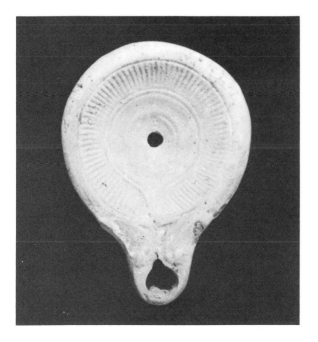

on this type of lamp is an early feature, and the flat base is late. *AJA* 50 (1946), p. 484, fig. 12. In J. B. Hennessey's article in *PBSR* 22 (1954): 22–23, fig. 7.6 shows a similar specimen, especially circles that point toward the nozzle. The shape of Szentléleky, *AL*, no. 108, is also quite similar.

153   Italian lamp

Length, 12.4 cm; width, 9 cm (C55–56/1/3)

Unusual red clay, partially misfired to gray; large round body; small, rounded nozzle; flat base with two grooves and a four-line inscription; flat discus decorated with a relief of a Gorgoneion; channel rim; a perforated lug on the right side, and indications of a matching lug (now lost) on the left; pierced handle with inscribed crescent handle shield.

This large clay lamp is an example of a terra-cotta specimen made in imitation of bronze forms. This is indicated by the crescent handle shield, which served as a reflector in bronze but had no such use in clay, and by the perforated lugs on the sides, which enabled bronze lamps to be suspended. *Athenian Agora VII*, p. 405; O. Broneer, *AJA* 31 (1927): 330 n. 4. Imitations of bronze lamps were among the most expensive type of clay lamp, since they were generally well executed, large, and had features impractical in clay. *Athenian Agora VII*, p. 5. The red clay of our lamp likely indicates Italian origin, and its Gorgoneion is reminiscent of the same head found on two Roman lamps of Bailey's Type P, both late first or early second century A.D. *BML*, vol. 2, pp. 321–22 and 325, pl. 66, no. Q1268, and pl. 67, no. Q1282. More striking is a similar crescent-shaped handle on a Type O lamp (ibid., vol. 2, pl. 62, no. Q1239), which has affinities to those of Type P and dates to the same general period. These lamps are marked by a circular body, a round nozzle without volutes, and usually the maker's name (or similar inscription) is impressed across the base. The Stovall lamp possesses precisely these traits, and thus should likely be dated to the early second century A.D., as is also a very famous lamp with somewhat analogous features, no. 157 in Szentléleky, *AL*. The unusual inscription on our base is probably a votive text. Cf. Bailey, *GRPL*, p. 24. That on the crescent handle is equally enigmatic; its first character looks like the symbol for a person freed by a Roman woman, followed by letters that perhaps read NOSTE. It may be added that

the crescent handle shield is believed to be symbolic of the goddess Diana. F. W. Robins, *The Story of the Lamp* (Bath, 1970), p. 57.

154   Italian lamp, likely Roman

Length, 10.8 cm; width, 7.5 cm (C82/9/1)

Buff clay, covered with an orange-red slip; circular body; short nozzle, separated from the body by a lateral groove; rounded and undecorated shoulder; discus with two circular grooves; pierced handle; flat base with one circular groove; stamped impression on the base, C.OPPI.RES, with a ring-and-dot mark below; air hole at the edge of the discus; broken and mended, several pieces missing.

This lamp, reported to have come from outside the Porta Salaria, is a standard example of Bailey's Type P, group i. *BML*, vol. 2, pp. 314–30. On the discus of the Stovall lamp there is a well-known scene: Cupid carries objects properly belonging to Hercules, e.g., in his left hand is a large club, to his right side a bow and arrow, while beneath his feet are either rocks or perhaps a lion skin. For this form cf. ibid., fig. 18 on

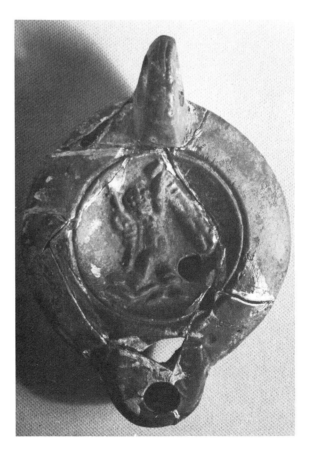

No. 153, Italian lamp (*top*). *Center*: underside. *Below*: handle.

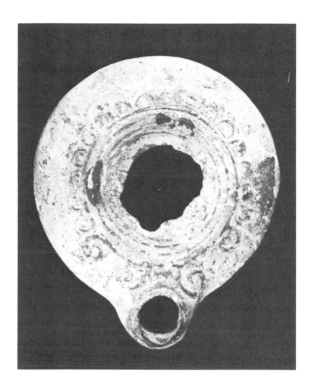

p. 20 and also pl. 68, no. Q1293. C. Oppius Restitutus was a prolific Italian lamp maker, whose signed products have long been known. Szentléleky, *AL*, lists two specimens (nos. 109 and 156), to which latter this lamp corresponds. Bailey in *BML*, vol. 2, p. 99, gives a full list and suggests that Restitutus had his workshop in Rome. The examples in *BML* by this lamp maker that correspond closely with ours are nos. Q1254, 1260, 1261, 1263, 1271, 1274, 1277, 1278, 1281, 1300, all Type P, group i. The lamps of Restitutus are invariably dated to the end of the first century and the beginning of the second century A.D. Ibid., p. 234.

155 Greek lamp

Length, 8.4 cm; width, 7 cm (C39–40/13)

Fine, hard, buff clay; unglazed (?); flat circular lamp on shallow ring foot; rim slopes inward toward the filling hole; short, round nozzle; a band of ovules surrounds the rim; spirals (late imitations of volutes?) near the nozzle.

This example may be Corinthian since it has a similar fabric. Its shape and nozzle indicate that it belongs to the period from the mid-first

through the second century A.D. Similar to this lamp is no. 133, pl. 5, in *Athenian Agora VII*.

156 Italian (?) lamp

Preserved length, 6.3 cm; preserved width, 6.9 cm (C57–58/11/28)

Fine, buff clay; unglazed; flat base with two grooves; sunken discus surrounded by two rings; moldmade handle; apparently a vine and grape

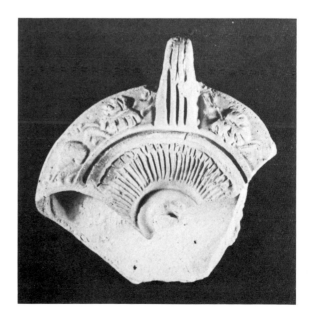

pattern on rim; ray pattern on disk; from the Athenian agora excavations.

The shoulder of this Italian lamp appears to have a vine and bunches of grapes pattern, similar to the kind shown in *BML*, vol. 2, fig. 101, p. 87, no. Q794, but cf. also nos. Q1387, 1397, 1416, and 1417. Our fragmentary lamp is similar to the *BML*, vol. 2, no. Q1327 (Type Q, group i), rather less to nos. Q1331–33 (Type Q, group ii). Since these all date to the second century A.D., the Stovall example will have the same date. This fragmentary lamp also has some analogy with Szentléleky, *AL*, no. 210, a lamp from Asia Minor dated to the fourth or fifth century A.D., but the examples in *BML* appear closer in style.

157 Italian (?) lamp

Length, 10.5 cm; width, 7.3 cm (C57–58/11/30)

Orange-red clay; red glaze; top half of lamp with kite-shaped nozzle; unpierced, grooved, mold-made handle; disk subject is a rosette; rim pattern is herringbone; from the Athenian agora excavations.

This lamp also corresponds to those described and illustrated in *BML*, vol. 2, Type Q,

groups i and ii (e.g., no. Q1333). The date, roughly, will be the second century A.D. Although the provenance of both this lamp and the preceding one (no. 156) is Athenian, comparison of these examples with those given in vols. 1 and 2 of *BML* suggests that their origin was likely Italian, not Greek.

158 Greek lamp

Length, 8.5 cm; width, 6 cm (C53–54/61/3)

Orange-red clay; red glaze; deep-bodied shape; ring base with bent-bar alpha in relief; remnants of a band handle; round, voluted nozzle; rim descending in two steps to a small filling hole; globules in a heavy but apparently orderly pattern all over the body; a few globules on the base and underside of the nozzle; curved ridge defining the underside of the nozzle; from the Athenian agora excavations.

This lamp is an example of the alpha globule lamp, a type that "formed the mainstay of Attic production during the second century" and was produced probably in the hundreds of thousands. *Athenian Agora VII*, pp. 13, 15. Their Hellenistic features include the plain disk, relief alpha on the base, and separately attached band handle, while the nozzle volutes indicate Roman influence. The meaning of the alpha on the base is unclear. The Stovall lamp is probably from the second century A.D., as indicated by several late features including its width and the lack of ribs on the body. The pervasiveness of simple lamps of this type is taken as a sign of the economic stagnation in Athens in the first and second centuries A.D. Ibid., pp. 11, 15–16. A mold that produced specimens such as these is seen on pl. 16(b) of Bailey, *GRPL* (= Walters, 1401).

159 Roman imperial lamp (Egypt)

Length, 7.5 cm; width, 7.2 cm (C41–42/6/1)

Fine, green clay; flat base with inscribed alpha; rounded body drawing inward and then continuing outward to form a nozzle; ridge around filling hole; unpierced air hole; vertical incisions down the side of the body where it draws inward to form the nozzle; two figures (monkeys or children?) are placed around the filling hole; decoration executed partly in relief and partly by incision.

It might be thought that the green color of this specimen was caused by lack of an inner coating of egg white or other substance, thereby allowing the olive-oil fuel to be absorbed into the clay. However, greenish unpainted clay is common in this type of lamp and may have been caused by the composition of the clay or the firing process. This example evidently belongs to a type called the "frog lamp," which was produced in Roman Egypt especially during the third and fourth centuries A.D. The frog was the symbol of resurrection for the Egyptians because it was the symbol of Heqet, the goddess of birth; as a sign of resurrection it was taken over by Christianity. In the fundamental type of "frog lamp" the figure of a frog was placed on the top of a lamp of almond shape, but the decoration soon became very stylized. A variant of this shape has a nozzle that projects out from a rounded body, as does that of this lamp; this variant was developed as early as the second century A.D. Additionally, an incised or relief alpha was quite common on "frog lamps." Cf. Szentléleky, *AL*, no. 227. The Stovall lamp is probably, but not necessarily, a late variant of this type, perhaps third or fourth century A.D. Ibid., pp. 121–24 with nos. 212–30.

160 Roman imperial lamp (Egypt?)

Length, 8 cm; width, 6.4 cm (C39–40/4)

Brownish-buff soft clay; very shallow ring foot; upper side slopes up to rim, and rim slopes inward toward filling hole; incised decoration on the upper side.

This is another very stylized "frog lamp" from the late Roman Empire, presumably from Egypt (see commentary on the preceding lamp, item no. 159). This example is rather similar to Szentléleky, *AL*, nos. 222–27, but the varieties of this type of lamp make it difficult to determine origin and date.

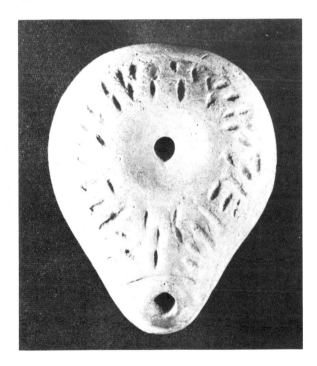

161 Greek lamp

Preserved length, 8 cm; width, 7.6 cm (C53–54/61/4)

Fine, light-buff clay; unglazed; fragment of top of a lamp; grooved base; moldmade handle; rim of four grooves surrounded by a band of globules; discus is decorated with a crescent; air hole near nozzle; filling hole near handle; from the Athenian agora excavations.

The subject of this disk relief was probably adopted from plastic lamp forms. The crescent was a common disk pattern, especially on lamps

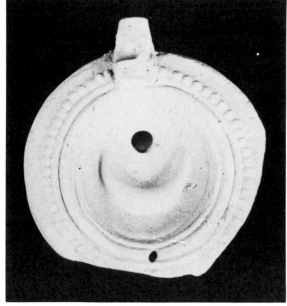

with U-shaped nozzles. Early in the third century A.D., Attic lamp makers began to produce specimens that were very different from, and far superior to, the simple lamps of the first and second century. Of different shapes from earlier Attic lamps, these new models carried many disk and rim patterns; the shapes, and often the accompanying patterns, were borrowed from Corinth and other unknown sources. Attic lamp makers also imitated the light clay of Corinth at the beginning of the process. In the years after A.D. 267, Attic lamp making was crippled by the Herulian invasion, a fact reflected in the quality of the lamps from the last part of the third century. Early in the fourth century the lamp-making industry had recovered, but by this time lamps were again usually glazed. The unglazed, light clay, and distinct disk and rim patterns indicate that this example was made in the early to mid-third century A.D. *Athenian Agora VII*, pp. 17–24.

162 Greek lamp

Preserved length, 7 cm (C53–54/61/5)

Light, yellowish-brown clay; unglazed; fragment of a discus from a lamp with a kite-shaped nozzle; plain rim with panels; disk subject is perhaps a boat; from the Athenian agora excavations.

The lamp with the kite-shaped nozzle was borrowed from Corinth in the early third century A.D. by Attic lamp makers. The disk on this

one seems to be part of a boat, with perhaps a lookout leaning over the edge. Attic lamps with this disk subject are not known before the late third century. No. 1023, pl. 21, in *Athenian Agora VII* seems very similar to the Stovall lamp and is dated to the late third century A.D. Furthermore, lamps with scenes similar to that on no. 1023 are dated to the late third or early fourth century A.D. Ibid., pp. 17, 132, pl. 21.

163 Greek or Roman imperial lamp

Preserved length, 8.6 cm (C53–54/61/6)

Brown clay, purple glaze; fragment of a round lamp disk with kite-shaped nozzle; plain rim with herringbone panels; disk subject is Pan to the right, with head to the left, playing the pan-pipes; air hole just above the nozzle; from the Athenian agora excavations.

The subject of this disk is Pan playing the panpipes or syrinx, which consisted of a set of graduated tubes joined together with each sounding one note. Curt Sachs, *The History of Musical Instruments* (New York, 1940), pp. 142–43. The glaze on this example indicates that it is not earlier than the fourth century A.D., and although it is possible that it was produced in the fifth century, it is much more likely that it dates to the fourth century. *Athenian Agora VII*, pp.

17–18, 21–22, 64–65. A lamp from Vari in Attica has a very similar disk. Samuel Bassett, *AJA* 7 (1903): pl. 13.

164 Greek/Late Roman imperial lamp

Preserved length, 7.8 cm; width, 6.6 cm (C57–58/11/29)

Fine, hard, reddish-brown clay; unglazed; lamp discus with relief of the Goddess with the Double Axe; grooved, unpierced, moldmade handle; kite-shaped nozzle; a hole on either side of the discus figure; from the Athenian agora excavations.

The Goddess with the Double Axe as a discus subject appeared in Athens after 276 A.D. This discus subject was once thought to be Mithras, because it appeared to be wearing a Phrygian cap. However, this peak has been recognized as the end of a long braid. Although this discus subject was very popular, the identity of the goddess is unknown. This lamp is probably from the fourth century A.D., to judge by the careless execution of the relief and the herringbone rim. The disk on this specimen is very similar to that on no. 770, pl. 17, in *Athenian Agora VII* (see also pp. 17–25 and 117).

165 Late Roman imperial lamp

Length, 9.6 cm; width, 6.1 cm (C39–40/11)

Coarse, rather soft, orange clay; depressed base with small raised circle in the center; angular shoulder; lug at the rear; high, rising upper side; relatively large filling hole; channel from filling hole to wick hole; herringbone pattern on the upper side.

This lamp is probably from the fourth century A.D. or later. The seventh-century shape of no. 2927, pl. 46, in *Athenian Agora VII* is similar to ours, which may be that late. Ibid., pp. 23–24, 64–65 with pl. 46. Also, the characteristics of our example fit quite well with the class of "Syrian-Palestinian Lamps" in Szentléleky, *AL*, especially nos. 244–50, of the late Roman Empire (fifth century A.D. and later).

166 Late Roman imperial lamp (?)

Length, 7.4 cm; width, 5.5 cm (C39–40/12)

Soft, brownish-buff clay; ring foot; shoulder rising to a ridge around the filling hole; lug at the rear; blunt, rather large nozzle; blurred band of pattern on the shoulder between two lines; on the back beneath the lug there is an **X**-shaped mark in relief.

The type and date of this lamp cannot be determined precisely. It may be late Hellenistic, or since it bears some resemblance to Szentléleky, *AL*, no. 246 ("Syrian-Palestinian Lamps"), perhaps it is late Roman imperial.

GLASS

Mold-blown Specimens

(A. J. HEISSERER)

Virtually all the glassware in the collection of classical antiquities at the Stovall Museum was purchased many years ago from the Khayat family. Something of the fortunes of this remarkable family is known, and in particular the localities of the Levant where the father, Azeez Khayat, conducted excavations for the purpose of selling artifacts through his New York City gallery. Sidney M. Bergman, "Azeez Khayat (1875–1943), a Noted Collector of Ancient Glass," *Bulletin of the Carnegie Institute* (June, 1974): 238–44. Thus, the provenance of many of our pieces is known and recorded below under the separate entries where such information was available; this knowledge, combined with the results of research on ancient glass, has allowed us to suggest a Syro-Palestinian origin for a number of interesting pieces. Wherever possible, we have supplied an approximate date for the glass; but since chronological development is very difficult to determine for glass from the Roman world (C. Isings, *Roman Glass from Dated Finds* [Groningen, 1957], pp. 163–65), we have avoided any attempt at exactitude. All our specimens are mold blown.

A great deal of study has been done in recent years on glass in antiquity. The bibliographical references that we give to each entry are not intended to be exhaustive but to provide the reader with aids to works that will have fuller discussion and bibliographies. The following abbreviations are employed:

Auth   Susan H. Auth, *Ancient Glass at the New-ark Museum* (Newark, N.J., 1976).
Hayes   John W. Hayes, *Roman and Pre-Roman Glass in the Royal Ontario Museum: A Catalogue* (Toronto, 1975).
Isings   C. Isings, *Roman Glass from Dated Finds* (Groningen, 1957).
Smith   R. W. Smith, *Glass from the Ancient World: The Ray Winfield Smith Collection* (Corning, N.Y., 1957).

167   Toilet bottle

First century A.D., Syro-Palestinian
Height, 8.1 cm; rim diameter, 1.5 cm; base diameter, 2.2 cm (C48–49/9)

Green, translucent glass, some iridescence on neck. Ovoid body, flat base; rather tall, narrow neck with slightly everted lip. No handles. The shoulder and lower portion are ornamented with a garland type of motif, within looping bands; midsection is a series of six panels each filled with a relief representation of a vase or other object. The molding of this intact specimen is quite lovely. Reported as "found near Sidon." See color plate.

The care taken in fashioning this exquisite toilet bottle suggests that it possibly derives from the workshop of Ennion. See the commentary to the following item (no. 168).

Very similar are the following: another Sidonian bottle is pictured in F. Kämpfer and Klaus G. Beyer, *Glass: A World History* (Greenwich, Conn., 1966), pl. 13; Auth, no. 328, shows a small vase with a midsection of panels of amphoras; Hayes, no. 84, pl. 7, has a similar midsection but also bears a handle; Frederic Neuburg, *Antikes Glas* (Darmstadt, 1962), Abb. 41–42, has two superb, handleless specimens, both dated to 200 A.D.;

105

Gisela M. A. Richter, *The Room of Ancient Glass* (New York, 1916), p. 15, fig. 13 (handleless). What are probably the finest handleless examples are those illustrated in Smith, nos. 76–78 and 80, pp. 62–63, all dated to the first or second century A.D.

168   Small jug

Likely first century A.D.
Max. height, 9.7 cm; maximum diameter, 5 cm (C46–47/5)

Original color uncertain owing to very heavy and brilliant iridescence, flaking overall. A mold-blown glass bottle of roughly cylindrical shape with rounded bottom and small circular base; convex shoulder; narrow neck with everted lip; single strap handle with vertical lug rising above lip. Shoulder and bottom marked with ribs; body with leaf pattern in relief. Vertical seams indicate the two halves of the mold; the handle added separately. Circle and sunk central dot on the base. One hole in bottom and a small hole in shoulder. Provenance not explicitly indicated.

The shape, decoration, and dimensions of this squat bottle are so close to those of Auth, no. 323, that it is quite possible both are by the same hand. There is also a similarity with Auth, no. 59, which also has a stylized garland for the midsec-

tion and which is believed to have come from the workshop of Ennion, probably the single most famous ancient glass maker. (On Ennion, see Auth's commentary to her item no. 58.) This Stovall small jug, therefore, is also likely from the workshop of Ennion; one characteristic it shares with these is its very thin walls. Accession records do not state that this purchase from Khayat came from the Levant, but notanda from other Khayat purchases strongly suggest that this vessel also is of Syro-Palestinian origin.

Also similar are: Hayes, no. 84, pl. 7; Axel von Saldern, *Ancient Glass in the Museum of Fine Arts, Boston* (Boston, Mass., 1968), pl. 31, presenting a squat bottle with similar shape and dimensions but with a midpanel of amphoras; Frederic Neuburg, *Antikes Glas* (Darmstadt, 1962), Abb. 36 with a leaf pattern; Smith, no. 79, p. 63 having vessels and other ornaments decorated on the body.

169   Small bottle

Perhaps first century A.D., Syro-Palestinian
Height, 7.8 cm; rim diameter, 2.5 cm; base diameter, 2 cm (C48–49/5)

Amber, translucent glass. Ovoid, mold-blown body with flat base (now cemented to plate glass); plain neck with flaring lip. Two handles extending from shoulder to midpoint of neck. Lower third of body decorated with vertical godroons; upper third (shoulder) with vertical ribs; middle third with horizontal tendril pattern. The two halves of the mold are visible; handles added

separately. One handle restored; chip at lip. Reported as "found near Sidon."

The tendril scroll in midportion, the vertical ribs on the shoulder, the vertical godroons on the lower portion, and the nearly identical dimensions are illustrated in another small vase, Auth, no. 66; her item no. 329 is also quite similar. This type, however, is a common design, sometimes designated "Sidonian." Cf. Hayes, pp. 32–33. Frederic Neuburg, *Antikes Glas* (Darmstadt, 1962), Abb. 38, shows a very similar bottle, also from Sidon; Gisela M. A. Richter, *The Room of Ancient Glass* (New York, 1916), p. 15, fig. 13, has a similar midpanel; Smith, no. 75, p. 61 (tendril scroll pattern), is dated to about the first or second century A.D.

170 Ribbed bowl

Likely first century A.D., Syro-Palestinian
Height, 4.5 cm; rim diameter, 13.5 cm (C49–50/7)

Shallow mold-blown bowl with vertical relief ribs on exterior; wheel-run incised grooves on interior. Pale green, some flaky, opaque white deposit on interior. A slight indented line encircles the exterior just below the rim. One chip at rim; some cracks on exterior at positions corresponding to the incised lines of the interior. Reported to have come "from near Sidon." Isings, form 3c, p. 21.

This is a very common Roman glass, specimens coming from virtually all areas of the Roman Empire. The Stovall specimen is interesting only because of its relatively intact state.

Similar cut rings on the interior of a ribbed bowl are seen in Axel von Saldern, *Ancient Glass in the Museum of Fine Arts, Boston* (Boston, 1968), pl. 11. Cf. also Auth, nos. 41 and 303; Hayes, no. 48, pl. 4.

171 Unguentarium

Probably first century A.D.
Height, 11.9 cm; rim diameter, 1.9 cm (C48–49/13)

Tall, slender vessel of translucent bluish-green glass. Drop-shaped body; faint constriction near the middle. Flat base; everted lip. Intact; some iridescence. Isings, form 8, p. 24.

This type of glass was extremely common to all parts of the Roman Empire, especially the littoral of the Mediterranean; unfortunately, nothing is known about either the provenance or origin of our piece. For unguentaria with this shape cf. Auth, nos. 410–13; Hayes, nos. 629–30, pl. 39; no. 664, pl. 42 (first century A.D.).

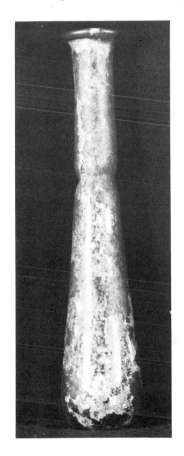

172 Flaring rim jar

Third century A.D., Syro-Palestinian
Height, 9.5 cm; rim diameter, 6.2 cm; maximum diameter, 7.6 cm (C45–46/16)

Brownish, translucent glass with almost no iridescence. Intact globular body with flattened base and shoulder. From the shoulder a low neck flares out into a wide mouth and plain lip; threads of glass are applied in a spiral pattern from neck

down toward the base. A finely executed urn, reported to have come "from Beth Shan." See color plate. Similar jars are found in Auth, nos. 464–66, and 153 (for the swirled design); Hayes, no. 154, pl. 12.

173   Grape flask

Probably third century A.D.
Height, 13.9 cm; rim diameter, 4 cm; base diameter, 3.6 cm (C45–46/8)

Golden-brown glass flask, mold blown with free-blown neck. Ovoid body ornamented with hobnailed pattern; cylindrical neck set off from body by flange. Vertical seams indicate a two-part mold; in the middle of each side of the mold, and at the top of the hobnailed pattern, is an inverted leaf pattern. Intact except for one small hole; another restored. Provenance unknown, likely Syro-Palestinian.

The shape and dimensions of this flask are virtually identical with two grape flasks in Auth, no. 72 ("late Roman") and no. 336, and another in Hayes, no. 91, pl. 7, the only difference being that the lip is thicker on the Ontario specimen; Hayes dates his to the third century A.D. Cf. another similar grape flask illustrated in Smith, no. 258, p. 133 ("Probably Syria, about 1st–2nd century A.D.").

174   Double-head flask

Probably third century A.D., likely Syro-Palestinian
Height, 7.6 cm; rim diameter, 2.1 cm; base diameter, 2.3 cm (C46–47/6)

Small bottle of white, opaque glass. The body is in the form of two male heads, back-to-back. Flat, circular base. Thin, tall neck with everted lip. Neck broken and repaired; otherwise intact. Provenance not stated, but likely Syro-Palestinian.

These small Janus-head flasks, which were quite common during the middle centuries of the Roman Empire, comprise an interesting class. The knobby hair seen here is typical, but the shape is rather unusual; the mold marks of the two vertical halves protrude to form the sides of the hair. Also, the smile on the one face, and the pout on the other, are very slight. Altogether, a fascinating specimen.

Others similar to this are: Auth, nos. 74–75 (the latter especially for the knobbed hair) and 340–41; Hayes, no. 94, pl. 7; Axel von Saldern, *Ancient Glass in the Museum of Fine Arts, Boston* (Boston, Mass., 1968), pl. 37; Anton Kisa, *Das Glas im Altertume*, vol. 3 (Leipzig, 1908), p. 737, Abb. 296; Smith, no. 283, p. 143, but the faces on the Stovall double-head flask compare more favorably with that on a single-head flask, no. 294, p. 147 ("Probably Syria, about 3rd–4th century A.D.").

175   Double-head flask

Probably third century A.D., Syro-Palestinian
Height, 13.1 cm; rim diameter, 3.3 cm; base diameter,
    4.7 cm (C48–49/10)

Clear glass with some opaque, whitish iridescence, especially on the neck. Rather globular
body, mold blown in two parts that form two
male heads, probably Bacchus, back-to-back. Tall
neck, free blown and widening toward the plain
rim. One face is smiling, the other pouting. Flat
base. Intact, except for broad cracks outlining
the left side of one face. Reported to have come
"from near Sidon." Form similar to Isings, form
104a, p. 123. Also similar are: Auth, no. 77;
Hayes, no. 92, pl. 7.

176   Dropper flask

Fourth century A.D., Syro-Palestinian
Height, 9 cm; rim diameter, 5 cm (C47–48/10)

Intact clear glass with heavy and brilliant iridescence. A mold-blown, globular body, decorated
with a faint leaf pattern, this dropper flask was
likely used to hold perfume. Rather wide neck
with gracefully flaring lip. At the base of the
neck the mouth of the body proper is nearly
closed over, an opening only about one-half cm
in diameter being left to provide access to the interior; the inner diameter of the neck above this
opening is about 2 cm. Punty mark. Reported to
have come from Sidon.

    D. B. Harden reported two groups of dated

glass in "Tomb-Groups of Glass of Roman Date
from Syria and Palestine," *Iraq* 11 (1949): 151–
59. His Group II came "from a cave in Galilee"
(p. 154) and is dated to the fourth century A.D.;
of this group, the flask illustrated in his plate
XLIX, 4 has the same dimensions and shape
as this dropper bottle, whose provenance is reported as being Sidonian. On this basis a date
of the fourth century A.D. is reasonable for the
Stovall flask.

    Similar examples are: Auth, nos. 80–82,
343; Hayes, nos. 303 and 305, pl. 21; D. B.
Harden, *Roman Glass from Karanis* (Ann Arbor,
Mich., 1936), no. 594, pl. VIII.

177   Cosmetic tube

Fourth century A.D., Syro-Palestinian
Height to rim, 10 cm, with handle, 15 cm; width including
    handles, 7.1 cm (C49–50/4)

Greenish translucent glass; handle of opaque
greenish glass. Heavy white iridescence over
most of body and handle. This cosmetic tube is
in the shape of a double-bodied unguentarium
with loop handle arching over the mouths of
both bodies; the loop handle has its ends fused
to the side handles. The body is wrapped spirally
with a fine thread of greenish glass. A bronze applicator is still inserted into one body, lodged
there by a pebble or bit of earth; the spatulate
end protrudes at top. Bottom is flattened, with
small punty mark. Reported as found "at Hamah
in northern Syria."

    This lovely and intact blown cosmetic tube is
a fine specimen of a type of glass that became
very popular throughout the Roman Empire. It

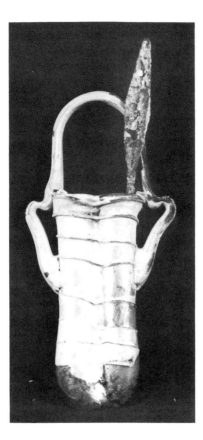

is thought that the bronze spatula was used to apply the ancient cosmetic kohl. Auth, p. 143. The double tubing was formed by pressing the glass and simultaneously indenting a ridge down the center.

The Stovall cosmetic tube is strikingly similar to no. 361, pl. 22, in Hayes, the only major difference being that no. 361 lacks the applicator. Cf. also his no. 360, pl. 28; Auth, nos. 482–83, and 485–86 (for similar threading); Frederic Neuburg, *Antikes Glas* (Darmstadt, 1962), Abb. 28 (dated to the second century A.D.) and 59 (with applicator, dated third–fourth century A.D.).

178   Cosmetic tube

Fourth century A.D.
Height, 11 cm; width at rim, 4.4 cm; width at base, 4.4 cm (C45–46/14)

Double unguentarium of light green glass with heavy silvery iridescence. One of the two handles is broken away; there was no handle at the top. Bottom flattened, with small punty mark. Provenance unknown. Similar are: Auth, nos. 482–483; Hayes, no. 359, pl. 28 (an especially good parallel).

179   Jug

Roman Palestine, fourth century A.D.
Height to lip, 17.7 cm; maximum diameter, 6.5 cm (C49–50/2)

A thin-walled jug with one handle, intact with little iridescence. Amber, transparent glass; strap handle same color and material. Threads of glass laid horizontally around neck, at midpoint, and at one outer edge of lip. Body has oblique wall supported on broad, low stem and flaring foot. Sloping shoulder and tall neck; flaring lip. Punty mark on the bottom. Reported to have come from "near Nazareth." See color plate. Isings, form 120b, p. 150.

Similar jugs are: Auth, no. 384; Hayes, no. 336, pl. 23 (although this has a threaded handle); F. Fremersdorf, *Römische Gläser aus Köln* (Cologne, 1928), Abb. 32 (a specimen, however, that comes from a different part of the Roman world).

180   Jug

Fourth century A.D.
Height, 23.4 cm; maximum diameter, 7.5 cm; diameter at base, 6 cm (C47–48/9)

One-handled jug of purplish-brown glass; strap handle, attached above midpoint of body and on undersurface of lip, of clear yellowish glass; thread of similar yellowish glass applied horizontally around neck and on undersurface of lip. Fusiform body; base concave with punty mark; tall neck; wide, flaring lip. Thin, vertical ribs extend up body from base to shoulder. Body is distorted at point of lower attachment. Reported to have come from Hauran in Syria, this glass is very likely to be of Syro-Palestinian origin. Variant of Isings, form 120b, p. 150. There are similar jugs in Auth, nos. 122 and 385.

181   Flagon
Likely fourth century A.D.
Height, 23 cm; maximum diameter, 7.2 cm (C45–46/9)

Intact clear glass with green and purple iridescence. Body in form of an elongated ovoid; tall neck and flaring lip. Markings on both shoulders and on each side of the neck show that originally this vessel possessed handles, and therefore that it was a two-handled flagon or flask; the base tapers to a blunt point with punty mark. Provenance is not given.

The shape of nos. 411 and 415, pl. 25, in Hayes, evokes similarities, although the Ontario vessels still preserve their handles and no. 415 bears indentations on its body. Glass of this type originated from many Syro-Palestinian workshops and is very common in the late Roman Empire. Cf. Hayes, pp. 86–87. An interesting comparison can be made by looking at Abb. 59 in Frederic Neuburg, *Antikes Glas* (Darmstadt, 1962); his flagon bears handles and is less bulbous but came from a grave in Palestine and is dated third–fourth century A.D.

182   Trefoil mouth jug with base
Fourth–fifth century A.D., likely Syro-Palestinian
Height, 13.3 cm; diameter at base, 3.5 cm (C49–50/1)

Pale green with yellowish tinge. Jug with globular body on small disk foot. Handle, with very slight ribs, extends from point of maximum diameter to lip. Rather tall neck, flaring lip. Threads of glass applied horizontally around neck at midpoint and on undersurface of lip. The goblet-style foot is warped, and carries oblique tooling marks on the outside (like Hayes, no. 397, pl. 19). Intact, except for a small part of the applied thread on the neck; some iridescence. Variant of Isings, form 124, p. 154. Provenance not known.

Similar jugs are: Auth, no. 126 (for a jug with trefoil mouth) and no. 382 (for one with a

goblet base); Hayes, no. 345, pl. 22; no. 397, pl. 19; Smith, no. 271, p. 139 (probably Syrian).

183   Deep bowl

Late Roman?
Maximum height, 5.7 cm; rim diameter, 10 cm; base diameter, 5.8 cm (C45–46/10)

Intact greenish glass with heavy silvery iridescence on the interior. Flat base, oblique wall, rounded rim; base ring formed by "squeezing" near the bottom. (No certain correspondence to Isings, form 41b, p. 57, which has a slightly concave wall.)

The size and shape of this deep bowl are similar to that shown at pl. III, no. 260, in D. B. Harden, *Roman Glass from Karanis* (Ann Arbor, 1936), who states (pp. 96–98) that these kinds of bowls are found in sites in Egypt and the Levant. This observation is borne out by the fact that the shape of our deep bowl corresponds closely to one described in Olof Vessberg and Alfred Westholm, *The Swedish Cyprus Expedition*, vol. 4, pt. 3, *The Hellenistic and Roman Periods in Cyprus* (Lund, 1956), p. 134, fig. 42, 30. But this same type of bowl is also found at the opposite end of the Empire, a circumstance reflected in Abb. 2, Fritz Fremersdorf, *Römische Gläser aus Köln* (Cologne, 1928), as well as in pl. 69 with p. 42 in the same author's *Römisches Buntglas in Köln* (Cologne,

1958). Furthermore, some specimens, which all predate A.D. 79 but which have analogies with our deep bowl, have been uncovered in the excavations at Pompeii. V. Spinazzola, *Le Arti Decorative in Pompei e nel Museo Nazionale di Napoli* (Rome, 1928), illustrations on pp. 222 and 228. Even an approximate date, therefore, cannot be obtained. With respect to origin, however, since the Stovall bowl was not a Khayat purchase, it is quite possible that it derives from the western half of the Roman Empire. Of course, certitude in such matters is out of the question.

184   Beaker

Byzantine?
Height, 11.4 cm; lip diameter, 9 cm (C48–49/15)

Clear glass with considerable coating of dirt and heavy, opaque white iridescence. An almost cylindrical body, flaring out slightly at the top to form a rim or lip. Flat base; a flange near the bottom of the wall. No indications for a handle on either side.

This interesting beaker poses a problem.

Neither origin nor provenance nor date was reported with its purchase, only the cryptic com-
ment, "Byzantine Beaker." Even this identification is uncertain, since there are no parallels to
the numerous beakers described and illustrated
in Isings, in Smith, in Axel von Saldern, *Ancient
and Byzantine Glass from Sardis* (Cambridge, Mass.,
1980), pp. 68–69, or in Olof Vessberg and Alfred Westholm, *The Swedish Cyprus Expedition*,
vol. 4, pt. 3, *The Hellenistic and Roman Periods in
Cyprus* (Lund, 1956), pp. 198–99, fig. 44, 1–42
and fig. 45, 1–16. We find nothing comparable
in other handbooks, and there is no authoritative
treatment of Byzantine glass.

COINAGE

The format used in describing the Stovall coins is as follows:

Number for this catalogue

Name of city or king or emperor, in which place or in whose reign the coin was minted (if applicable and known; not necessarily the person who appears on the coin): place of mintage, date of mintage (if known)

Stovall Museum's accession number for the coin

Description of obverse of coin

Description of reverse. (Note: That portion of the legend which is in brackets represents modern restoration of the lost ancient letters. A dash indicates that the legend is interrupted by some part of the coin's decoration, e.g., HA-DRIANVS and not HADRIANVS on no. 254. Roman coins of the Republic and early Empire customarily show interpuncts, small dots which signify syllabic or word division; for ease of reading, these interpuncts have been omitted from the descriptions.)

Approximate die-axis. Weight in grams. Approximate average diameter in millimeters. Composition and denomination (if known). Bibliographical references. (Note: The die-axis of Jewish coins cannot be indicated in modern texts, owing to the ancient prohibition against depicting human or divine images.)

Explanation of significance of the coin and information relating to identification, wherever necessary. (Photographs of a coin, wherever included, represent actual size or an extremely close approximation.)

The coins are arranged chronologically within the following categories: Greek, Jewish, Roman, and African.

The following general abbreviations are used in the descriptions:

AE copper or copper alloy (usually bronze)
AR silver
ca. about
ex from
l. left
r. right
obv. obverse
rev. reverse

We have been concerned with determining wherever possible the provenance of the Stovall Museum's ancient coins, or providing some information about where the coins were obtained. We have entered data of this kind on only a few of the individual entries, but close examination of the accession records and correspondence with several helpful scholars have allowed us to make the following notations:

Nos. 270 and 297: (C49–50/9/1–2)	Accession records state "acquired in Bath, England."
Nos. 224, 227, 228, 230–32, 246, 255, 256, 258, 259, 262, 265, 271, 272, 313, 314, 332–42: (C51–52/1/1–32)	Accession records show that the donor obtained all these coins "from the ruins of Carthage."
Nos. 236, 238, 240, 242, 245, 251–54, 311, 323: (C56–57/9/1–12)	The donor acquired all these coins from famous collections in England that were broken up after World War II, e.g., the V. J. E. Ryan Collection, the L. G. P. Messenger Collection, the

Nos. 186, 188, 190–92, 199–201, 203–208, 210–14, 216–22, 249, 250, 261, 264: (C81/1/1–29)

Duke of Argyll Collection; as well as from the British Museum Exchange. When the specific collection is known, it is indicated in the entry.

Our donor received these coins from one of his university professors, who in turn had obtained them from a divinity scholar; the provenance of most is apparently Judaea, since many came in old paper wrappers handwritten in French, "Museum of St. Anne, Jerusalem."

Nos. 233, 330, 331: (C84/4/16–18)

Obtained by the donor in Tunisia, 50 miles inland from modern Tunis.

Nos. 185, 189, 194, 197, 223, 225, 239, 243, 244, 247, 248, 257, 260, 263, 266, 268, 269, 273, 296, 302–305, 307–310, 312, 315–320, 324, 329: (C82/2/1–54)

Our donor received these coins from a friend of his, George D. Chase, emeritus dean of the College of Arts & Sciences at the University of Maine.

No. 234: (C82/3/1)

Purchased from Harlan Berk, Joliet, Ill., 21st sale bid.

Nos. 187, 193, 198, 202, 209, 215, 226, 235, 237, 241, 274–95, 298–301, 306, 321, 322, 325, 326, 328: (C82/7/1–51)

Gift exchange with Mabee-Gerrer Museum, St. Gregory's College, Shawnee, Oklahoma. Previously obtained many years ago by Rev. Gregory Gerrer. Provenance is unknown.

Nos. 204, 229: (C83/1/1–2)

Purchased from Tom Cederlind, Portland, Oregon, Sale Catalogue no. 27.

Abbreviations used for Greek and Jewish coins in bibliographical references:

BMCG   Reginald S. Poole et al., *A Catalogue of Greek Coins in the British Museum*, 29 vols. (London, 1873–1927; reprint; Bologna, 1963–65).

Hendin   David Hendin, *Guide to Ancient Jewish Coins* (New York, 1976).

Kindler   Arie Kindler, *Coins of the Land of Israel* (Jerusalem, 1974).

Meshorer   Ya'akov Meshorer, *Jewish Coins of the Second Temple Period* (Tel Aviv, 1967).

Reifenberg   A. Reifenberg, *Ancient Jewish Coins*, 2d ed. (Jerusalem, 1947).

Reinach   Theodore Reinach, *Jewish Coins* (London, 1903).

Greek

(A. J. HEISSERER)

185

Tarentum, 380–345 B.C.
(C82/2/45)

Obv. Naked boy on horseback, cantering, r., r. arm hanging at side; under horse's body, Θ.

Rev. Taras astride dolphin r., r. arm stretched forward with open palm, l. arm on animal's tail, outline of r. shin and foot in front of animal's head; below dolphin, inscription, TAPA[Σ].

↓ 7.85 g. 19.75 mm. AR didrachm. *BMCG*, vol. 1, Tarentum, no. 110; A. J. Evans, *Numismatic Chronicle*, 3d ser., 9 (1889): 1–228 (period III, type P).

The reverse type refers to the Phoenician legend in which Taras, the founder of the city, landed in Italy on a dolphin. The horse type on the obverse perhaps makes reference to Taras's father, Poseidon, whose cult had great importance in Tarentum. Evans, *Numismatic Chronicle*, pp. 14–15. Unlike many Tarentine issues, neither of the figures on this issue bears any arms, an indication of the period of peace during which it was minted. Ibid., p. 46. The dates given above are also from ibid.

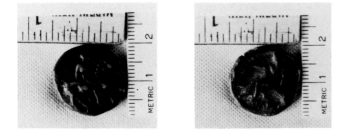

186

Alexander the Great (336–323 B.C.): Miletus?, ca. 325–293 B.C.
(C81/1/10)

Obv. Head of youthful Heracles r. with lion's skin covering.

Rev. ΑΛΕΞΑΝΔΡ[ΟΥ] downward in field r. Zeus seated l., holding eagle in outstretched r. hand and leaning with l. hand on long scepter. Monogram l. is obscure, but a form of **M** is visible with a magnifying glass.

↑ 3.43 g. 18 mm. AR drachm. M. Thompson and A. Bellinger, *Yale Classical Studies* 14 (1955): 3–45; A. Bellinger, *Essays on the Coinage of Alexander the Great* (New York, 1963).

This coin is representative of the large number of drachms issued by the various mints of Asia Minor during and after the period of Alexander the Great; these drachms supplemented the king's own silver. The name "Alexander" on the coin is no certain clue to dating, for the successors also minted silver with the conqueror's name. Thompson and Bellinger, *Yale Classical Studies*, pp. 10–12. The lack of uniformity of procedure in the mints of Alexander's empire makes it difficult to assign this specimen to a particular city, but its style and monogram suggest similarities with issues from Miletus. Cf. ibid., p. 32 with pls. 68 and 74. The dates given above correspond to those supplied by these two authors; if the Stovall coin was produced by the same moneyer as that in their pl. 74, it is one of the "autonomous" issue of 293 B.C. at Miletus.

117

The Greek cities minted autonomous drachms of ca. 2.5 to 3.5 grams, while Alexander produced drachms on the Attic standard that weighed 4.3 grams; this coin, therefore, reflects the problem of the "simultaneous issue of autonomous coins on one standard and drachms of Alexander on another." Bellinger, *Essays*, p. 45 n. 44.

187

Alexander the Great: Lampsacus, 310 B.C.
(C82/7/1)

Obv. Same as no. 186 above.

Rev. Same as no. 186 above, inscription AΛE-ΞAN[ΔPOY]. Forepart of Pegasus l.; monogram below illegible.

→ 3.88 g. 16 mm. AR drachm. (Bibliography as in no. 186.)

The remarks on the previous Alexander drachm apply here also, except that the use of the forepart of Pegasus indicates Lampsacus as the mint, and the presumed activity of Antigonus after the Peace of 311 B.C. has suggested the date of 310 B.C.. Cf. Thompson and Bellinger, *Yale Classical Studies*, pp. 14–15 with pls. 6b–e.

188

Ptolemy II Philadelphus (285–246 B.C.): mint uncertain, ca. 285–266 B.C.
(C81/1/12)

Obv. Head of Zeus to r., laureate.

Rev. Inscription obliterated; eagle to l. on thunderbolt, wings open; apparently plain border.

↑ 15.83 g. 22.5 mm. AE. *BMCG*, vol. 6, no. 20; L. Forrer, *The Weber Collection*, vol. 3, pt. 2 (London, 1929), nos. 8251–55, pl. 305.

Both surfaces are badly worn, but the obverse and reverse types most closely resemble the large bronzes issued by Ptolemy II Philadelphus in about the years 285–266 B.C.

189

Hieron II (274–216 B.C.): Syracuse
(C82/2/54)

Obv. Obliterated remains of head of Poseidon l., wearing tainia.

Rev. Ornamented trident with a dolphin on each side; inscription, IEPΩ[NOΣ]; in field, A or Λ.
Die-axis cannot be determined. 9.25 g. 20 mm. AE. *BMCG*, vol. 2, no. 598; S. W. Grose, *Catalogue of the McClean Collection of Greek Coins*, vol. 1 (Cambridge, 1923), nos. 2929–38.

190

Antiochus IV Epiphanes (175–164 B.C.): mint uncertain
(C81/1/14)

Obv. Head of Antiochus r., radiate; serrated edge; struck off-center.

Rev. Inscription obliterated; female figure, facing, wearing long garment; holds in r. hand long scepter.

↑ 1.87 g. 14 mm. AE. *BMCG*, vol. 4, no. 41.

191

Antiochus IV Epiphanes or Antiochus V Eupator (164–162 B.C.): mint uncertain.
(C81/1/13)

Obv. Head of Apollo r., laureate; in field to l., letter A with bent Y in place of crossbar; border of dots; serrated edge; struck off-center.

Rev. BAΣIΛE[ΩΣ ANTIOXOY]. Apollo seated l. on omphalos; holds bow and arrow.

↑ 2.78 g. 14 mm. AE. *BMCG*, vol. 4, nos. 5–6.

192

Demetrius II Nicator (146–138 B.C.): mint uncertain.
(C81/1/20)

Obv. Head of Demetrius r., diademed; serrated edge.

Rev. [BA]ΣIΛE[ΩΣ] ΔHMHT[PIOY]. Goddess (Demeter?) facing, veiled; holds in r. hand long torch or scepter.

↖ 3.15 g. 15 mm. AE. *BMCG*, vol. 4, no. 28.

193

Artabanus II (ca. A.D. 10–38): perhaps Ecbatana
(C82/7/2)

Obv. Diademed bust of Artabanus.

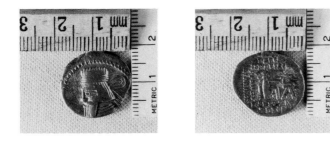

Rev.   Archer enthroned, holding bow; to r. form of A with topbar and dot below crossbar; inscription ΒΑΣΙΛΕ[ΩΣ] ΒΑΣΙ-ΛΕΩΝ[ΑΡ]ΣΑ[ΚΟΥΕ]ΥΕΡΓΕΤΟ[Υ] ΔΙ-ΚΑΙΟΥ ΕΠΙΦΑΝΟΥΣ ΦΙΛΕΛΛΗΝΟΣ.

↑   3.07 g.   19 mm.   AR drachm.   D. Sellwood, *An Introduction to the Coinage of Parthia* (London, 1971), no. 63/6.

194

Nero (A.D. 54–68): Alexandria, A.D. 64/65
(C82/2/48)

Obv.   [Ν]ΕΡΩ[ΚΛΑΥΚΑΙΣΣΕΒΓ]ΕΡ,   around bust r.

Rev.   [ΑΥΤ]ΟΚΡΑ. Eagle standing l., on thunderbolt; to l., ‖Α (= Year 11).

↑   11.89 g.   24 mm.   Billon tetradrachm. *BMCG*, vol. 16, nos. 165–67; J. G. Milne, *Catalogue of Alexandrian Coins* (Oxford, 1933; reprint with supplement by C. M. Kraay: Oxford, 1971), nos. 228–35.

195

Philip I (A.D. 244–249): Antioch ad Orontem
(C82/5/1)

Obv.   ΑΥΤΟΚΚΜΙΟΥΛΙΦΙΛΙ[ΠΠΟΣΣΕΒ], around from l.; draped bust of Philip I, r., radiate; border of dots.

Rev.   ΑΝΤΙΟΧΕΩΝΜΗΤΡΟΚΟΛΩΝ, around from l.; draped, veiled, and turreted bust of Tyche of Antioch, r.; above, ram running r., head l.; in field, Δ Ε and S C; star below neck; border of dots.

↓   15.38 g.   29.75 mm.   AE.   *BMCG*, vol. 20, nos. 524–32; S. W. Grose, *Catalogue of the McClean Collection of Greek Coins*, vol. 3 (Cambridge, 1929), nos. 9404–9408, pl. 347.1 and 4.

196

Philip I
(C82/5/2)

Obv.   Same as no. 195 above, but inscription faint.

Rev.   Same as no. 195 above, but inscription faint.

↑   13.35 g.   28 mm.   AE.   (Bibliography as in no. 195.)

197

Philip I: Alexandria, A.D. 245/46
(C82/2/47)

Obv.   ΑΚΜΙΟΥΦΙΛΙΠΠΟΣΕΥΣΕΒ.   Bust r., laureate; wears cuirass.

Rev.   Sarapis standing, facing, head r., rests with r. hand on sceptre; in field, L Γ (= Year 3).

↖   9.18 g.   22 mm.   Billon tetradrachm. *BMCG*, vol. 16, no. 1980; J. G. Milne, *Catalogue of Alexandrian Coins* (Oxford, 1933; reprint with supplement by C. M. Kraay: Oxford, 1971), nos. 3617–19.

Jewish and Related Issues

(A. J. HEISSERER)

198

Antiochus VII Sidetes (138–129 B.C.): likely Jerusalem, 132–130 B.C.
(C82/7/3)

Obv.   Anchor upside down flanked by Greek inscription in three lines, ΒΑΣΙΛΕ[ΩΣ] ΑΝΤΙΟΧ[ΟΥ ΕΥΕΡΓΕΤΟΥ]. Date below anchor, ΑΠ[Ρ] (Year 181 = 132/1 B.C.).
Rev.   Lily; border of dots.
←   2.57 g. 14 mm. AE. *BMCG*, vol. 4, no. 69; Kindler, no. 3; Hendin, no. 6.

199

Antiochus VII Sidetes
(C81/1/16)

Obv.   Same as no. 198 above, but date is obliterated and only faint remains of the inscription are visible; date will be either 132/1 or 131/0 B.C.
Rev.   Same as no. 198 above.
↗   2.79 g. 14.5 mm. AE. (Bibliography as in no. 198.)

200

Antiochus VII Sidetes
(C81/1/21)

Obv.   Same as no. 198 above, but date is obliterated and only faint remains of the inscription are visible; date will be either 132/1 or 131/0 B.C.
Rev.   Same as no. 198 above.
↗   2.48 g. 15 mm. AE. (Bibliography as in no. 198.)

These three Seleucid coins represent the prototype for a series later issued by the Jewish king Alexander Jannaeus (see no. 201); one may observe the similarity in the anchor and flower emblems. It seems that Antiochus allowed this type of coin to be minted at Jerusalem and circulated in the surrounding region, for these coins are mainly found in Judaea. Meshorer, pp. 57–58. The date on the first of these specimens refers to the year of the campaign of Antiochus in Judaea, when he captured Jerusalem. Probably these coins were intended by Antiochus to be used in the lands held by the Jewish ruler, John Hyrcanus I. Cf. Kindler, p. 11.

201

Alexander Jannaeus (103–76 B.C.): mint unknown
(C81/1/19)

Obv.   Anchor surrounded by Greek inscription, ΒΑΣΙΛΕΩ[Σ ΑΛΕΞ]ΑΝΔ[ΡΟΥ]; border of dots.
Rev.   Star with eight rays; between rays, faint remains of Hebrew inscription visible (presumably, "Yehonatan the king").
       4.39 g. 16 mm. AE. *BMCG*, vol. 27, nos. 61–88; Meshorer, no. 8; Reinach, pl. III.1; Kindler, no. 8; Reifenberg, no. 14.

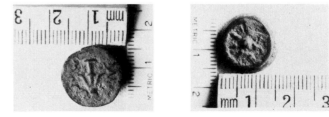

This is an interesting specimen of the major bronze issue of Alexander Jannaeus, king of the revived and independent Judaea and very likely first Hasmonaean monarch to mint coins. It illustrates Meshorer's observation (p. 59) that this bronze issue produced large and beautiful specimens at the beginning of the king's reign, but later the weight fell to as little as ca. 0.50 g. The Stovall coin, therefore, dates from some time in the early part of this king's reign.

202

Alexander Jannaeus
(C82/7/4)

Obv. Same as no. 201 above, but inscription, ΒΑΣΙΛΕ[ΩΣ] ΑΛ [ΕΞΑΝΔΡΟΥ].
Rev. Same as no. 201 above.
1.99 g. 14 mm. AE. (Bibliography as in no. 201.)

203

John Hyrcanus II (67 and 63–40 B.C.) or Judah Aristobulus II (67–63 B.C.): mint unknown, 67–40 B.C.
(C81/1/18)

Obv. Faint remains of Hebrew inscription, surrounded by wreath.
Rev. Faint remains of double cornucopiae, with pomegranate between horns; border of dots.
2.65 g. 14 mm. AE. *BMCG*, vol. 27, nos. 15–47, and p. 197, nos. 1–3; Meshorer, nos. 18–20A, 22–23, 26–29; Kindler, nos. 18–19.

Both surfaces are badly worn, and the reverse strike appears off-center; consequently, certain identification is not possible, but comparison with the numismatic styles of the Hasmonaean house suggests that this coin was very likely minted by one of these two rulers, and more probably John Hyrcanus II inasmuch as a greater number of his coins are extant. Compare also *BMCG*, vol. 27, pl. XX, no. 21. During the nineteenth century scholars ascribed this type of issue to John Hyrcanus I (135–104 B.C.), e.g., Reinach, pp. 22–24 with pl. II.4 and 5; and *BMCG*, vol. 27, pp. 188–97. But since Meshorer's revolutionary study (esp. pp. 41–56), the view has gained prominence that Alexander Jannaeus was the first Hasmonaean to strike coins. It may be mentioned, however, that Kindler (pp. 9–11) retains the traditional point of view.

204

Herod I (37–4 B.C.): mint unknown (Jerusalem?)
(C83/1/1)

Obv. Anchor surrounded by Greek inscription, much obliterated; border of dots.
Rev. Double cornucopiae, with caduceus between horns; dots or pellets above; border of dots.
1.66 g. 15 mm. AE. Meshorer, no. 53; Kindler, no. 35; Reifenberg, no. 33; Hendin, no. 54.

This coin is one of the most common types issued by Herod the Great and thus cannot be given any specific date during his reign. The inscriptions on all his coins are in Greek only, without a single specifically Jewish design apparent. Meshorer, pp. 64–67.

205

Aretas IV Philopatris (9 B.C.–A.D. 40): likely Petra
(C81/1/29)

Obv. Busts of Aretas and his sister and wife Shaqilath, conjoined, to 'r.; both wear ornaments on top of head; border of dots.
Rev. Two cornucopiae crossed and filleted; between them, above in two lines and below in one, a Nabataean inscription ("Aretas," "Shaqilath"); border of dots.
↑ 3.45 g. 17.5 mm. AE. *BMCG*, vol. 28, nos. 14–22; L. Forrer, *The Weber Collection*, vol. 3, pt. 2 (London, 1929), no. 8147 (pl. 300).

The territory of the Nabataeans was centered on its capital at Petra, but occasionally it incorporated areas toward the north. Aretas IV, for example, appears to have been in control of Damascus for a while. 2 Cor. 11.32. Aretas IV is well known as the father-in-law of Herod Antipas, son of Herod the Great.

206

Herod Agrippa I (A.D. 37–44): likely Jerusalem, A.D. 42/43
(C81/1/22)

Obv. Umbrella or canopy with fringes; Greek inscription around, ΒΑΣΙ [ΛΕΩΣ ΑΓΡ]ΙΠΠΑ; border of dots.
Rev. Three ears of barley growing between two leaves; in field, the date [L]S (Year 6 = A.D. 42/43); border of dots.
2.62 g. 17.5 mm. AE. *BMCG*, vol. 27, nos. 1–19; Meshorer, no. 88; Reinach, pl.

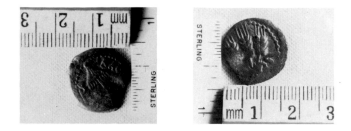

IV.5 and 6; Kindler, no. 51; Reifenberg, no. 59.

The reference to Year 6 indicates that this coin was struck in A.D. 42/43, the sixth year of the reign of Herod Agrippa I, grandson of Herod the Great. Meshorer, pp. 78–80. The grandson was educated at Rome and became a close friend to Caligula and Claudius. As a consequence, when Caligula became emperor in 37, he appointed his friend to be king of some of the territories of Herod the Great that had not formed the Roman province of Judaea. When Claudius in 41 succeeded Caligula, he assigned virtually the entire area previously ruled by Herod the Great. From 41 to 44 there was no province of Judaea; when Herod Agrippa I died in 44, Claudius reverted the area to its former provincial status and appointed a new governor.

207

Coponius (prefect of Judaea, A.D. 6–9) or Marcus Ambibulus (prefect of Judaea, A.D. 9–12): Caesarea, A.D. 6 or 9–11
(C81/1/3)

Obv. Ear of barley curved to r.; around, Greek inscription [K]AIΣA-PO[Σ].
Rev. Palm tree with eight branches and two bunches of fruit; the date in field is illegible.
2.02 g. 16 mm. AE. *BMCG*, vol. 27, nos. 1–27; Meshorer, pp. 102–106 with nos. 216–19; Reinach, pl. V.3; Kindler, nos. 143–45; Reifenberg, nos. 118–21.

208

Coponius or Marcus Ambibulus
(C81/1/4)

Obv. Same as no. 207 above with [K]AIΣA-[P]OΣ.
Rev. Same as no. 207 above.
1.72 g. 14.5 mm. AE. (Bibliography as in no. 207.)

These two coins both carry emblems that assign them to either of the prefects given above. The precise dates for their issues are known, but unfortunately the letters on the obverse indicating this fact are worn away.

The coins of all the Roman governors were not issued under the authority of the Roman senate, like the usual imperial bronze. Since Judaea was an imperial province, these small bronzes usually carry the name of the Roman emperor in Greek and a monogram indicating the regnal year of that emperor. Because these coins invariably present only inanimate objects, it is felt that they were struck by Jewish workmen and were intended for circulation only in Judaea. Reinach, pp. 40–41. Some coins, however, such as those of Pilate (see no. 209) were abhorrent to the Jewish people.

209

Pontius Pilatus (prefect of Judaea, A.D. 26–36): Caesarea, A.D. 30–31
(C82/7/5)

Obv. Lituus surrounded by Greek inscription, [T]IBEPIO[Y] KAI[ΣAPOΣ].
Rev. Wreath tied at bottom with an ×; within wreath the date [LI]Z (Year 17 = A.D. 30).
1.38 g. 15 mm. AE. *BMCG*, vol. 27, nos. 69–73; Meshorer, no. 230; Kindler, no. 158; Reifenberg, no. 132.

210

Pontius Pilatus
(C81/1/5)

Obv. Same as no. 209 above, TIBEPIOY [KAIΣ]APO[Σ].
Rev. Same as no. 209 above, the date LIH (Year 18 = A.D. 31).
1.63 g. 15 mm. AE. *BMCG*, vol. 27, nos. 78–82; Meshorer, no. 231; Reinach, pl. V.2; Kindler, no. 159; Reifenberg, no. 133.

211

Pontius Pilatus
(C81/1/23)

Obv. Same as no. 209 above, [T]IBEPI[OY KAIΣAPOΣ].
Rev. Same as no. 209 above, date illegible.
1.94 g. 14 mm. AE. (Bibliography as in no. 209.)

212

Pontius Pilatus
(C81/1/24)

Obv.   Same as no. 209 above, [TIBEPIO]Y ΚΑΙΣΑΡ[ΟΣ].
Rev.   Same as no. 209 above, date illegible.
1.93 g. 14 mm. AE. (Bibliography as in no. 209.)

213

Pontius Pilatus
(C81/1/25)

Obv.   Same as no. 209 above, lettering illegible.
Rev.   Same as no. 209 above, date illegible.
1.44 g. 14.5 mm. AE. (Bibliography as in no. 209.)

All the above coins of Pontius Pilatus are dated by Greek letters indicating the regnal year of the emperor Tiberius, which began in A.D. 14; and all specimens of the Stovall type fall in either the Year 17 (A.D. 30) or Year 18 (A.D. 31).

The coins of Pontius Pilatus are interesting because, unlike those of his predecessors, they often represent Roman pagan objects like the augur's wand (*lituus*) that were despised by the Jews.

The title of equestrian governors of imperial provinces under Augustus and Tiberius was *praefectus*, which was changed by Claudius to that of *procurator*. Thus, in the inscription of Pontius Pilatus from Caesarea, that governor is designated *praefectus*. Cf. H. H. Scullard, *From the Gracchi to Nero*, 2d ed. (London, 1963), p. 429 n. 24, and p. 444 n. 18.

214

Antonius Felix (procurator of Judaea, A.D. 52–58): Caesarea, A.D. 58
(C81/1/6)

Obv.   Wreath tied at bottom with an ×; within wreath, Greek inscription, ΝΕΡ/ΩΝΟ/Σ.
Rev.   Palm branch surrounded by date and Greek inscription, LE ΚΑΙΣ-ΑΡ[ΟΣ] (Year 5 = A.D. 58).
2.39 g. 16 mm. AE. *BMCG*, vol. 27, nos. 1–28; Meshorer, no. 234; Kindler, no. 163; Reifenberg, no. 136.

215

Antonius Felix
(C82/7/6)

Obv.   Same as no. 214 above, [ΝΕ]Ρ/ΩΝΟ/Σ.

Rev.   Same as no. 214 above, LE ΚΑΙΣ-[ΑΡΟΣ] (Year 5 = A.D. 58).
1.57 g. 14.5 mm. AE. (Bibliography same as in no. 214.)

The monogram LE indicates that the coin was struck in A.D. 58, because "Year 5" is calculated according to Nero's reign, which began in A.D. 54. Meshorer, pp. 102–106 and 174–75. This is the last year in which Roman governors of Judaea struck coins, and also the year of heaviest issue for any governor.

216

The First Revolt (A.D. 66–70): Jerusalem, A.D. 67
(C81/1/1)

Obv.   Amphora with wide brim and two handles; around, Hebrew inscription ("Year Two").
Rev.   Vine leaf with small branch and tendril; around, Hebrew inscription ("The freedom of Zion").
3.25 g. 17 mm. AE. *BMCG*, vol. 27, nos. 22–41; Meshorer, no. 153; Reinach, pl. V.4; Kindler, no. 73; Reifenberg, no. 147.

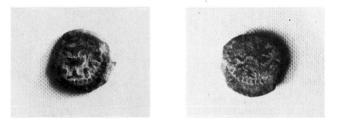

217

The First Revolt
(C81/1/26)

Obv.   Same as no. 216 above, but with faint remains of the Hebrew inscription.
Rev.   Same as no. 216 above, but with faint remains of the Hebrew inscription.
3.50 g. 18 mm. AE. (Bibliography as in no. 216.)

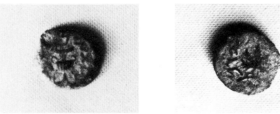

218

The First Revolt
(C81/1/28)

Obv.   Same as no. 216 above, but with faint re-
        mains of the Hebrew inscription.
Rev.   Same as no. 216 above, but with faint re-
        mains of the Hebrew inscription.
        2.89 g.   18 mm.   AE.   (Bibliography as
        in no. 216.)

219

The First Revolt: Jerusalem, A.D. 68
(C81/1/27)

Obv.   Amphora with wide rim, decorated lid,
        and two handles; around, Hebrew in-
        scription ("Year Three").
Rev.   Vine leaf with small branch and tendril;
        around, Hebrew inscription ("The free-
        dom of Zion").
        2.89 g.   16 mm.   AE.   *BMCG*, vol. 27,
        nos. 42–54; Meshorer, no. 156; Kindler,
        no. 76; Reifenberg, no. 148.

220

Bar Kochba Revolt (A.D. 132–35): Jerusalem, A.D. 133/34
(C81/1/2)

Obv.   Seven-branched palm tree with two
        bunches of fruit; below, Hebrew inscrip-
        tion ("Shimon").
Rev.   Vine leaf; around, Hebrew inscription
        ("Year Two of the freedom of Israel").
        9.02 g.   23.5 mm.   AE.   *BMCG*, vol.
        27, nos. 29–37; cf. Meshorer, no. 195;
        Reinach, pp. 56–57 with pl. IX.3; Hen-
        din, no. 160b; Kindler, nos. 107 and 114.

This beautiful coin was issued by Simon Bar
Kochba during the second year of the Second
Jewish War against Rome. The name "Shimon"
that appears on so many coins of this war is a real
name, not merely a slogan name or the like; the
letters written during the second war that were
discovered not long ago in the Judaean caves re-

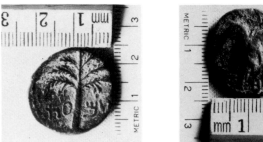

fer to him as "Shimon Bar Koseva." Meshorer,
p. 96.

221

Tyre, second era of autonomous coinage (125 B.C.–A.D. 70)
(C81/1/17)

Obv.   Head of Tyche r., wearing turreted
        crown, veil, and earring; border of dots.
Rev.   Galley l., with prow terminating in volute,
        and aphlastron at stern; above, date and
        monogram obliterated; Greek inscrip-
        tion ΙΕΡΑΣ ΑΣΥΛΟΥ; below, remains of
        Phoenician inscription ("of Tyre").
↑   5.04 g.   18.5 mm.   AE.   *BMCG*, vol.
        26, nos. 252–67; cf. B. V. Head, *Historia
        Numorum* (London, 1911), p. 800.

222

Vespasian?: Ascalon?, A.D. 78–79?
(C81/1/8)

Obv.   (No lettering visible). Male bust r., laure-
        ate, probably Vespasian.
Rev.   (No lettering visible). Female figure stand-
        ing l., draped, holding standard in r.
        hand, aphlaston in l., on prow.
↗   10.07 g.   21 mm.   AE.

This coin closely resembles two examples in the
BMCG of coins struck by Vespasian at Ascalon,
Judaea, (vol. 27, Ascalon, nos. 108–109); however, the absence of any legible lettering prevents this identification from being certain.

Roman

(FREDERICK L. BROWN)

Abbreviations used in bibliographical references:

Babelon — Ernest C. F. Babelon, *Description historique et chronologique des monnaies de la république romaine*, 2 vols. (Paris, 1885–86; reprint: Bologna, 1963).

BMC — Harold Mattingly et al., *Coins of the Roman Empire in the British Museum*, 6 vols. (London, 1923–62. Vols. 1–4 reprinted [vols. 3 and 4 with alterations]: London, 1965–68).

BMCG — Reginald S. Poole et al., *A Catalogue of Greek Coins in the British Museum*, 29 vols. (London, 1873–1927; reprint: Bologna, 1963–65).

BMCRR — H. A. Grueber, *Coins of the Roman Republic in the British Museum*, 3 vols. (London, 1910).

Cohen — Henry Cohen, *Description historique des monnaies frappées sous l'empire romain communément appelées médailles imperiales*, 8 vols. (Paris, 1880; reprint: Graz, 1955).

Crawford — Michael H. Crawford, *Roman Republican Coinage*, 2 vols. (Cambridge, 1974).

LRBC — P. V. Hill and J. P. C. Kent, *Late Roman Bronze Coinage A.D. 324–498* (London, 1965).

RIC — Harold Mattingly et al., *Roman Imperial Coinage*, 10 vols. (London, 1926–81).

Sydenham — Edward A. Sydenham, *The Coinage of the Roman Republic* (London, 1952).

For the date and place of mintage of the Stovall Roman coins, the following sources were generally used: Michael Crawford's *Roman Republican Coinage* (Cambridge, 1974) for the Republic (until 27 B.C.); *Coins of the Roman Empire in the British Museum* by Harold Mattingly and others (London, 1923–62) for the period 27 B.C. to A.D. 238; *Roman Imperial Coinage* by Mattingly and others (London, 1926–81) for the rest of the empire. However, P. V. Hill and J. P. C. Kent, *Late Roman Bronze Coinage* (London, 1965), was consulted for some of our fourth-century coinage, which cannot be identified specifically. Dates and places of mintage taken from other sources have been mentioned in the text.

Roman Republican

223

Rome, 275–270 B.C.
(C82/2/7)

Obv. Pegasus r.; below, ꝛ.
Rev. Pegasus l.; below, [S].
↑   141.72 g.   49 mm.   AE semis. *BMCG*, vol. 1, no. 12; Crawford, no. 18.2; Sydenham, no. 16.

This is one of the first Roman examples of what can truly be called coinage, since, in this period, coins have both indications of their value and fairly uniform weight. The S's on this issue indicate that the coins are semisses, worth half of an *as*.

224

Rome?, 211–209 B.C.?
(C51–2/1/17)

Obv.   Laureate head of Jupiter r.
Rev.   Victory r., crowning trophy; in exergue, ROMA.
↗   2.96 g.   17 mm.   AR victoriatus.

This victoriatus is apparently part of an anonymous issue. However, tarnish and wear might have merely hidden the moneyer's monogram, which would appear between Victory and the trophy. Crawford says that anonymous victoriati were minted from 211 to 170 B.C. at various mints. Of these anonymous issues, one example of issue 44 (pl. IX.1) most closely resembles the Stovall coin, especially in the base of the trophy, which neither widens nor narrows, the rough

portrait of Jupiter, and the lettering of ROMA with the "O" smaller than the other letters. Membership in this issue would give the coin the date and mint shown above. This anonymous issue developed into the issues signed with an anchor, an M, and an *apex* in 209 B.C. Crawford, p. 10 with nos. 50–52. However, the Stovall coin could belong to other issues of the period 211–170 B.C.

225

Rome?, 211–207 B.C.
(C82/2/8)

Obv.   Helmeted head of Roma r.; behind, X.
Rev.   Dioscuri on horseback r., each holding a spear; in exergue, ROMA (with archaic A, see photograph).
↘   4.18 g.   20 mm.   AR denarius.

Anonymous denarii like this one, having the mounted Dioscuri on the reverse, were minted from 211 to 156 B.C., primarily in Rome, according to Crawford. Of these anonymous issues, this denarius most closely resembles and probably belongs to the same issue as one example of Crawford, no. 53/2 (pl. X.13). It resembles this example especially in the style of Roma's helmet, the lettering of ROMA, the position of the horses, and the stars above the Dioscuri's heads, faintly visible on our coin. Such an identification would place the coin in the anonymous issue which developed into the issues signed by a crescent and a cornucopia in 207 B.C. and would place its mint at Rome. Crawford, p. 10 with nos. 57–58. However, this specific identification based on style cannot be certain.

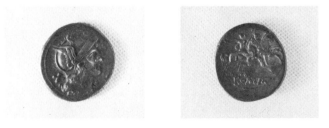

226

Probably Rome, 211–86 B.C.
(C82/7/8)

Obv.   Laureate head of Saturn r.; behind, S.
Rev.   Prow r.; below, ROMA; above, S.
←   10.94 g.   24 mm.   AE semis.

Crawford indicates in his index that the laureate head of Saturn, facing r., was the standard obverse type for semisses from 211 to 86 B.C. (nos. 56–350B). The first issue that has a weight standard which could reasonably be considered right for this coin is no. 97 with a standard of 23.5 g. for an *as* (a semis having half the weight of an *as*). The date Crawford suggests for no. 97 is 211–208 B.C., which means the Stovall coin could have been produced at any time during the period in which this type of semisses was being produced. Since no moneyer's mark is visible, no exact identification can be made as to the date or place of minting. This coin may be either an anonymous issue, or an issue on which the moneyer's mark has been worn away. Crawford (p. 601) indicates that almost all coinage from the end of the Second Punic War to the time of Sulla was minted at Rome, so the Stovall coin was most probably struck there.

227

Rome, 155 B.C.
(C51–52/1/13)

Obv.   Helmeted head of Roma r.; below chin, X.
Rev.   SAR (the letter Λ has a *v* in place of the crossbar). Victory in biga r., holding whip in r. hand, reins in l.; in exergue, ROMA.
↗   3.64 g. 17.5 mm. AR denarius. Babelon, Atilia, no. 1; *BMCRR*, Rome, no. 744; Crawford, no. 199.1a; Sydenham, no. 377.

The moneyer is perhaps Sex. Atilius Saranus, consul in 136 B.C.

228

Rome, 148 B.C.
(C51–52/1/12)

Obv.   LIBO. Helmeted head of Roma r.; below chin, X.
Rev.   Q MRC (with crossbar within the upper left portion of the M). Dioscuri on horseback r., with spears; in exergue, ROMA.
↓   3.59 g. 17.5 mm. AR denarius. Babelon, Marcia, no. 1; *BMCRR*, Rome, nos. 700, 701; Crawford, no. 215.1; Sydenham, no. 395 (all these examples show M with crossbar within the upper right portion of the letter).

Sydenham identifies the moneyer as Q. Marcius Libo.

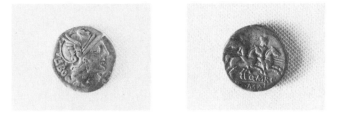

229

Rome, 138 B.C.
(C83/1/2)

Obv.   Helmeted head of Roma r.; behind her, X.
Rev.   Dioscuri on horseback r.; below, P PAETVS; in exergue, ROMA.
↙   4.02 g. 18 mm. AR denarius. Babelon, Aelia, no. 3; *BMCRR*, Rome, no. 877; Crawford, no. 233; Sydenham, no. 455.

The moneyer probably belonged to the Aelia *gens*, three members of which had been consuls in 201, 198, and 167 B.C. Crawford, p. 266.

230

Rome, 131 B.C.
(C51–52/1/16)

Obv.   Helmeted head of Roma r., behind, *apex* (flamen's cap); below chin, X.
Rev.   L POST A. B. Mars in quadriga r., holding shield and spear (the trophy visible in r. hand of Mars on some specimens is worn away here); in exergue, ROMA.
↙   3.82 g. 18.5 mm. AR denarius. Babelon, Postumia, no. 1; *BMCRR*, Rome, nos. 1130–32; Crawford, no. 252.1; Sydenham, no. 472.

Sydenham identifies the moneyer as L. Postumius Albinus. The flamen's cap probably indicates that he was the son of L. Postumius Albinus, flamen martialis in 168 B.C., curule aedile in 161 B.C., and consul in 154 B.C.

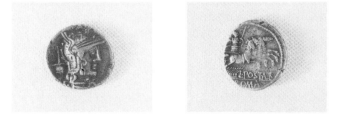

231

Rome, 111–110 B.C.
(C51–52/1/14)

Obv. Helmeted head of Roma r.; behind, a quadrangular design faintly visible.

Rev. Victory in triga r., holding reins in both hands; in exergue, T M̷ AP CL Q [V̷R] (with a small crossbar in the upper right portion of the letter M).

↙ 3.80 g. 17 mm. AR denarius. Babelon, Mallia, no. 2, Claudia, no. 3; *BMCRR*, Rome, no. 1293; Crawford, no. 299.1b; Sydenham, no. 570a.

232

Rome, 111–110 B.C.
(C51–52/1/15)

Obv. Same as no. 231 above, but quadrangular design is off flan.

Rev. Same as no. 231 above; in exergue, AP CL T M̷ Q V̷R (with a small crossbar in the upper right portion of the letter M).

↓ 3.92 g. 17 mm. AR denarius. Babelon, Mallia, no. 1, Claudia, no. 2; *BMCRR*, Rome, no. 1290; Crawford, no. 299.1a; Sydenham, no. 570.

The above two denarii were struck by the same triumvirate of moneyers, who merely changed the order of their names. AP CL is perhaps Ap. Claudius Pulcher, praetor in 89 B.C. and consul in 79. Crawford thinks that T M̷ could be T. Maloleius or T. Mallius (Babelon's interpretation) if M̷ is taken as a monogram for MAL, or T. Manlius Macinus, tribunis plebis in 107 B.C., if it is taken as a monogram for MANL. He interprets the last three letters of the legend as Q. Urbinius, although Babelon and others have taken it to mean "Quaestores Urbani."

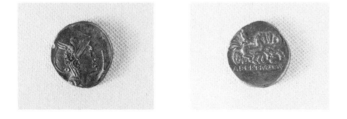

233

Spain or Sicily, 45–44 B.C.
(C84/4/17)

Obv. Laureate head of Janus; above, [some form of MAGNVS].

Rev. Prow r.; below, IMP; above, [PIVS].

↑ 22.26 g. 28 mm. AE *as*. Babelon, Pompeia, no. 20; *BMCRR*, Spain, nos. 95–103; Crawford, no. 479.1; Sydenham, nos. 1044–44b.

This coin was struck by Sextus Pompey during the period in which he moved from Spain to Sicily, the first part of the issue being struck in Spain, the last part in Sicily. This *as* can be distinguished from other coins of the denomination by Sextus's replacing of the standard exergual legend, ROMA, with his own title, IMP(erator), and by the absence of the sign of value, I, above Janus's head, which he replaced with some form of his title, MAGNVS. Crawford and Sydenham both note that Janus has the features of Sextus's father, Pompey the Great.

234

Vienna, 40–28 B.C.
(C82/3/1)

Obv. DIVI IVLI IMP CAESA[R DIVI F]. The bare heads of Julius Caesar (on left) and Octavian, back-to-back.

Rev. The prow of a ship with superstructure r.; above, [C I V].

↙ 20.78 g. 31.25 mm. AE *as*. Cohen, Julius Caesar and Octavian, no. 7; *RIC*, vol. 1, p. 43.

The date is from *RIC*. The name of the town, Vienna, was that of a Roman colony in southeastern Gaul.

Early Roman Imperial

The two forms of the letter A (A and Λ) are common on the coinage of the first 150 years of the Roman Empire, sometimes both appearing on the same coin. In the following legends, both have been represented with A.

The question arises whether certain antoniniani of the period from Valerian to Diocletian should be called silver, base silver, or bronze. We have generally labeled them "AE," since in their present state they are almost wholly base metal. Actually, however, when these coins were minted, they probably had a coating of silver wash, which has since worn off. David R. Sear, *Roman Coins and their Values* (London, 1981), p. 246. Sear states that this practice started about A.D. 258, when the real silver content of this coin fell dramatically. Rarely in the period A.D. 258–96 did the antoninianus have a silver content greater than 4 percent. From this time to the reform of Diocletian, the antoninianus, first issued as a silver coin by Caracalla in A.D. 214, really became the principal bronze coin of the empire. Diocletian ceased minting the antoninianus around A.D. 296, replacing it with the "postreform radiate" (which was minted for only about ten years) and the follis. The folles were usually silver-washed too, although they appear to be merely base metal today. The Stovall's collection contains several examples of these antoniniani and folles which were once silver-washed.

235

Augustus: Rome, 23 B.C.
(C82/7/9)

Obv.   [AVG]V[STVS] TRIBVNIC POTEST, inside an oak wreath.
Rev.   CN PISO CN [F III] VIR A A [A F F], with large S C in center.
↗   13.07 g.   26.5 mm.   AE dupondius. *BMC*, nos. 135, 136; Cohen, no. 378; *RIC*, no. 71.

This coin was issued by the moneyer Cn. Calpurnius Piso, consul in 7 B.C. *BMC*, vol. 1, p. xcv.

236

Augustus: Nemausus, 18 B.C.
(C56–57/9/2)

Obv.   IMP-DIVI F. Heads of Augustus on r.; laureate and Agrippa with rostral crown (see commentary to nos. 239–40 below), back to back.

Rev.   COL-NEM. Crocodile r., chained to palm tree.
↘   12.53 g.   26.5 mm.   AE *as*. Cohen, Augustus and Agrippa, no. 10; *RIC*, vol. 1, p. 44. Ex L. G. P. Messenger Collection (London).

The reverse legend refers to the Roman colony of Nemausus (modern Nîmes, France), founded ca. 22 B.C. E. A. Sydenham (*Historical References to Coins of the Roman Empire* [London, 1917; reprint, 1968], p. 20) dates this coin to 18 B.C., because that was the only year after the founding of Nemausus during which Augustus and Agrippa were partners in government. He identifies the moneyer as C. Sulpicius Platorinus, and also states, "The crocodile cannot well be associated with southern Gaul but must refer to the subjection of Egypt." Ibid.

237

Augustus: Rome, 7 B.C.
(C82/7/10)

Obv.   [CAESAR AVGVST PONT MAX TRIBVNIC POT]. Head of Augustus, bare l.
Rev.   M SALVIVS OTHO III [VIR] A A A F F Large S C in center.
↖   9.79 g.   26.5 mm.   AE *as*. *BMC*, nos. 233–34; Cohen, no. 516; *RIC*, no. 190.

This coin was minted by the moneyer M. Salvius Otho.

238

Tiberius: Rome, A.D. 22–23
(C56–57/9/3)

Obv.   PIETAS. Bust of Livia r., draped, veiled, and wearing a stephane.
Rev.   DRVSVS CAESAR TI AVGVSTI F TR POT ITER. Large S C in center.
↓   14.12 g.   30 mm.   AE dupondius. *BMC*, Tiberius, no. 98; Cohen, Livia, no. 1; *RIC*, Tiberius, no. 24.

This coin is a member of one of a series of three issues in which the senate honored Livia as the personification of *Pietas*, *Justitia*, and *Salus*.

239

Tiberius or Caligula: Rome, ca. A.D. 30–41
(C82/2/9)

Obv.   M AGRIPPA L-F COS III. Head of Agrippa l., wearing rostral crown.
Rev.   Neptune standing l., naked except for cloak over l. shoulder, holding trident in l. hand, small dolphin in r.; in field, S-C.
↓   10.50 g. 27 mm. AE *as*. *BMC*, Tiberius, no. 161; Cohen, Agrippa, no. 3; *RIC*, Tiberius, no. 32.

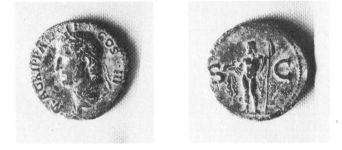

240

Tiberius or Caligula
(C56–57/9/1)

Obv.   Same as no. 239 above.
Rev.   Same as no. 239 above, but dolphin has been worn away.
↙   9.73 g. 29 mm. AE *as*. (Bibliography as in no. 239.) Ex Messenger Coll.

The *BMC* identifies these as asses minted after the death of Agrippa; thus, the COS III is of no aid in dating them. Mattingly states that "a study of the hybrids formed by the obverse of this as with other reverses rather suggests a date near the close of the reign of Tiberius." *BMC*, vol. 1, p. cxxxiii. But he also mentions an article by Laffranchi (*Rivista Italiana di Numismatica*, 1910, pp. 26 ff), which suggests a date in Caligula's reign.

The Neptune reverse is obviously a reference to Agrippa's brilliant naval career, as is the rostral crown, "a circlet of gold, relieved with figures of the prows and sterns of ships," which identifies Agrippa as a *praefectus classis*, or high admiral. Seth Stevenson et al., *A Dictionary of Roman Coins* (London, 1889; reprint, 1964), p. 27.

241

Claudius: Rome, A.D. 41
(C82/7/11)

Obv.   [TI CLA]VDIVS CAES[AR AVG]. Hand l., holding pair of scales; below, [P N R].
Rev.   PON M [TR P IMP C]OS DES IT. Large S C in center.
↙   2.43 g. 17 mm. AE quadrans. *BMC*, no. 174; Cohen, no. 71; *RIC*, no. 74.

The "P N R" probably stands for "pondus nummorum restitutum." *BMC*, vol. 1, p. clviii.

242

Nero: Lugdunum, A.D. 64–66
(C56–57/9/4)

Obv.   IMP NERO CAESAR AVG PONT MAX TR POT P P. Laureate bust of Nero l., with small globe at point of bust.
Rev.   View of a triumphal arch, showing the front and l. side; above, the emperor in a facing quadriga, Victory standing facing on r., Pax standing facing on l., two small soldiers on either side of Victory and Pax; in niche on l., Mars standing facing; the arch is also covered with ornate relief; in field, S-C.
↙   25.30 g. 33.5 mm. AE sestertius. *BMC*, nos. 333–34; Cohen, no. 309; *RIC*, no. 156. Ex British Museum exchange.

Mattingly says that this arch is the one mentioned in Tacitus (*Annales* 13.4.1), decreed after Nero's victories in the East in A.D. 58. *BMC*, vol. 1, p. clxxviii.

243

Nero: Rome, A.D. 64–66
(C82/2/22)

Obv.   [NERO CLAVDIVS] CAESAR AVG

GERM P M T[R P IMP P P]. Radiate
head of Nero r.

Rev.   VICTORIA [AVGVSTI] Winged Victory
advancing l., draped, holding wreath in
r. hand, palm in l.; in field, S-C; in exergue, $\overline{II}$.

↓   13.50 g.   27 mm.   AE dupondius.
BMC, no. 220; *RIC*, no. 311.

The $\overline{II}$ on the reverse indicates the coin's worth,
two asses. The reverse type of Victory probably
refers to the Parthian victory of A.D. 63. *BMC*,
vol. 1, p. clxxx.

244

Galba: Mint of Rome or Gaul, A.D. 68–69
(C82/2/23)

Obv.   [IMP SER G]ALBA [CAE]SAR AVG TR
[P]. Bare head of Galba r.

Rev.   Vesta seated l., draped, holding palla-
dium in r. hand, spear in l.; in exergue,
VEST[A]; in field, S-[C].

↙   10.54 g.   26.75 mm.   AE *as*. *BMC*, no.
160; Cohen, no. 310; *RIC*, no. 72.

245

Vitellius: Rome, July 18–December 20, A.D. 69
(C56–57/9/5)

Obv.   A VITELLIVS GERMA-N IMP AVG P M
TR [P]. Laureate bust of Vitellius r.,
draped.

Rev.   MARS-VICTOR. Mars advancing l., helmeted and in military dress, holding Victory in r. hand and a trophy in l., with a
short sword at l. side; in field, S-C.

↙   24.76 g.   34.5 mm.   AE sestertius.
BMC, no. 52 shows GERMAN, instead
of GERMA-N. Ex British Museum exchange.

This coin can be dated to the latter part of Vitellius's short reign, because he did not strike bronze
coinage until he entered Rome on about July 18;

he also did not accept the title AVG(ustus) until
that time. This issue continued to be struck until
his death. *BMC*, vol. 1, p. ccxxii.

246

Titus: Rome, A.D. 80–81
(C51–52/1/22)

Obv.   [DIVVS AVGVST]VS VESPASI[ANVS].
Laureate head of Vespasian r.

Rev.   Spes advancing l. (and, as less worn examples show, holding a flower in r. hand,
while raising dress with l.); in exergue,
[S-C].

↓   21.30 g.   35 mm.   AE sestertius. *BMC*,
Titus, no. 249; Cohen, Vespasian, no.
461; *RIC*, Titus, no. 147.

This is a commemorative issue struck by Titus
for his father after his death.

247

Domitian: Rome, A.D. 85–96
(C82/2/24)

Obv.   IMP [CAES] DOMIT AVG GERM COS
X . . . [CENS PER P P]. Laureate head of
Domitian r.

Rev.   VIRTV[TI]-AVGVSTI. Virtus standing
r., draped, holding a spear in r. hand,
short sword in l., with l. foot resting on
globe; in field, S-C.

↓   10.56 g.   27.5 mm.   AE dupondius.

248

Domitian
(C82/2/25)

Obv.   [IMP CAES DOMIT AVG] GERM COS
. . . [CENS PER P P]. Same as no. 247
above.

Rev.   [VIRTVTI]-AVG[VSTI]. Same as no. 247
above; in field, S-C.

↓   10.37 g.   27.5 mm.   AE dupondius.

These two coins could belong to any of several
issues which Domitian minted, having consular

numbers from XI to XVI; however, since the number of Domitian's consulship is not completely legible on either coin, we cannot date them specifically.

Mattingly (*BMC*, vol. 2, p. xci) describes Virtus as "the spirit of martial valour, the symbol of that forward military policy which ruled Domitian from A.D. 83 to almost the close of his reign."

249

Domitian
(C81/1/9)

Obv. [IMP CAES] DO[MIT] AVG-GERM. . . . Laureate bust of Domitian r.
Rev. [I]M[P]. . . . Minerva standing r., draped, helmeted, throwing spear with r. hand, holding a round shield in l., on the prow of a ship with an owl at her feet.
↙ 2.66 g. 18.5 mm. AR denarius.

This is a common type of coin throughout Domitian's reign. The date can be specified only somewhat by the title, GERM(anicus), which he did not receive until A.D. 83 or 84, and by the abbreviation, DOMIT, which he did not use until A.D. 85.

Mattingly (*BMC*, vol. 2, pp. lxxxv–lxxxvi) states that Minerva was "the goddess to whom Domitian referred all his activities," citing Dio Cassius, Martial, and Quintilian as literary proof. In the type on this coin, she stands as the goddess of the fleet.

250

Trajan: Rome, A.D. 103–11
(C81/1/11)

Obv. [IMP TRAIA]NO AVG GER DAC [P M TR P]. Laureate bust of Trajan r., with slight drapery over l. shoulder.
Rev. COS V P [P S P Q R OPTI]MO PRINC. Goddess standing l., draped, holding object in r. hand, resting l. arm on column.
↙ 2.79 g. 17.5 mm. AR denarius.

Since the object in the goddess's right hand is not visible, it is impossible to determine whether she is Felicitas holding a caduceus (as in *BMC*, no. 305) or Pax holding a branch (as in *BMC*, no. 315).

251

Trajan: Rome, A.D. ca. 107–11
(C56–57/9/6)

Obv. IMP CAES NERVAE TRAIANO AVG GER DAC P M TR P COS V P P. Laureate bust of Trajan r., draped.
Rev. S P Q R OPTIMO PRINCIPI. Front view of temple with eight columns, on podium of five steps; in center of columns, a seated figure; to l. and r., arcades of five columns; in exergue, S C.
↓ 23.34 g. 34.5 mm. AE sestertius. *BMC*, nos. 863–65; Cohen, no. 549; *RIC*, no. 577. Ex V. J. E. Ryan collection (Jersey).

Mattingly (*BMC*, vol. 3, p. cii) says that any positive identification of the temple is impossible; Cohen, however, (vol. 2, p. 75) describes the seated figure in the temple as Jupiter. For the dates given above see *BMC*, vol. 3, p. ci.

252

Hadrian: Rome, A.D. 119–21
(C56–57/9/8)

Obv. [IMP] CAESAR TRAIAN HADRIANVS-VG P M TR P COS III. Laureate bust of Hadrian r., with drapery over l. shoulder.
Rev. PIETAS-AVGVSTI. Pietas standing r., veiled, draped, raising r. hand, holding box of incense in l., before altar; in field, S-C.
↓ 26.69 g. 34 mm. AE sestertius. *BMC*, no. 1198.

Mattingly says that the obverse legend ends with P P, but the plates for this section of *BMC* show no P P. The drapery of Hadrian matches the variant from the Tinchant collection mentioned in Mattingly's note.

253

Hadrian: Rome, A.D. 119–38
(C56–57/9/9)

Obv. HADRIANVS-AVG COS III P P. Laure-

ate bust of Hadrian r., with slight drapery over l. shoulder.

Rev.   S-ALVS-AVG. Salus standing l., draped, feeding snake on altar out of patera in r. hand, holding scepter in l.; in field, S-C.

↘   26.63 g.   31.5 mm.   AE sestertius. *BMC*, no. 1558 (this example shows SALVS, not S-ALVS); Cohen, no. 1333 (breaks not mentioned); *RIC*, no. 786 (breaks not mentioned).

254

Hadrian: Rome, A.D. 121–ca. 125
(C56–57/9/7)

Obv.   IMP CAESAR TRAIAN HA-DRIANVS AVG. Laureate bust of Hadrian r., with drapery over l. shoulder.

Rev.   P M TR P-COS III. Spes advancing l., draped, holding up a flower in r. hand, raising her skirt with l.; in field, S-C.

↓   26.71 g.   34 mm.   AE sestertius. *BMC*, no. 1255 (this example shows the break after TRAIAN, instead of HA-DR . . .); *RIC*, no. 612a (break not mentioned).

See *BMC*, vol. 3, p. clxiii for the dates given above.

255

Hadrian: Rome, A.D. 125–28
(C51–52/1/18)

Obv.   HADRIANVS-[AVGVSTVS]. Laureate bust of Hadrian r., with drapery on l. shoulder.

Rev.   COS-[I]II. Diana standing facing, head to r., holding arrow in r. hand, bow in l.

↙   3.01 g.   17 mm.   AR denarius. *BMC*, nos. 334–36; Cohen, no. 315; *RIC*, no. 147.

Mattingly (*BMC*, vol. 3, p. cxxxiv) states, "Diana, the archeress with bow and arrow, is the patroness of Hadrian, who, like Trajan, was a passionate hunter."

256

Antoninus Pius?: Rome?, A.D. 140–44?
(C51–52/1/23)

Obv.   (No lettering visible). Bust of youthful man r., draped, probably Marcus Aurelius.

Rev.   . . . O. . . . Female figure standing facing, draped, with head to l., r. arm extended, l. arm raised; possibly Honos (as *BMC*, no. 1395); in field, S-C.

↑   19.10 g.   28 mm.   AE sestertius.

The portrait on the obverse of our coin closely resembles other youthful portraits of Marcus Aurelius, and the reverse type resembles those found on the early coins of Marcus Aurelius. If the coin does belong to him, it certainly must have been struck when he was a consul under Antoninus Pius, since the portrait shows that he is still clean-shaven. He was consul for the first time in A.D. 140, and his beard first appears on his coins in A.D. 145; thus, we have for the coin the possible dates given above. However, since no obverse legend is visible, this identification cannot be certain.

257

Antoninus Pius: Rome, A.D. 145–61
(C82/2/26)

Obv.   ANTONINVS AVG-[PIVS P P TR P COS IIII]. Laureate head of Antoninus Pius r.

Rev.   Mars advancing r., naked except for drape floating behind him, holding spear in r. hand, trophy over l. shoulder in l.; in field, S-C.

✓   10.41 g. 24.5 mm. AE *as*. *BMC*, no. 1758; *RIC*, no. 825.

258

Antoninus Pius: Rome, A.D. ca. 147–61
(C51–52/1/19)

Obv. DIVA-FAV[STINA]. Draped bust of Faustina I r., with hair curled on top of head.

Rev. AVGV-[STA]. Ceres standing r., draped, veiled, holding scepter in r. hand, two ears of corn in l.

✓   2.69 g. 17 mm. AR denarius. *BMC*, no. 389; *RIC*, no. 358.

This is one of many issues of coins that Antoninus Pius used to honor his wife, who died in A.D. 141. These issues, emphasizing her divinity and immortality, continued to the end of his reign. See *BMC*, vol. 4, p. xliii for the dates of this issue given above.

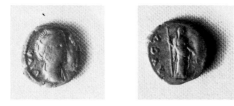

259

Marcus Aurelius: Rome, December, A.D. 170–December, 171
(C51–52/1/24)

Obv. M ANTONINVS-[AVG TR P X]XV. Laureate head of Marcus r.

Rev. [IMP VI COS III]. Winged Victory standing facing, with head to r., draped, l. hand on round shield, inscribed VIC/GER, resting on the trunk of a tree; in field, [S-C].

↖   24.59 g. 33 mm. AE sestertius. *BMC*, nos. 1388–89; Cohen, no. 269; *RIC*, no. 1001.

This coin called to the Roman people's attention a certain victory in the war in Germany, where fighting was to continue until the end of Marcus Aurelius's reign.

260

Marcus Aurelius: Rome, A.D. 176–80
(C82/2/27)

Obv. [DIVA]FAV-STINA PIA. Bust of Faustina II r., draped, hair elaborately waved and put into a bun.

Rev. [AETERNITAS]. Aeternitas standing front, head to l., veiled, draped, holding phoenix on globe in r. hand, resting l. arm on column; in field, S-C.

↗   19.71 g. 28.5 mm. AE sestertius. *BMC*, Marcus Aurelius, nos. 1563–65; Cohen, Faustina the Younger, no. 7; *RIC*, Marcus Aurelius, no. 1693.

This coin is a memorial to the wife of Marcus Aurelius, who died in the winter of A.D. 175–76; it emphasizes her divinity and immortality.

261

Pescennius Niger: Antioch?, A.D. 193–94
(C81/1/15)

Obv. IMP CAES C PESC-NIGER IVS. . . . Head of Pescennius Niger r., laureate.

Rev. FOR-TVN[AE] REDVCI. Fortuna standing l., draped, holding rudder in r. hand, cornucopia in l.

↑   3.01 g. 18 mm. AR?

Although at first glance this coin appears to be bronze, a closer inspection reveals silver showing through on the highest detail, which leads one to believe this is a silver denarius covered with corrosion because of its base metal content or because of contact with bronze coins in a hoard. The Stovall coin resembles the coin mentioned in the footnote. *BMC*, vol. 5, p. 76 (L. Vierordt Sale, Schulman, Amsterdam, 5 March 1923; lot 1798). If this coin is bronze, it would have to be a forgery, since Pescennius Niger, never having been recognized by the senate, struck no money in base metal.

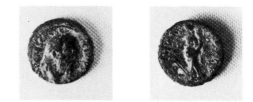

262

Septimius Severus: Rome, A.D. 203
(C51–52/1/20)

Obv.   SEVERVS-PIVS AVG. Laureate head of
Septimius r.

Rev.   P M TR P XI–COS III P P. Fortuna
seated l., draped, holding rudder in r.
hand, cornucopia in l.; under chair,
wheel.

↙   3.50 g.   18.5 mm.   AR denarius.
BMC, no. 432; Cohen, no. 461; *RIC*,
no. 189b.

With this coin, Septimius honors Fortuna Redux
for her help in guiding him back to Rome from
the campaign in Britain.

263

Elagabalus?: mint uncertain, A.D. 218–22?
(C82/2/5)

Obv.   . . . AV(R?) AN[T]ONINVS. . . . Laureate male head r., possibly Elagabalus.

Rev.   (No lettering legible). Figure seated l.

↓   5.16 g.   20 mm.   AE.

A number of Roman emperors used AN-
TONINVS as part of their name on their coinage, the most important being Antoninus Pius,
Marcus Aurelius, Commodus, Caracalla, and
Elagabalus; of these men, the portrait on the
Stovall coin most closely resembles Elagabalus.
The size and weight of this coin are, however,
much too small for any of his bronze coinage,
which may indicate that it is a forgery of a silver
coin, struck in base metal. The worn condition of
this specimen prevents any certainty about this
judgment.

264

Severus Alexander?: mint uncertain, A.D. 226?
(C81/1/7)

Obv.   (No visible lettering). Laureate male bust
r., draped, possibly that of Severus
Alexander.

Rev.   (No visible lettering). Some sort of struc-
ture, possibly the Nymphaeum of
Alexander.

↗   5.67 g.   19 mm.   AE.

The French gentleman who owned this coin
about a century ago identified it as belonging to
Severus Alexander, an identification which cannot be certain given the worn condition of the
coin and the absence of any legible lettering. If
the coin does belong to Alexander, it must be an
ancient forgery of one of his denarii (*BMC*,
no. 323) struck either in base metal or in base
metal with a silver-wash coating, which has since
worn off. See *BMC*, vol. 6, pp. 24–25. Alexander
struck no bronze coinage that resembles this coin
in both size and type.

265

Severus Alexander: Rome, A.D. 228
(C51–52/1/25)

Obv.   [IMP CAE]S M AVR SEV-ALEXANDE[R
AVG]. Laureate bust of Alexander r.,
draped.

Rev.   [P M TR P VII] COS [II P P]. Severus
Alexander, as Romulus, in military dress,
advancing r., holding spear in r. hand,
trophy over l. shoulder with l. hand; in
field, S-C.

↑   22.62 g.   29 mm.   AE sestertius.   *BMC*,
no. 474; Cohen, no. 352; *RIC*, no. 481.

This coin is too corroded to be able to determine
whether the reverse legend is divided like *BMC*,
no. 474 (i.e., CO-S-II).

266

Severus Alexander: Rome, A.D. 228
(C82/2/10)

Obv.   IVLIA MAMA-[E]A AVGVSTA. Bust of
Mamaea r., draped, wearing stephane.

Rev.   [FELICITAS P]V[B]LICA. Felicitas
standing facing, draped, head to l., legs
crossed, leaning on column to l. (less
worn examples show that she holds a caduceus in her r. hand); in field, S-C.

↓   15.95 g.   23.5 mm.   AE sestertius.
BMC, Severus Alexander, nos. 487–92;
Cohen, Julia Mamaea, no. 21; *RIC*,
Severus Alexander, no. 676.

With this coin, as with various issues throughout
his reign, Alexander honors his mother, who
helped him in obtaining the throne and in ruling.

267

Severus Alexander: Rome, A.D. 231
(C81/3/1)

Obv. IMP ALE[X]AN[DER PIV]S AVG.
      Laureate bust of Alexander r., draped,
      cuirassed.
Rev. IOVI [PR]O-P-VGNATORI. Jupiter
      standing facing, with head to r., naked
      except for drapery over l. shoulder and
      arm, holding a thunderbolt in r. hand.
↗   2.59 g.   17.5 mm.   AR denarius.
      BMC, nos. 790–93 (Carson gives the re-
      verse legend as IOVI PRO-PVGNATORI,
      but his plate for coin no. 793 quite clearly
      shows that the division is IOVI PRO-P-
      VGNATORI, as on this coin); Cohen,
      no. 76 (breaks not mentioned).

Carson states that Jupiter's importance on this
coin is as the defender of Alexander in the Persian War. *BMC*, vol. 6, p. 80. His presence also
points to Alexander's attempt to purge Rome of
Eastern cults and to restore the worship of the
Roman gods. Edward A. Sydenham, *Historical
References to Coins of the Roman Empire*, (London,
1917; reprint, 1968), p. 133.

268

Severus Alexander: Rome, A.D. 232
(C82/2/28)

Obv. IMP ALEXANDER PIVS AVG. Laureate
      bust of Severus Alexander r., draped,
      cuirassed.
Rev. [PROVIDENTIA AVG]. Providentia
      standing front, head to l., draped, hold-
      ing corn ears over modius with r. hand,
      cornucopia with l.; in field, S-C.
↗   18.36 g.   27.5 mm.   AE sestertius.
      BMC, no. 881.

Carson (*BMC*, vol. 6, p. 80) states that Providentia's importance here is as the supplier of the
army and of the fleet.

269

Gordian III: Rome, A.D., July, 238–July, 239
(C82/2/29)

Obv. [IMP] CAES M ANT GOR[DIANVS
      AVG]. Laureate bust of Gordian r.,
      draped, cuirassed.
Rev. [VI]CTO-RIA [AVG]. Victory advancing
      l., draped, holding wreath in r. hand,
      palm in l.; in field, S-[C].
↗   11.87 g.   25 mm. (edge broken away).
      AE *as*. Cohen, no. 359; *RIC*, no. 258b.

Mattingly (*RIC*, vol. 4, pt. 3, p. 8) states that this
Victory refers not to any specific military victory,
but to Gordian's ability to maintain the "tri-
umphant peace of Rome."

270

Gordian III: Rome, A.D. 240–44
(C49–50/9/1)

Obv. IM[P GOR]DIANVS PIVS FEL AVG.
      Laureate bust of Gordian r., draped.
Rev. P A X-AETERNA. Pax running l.,
      draped, holding branch in r. hand,
      scepter in l.; in exergue, S-C.
↑   17.87 g.   28.5 mm.   AE sestertius.
      Cohen, no. 169; *RIC*, no. 319a.

RIC does not date this issue; thus, we can only
specify the date somewhat by the fact that Gordian did not take the title PIVS until A.D. 240.

271

Gordian III: Rome, A.D. 241–43
(C51–52/1/21)

Obv. IMP GORDIANVS PIVS FEL AVG.
      Radiate bust of Gordian r., draped,
      cuirassed.
Rev. [LAET]ITIA AVG N. Laetitia standing l.,
      draped, holding wreath in r. hand, an-
      chor in l.
↓   4.08 g.   23 mm.   AR antoninianus.
      Cohen, no. 121; *RIC*, no. 86.

The *Laetitia* of Augustus probably refers to his
marriage in A.D. 241 to Sabinia Tranquillina,
daughter of Timisitheus, the prefect of the
praetorian guard. *RIC*, vol. 4, pt. 3, pp. 10–11.

272

Philip I: Rome, A.D. 244–49
(C51–52/1/26)

Obv. IMP M IVL PHILIPPVS AVG. Laureate
      bust of Philip r., draped, cuirassed.

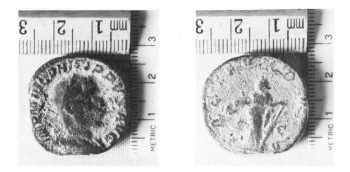

Rev.   LAET [F]V[N]D[AT]A. Laetitia standing
        l., draped, holding rudder in l. hand,
        wreath in r.; in field, S-C.
↗   20.62 g.   28 mm.   AE sestertius. *RIC*,
        no. 175a; Cohen, no. 73.

273

Philip I: Rome, A.D. 248–49
(C82/2/30)

Obv.   IMP M IVL PHIL[IPVS] AVG. Laureate
        bust of Philip II r., draped, cuirassed.
Rev.   LIB[ERA]LITAS AVGG III. Philip I (on
        r.) and Philip II seated l. on curule chairs,
        with r. hands extended; Philip I holds a
        short scepter in l. hand; in exergue, S C.
↑   16.82 g.   27.5 mm.   AE sestertius.
        Cohen, no. 18; *RIC*, no. 267a.

This issue celebrates the third largesse of Philip I
and his co-Augustus and son, Philip II.

274

Gallienus: Rome, A.D. 260–68
(C82/7/12)

Obv.   IMP GALLIENVS AVG. Radiate head of
        Gallienus r.
Rev.   DIANAE CONS AV[G]. Stag walking r.,
        looking backward; in exergue, unclear
        mint mark, apparently Є.

↗   2.52 g.   21 mm.   AE antoninianus.
        RIC, no. 178 (sole reign).

275

Gallienus: Siscia, A.D. 260–68
(C82/7/13)

Obv.   GAL[L]IENVS AVG. Radiate head of
        Gallienus r.
Rev.   [FOR]TVNA [REDVX]. Draped Fortuna
        standing l., holding uncertain object in r.
        hand, cornucopia in l.; in field r., S; (pos-
        sibly * in field l., but the coin is too worn
        to be certain).
↓   1.98 g.   20.5 mm.   AE antoninianus.
        RIC, no. 572 (sole reign).

276

Gallienus: Mediolanum, A.D. 260–68
(C82/7/15)

Obv.   SALO[NINA] AVG. Diademed bust of
        Salonina r., draped.
Rev.   VENV[S F]EL[IX]. Draped Venus stand-
        ing l., holding child in extended r. hand,
        scepter in l.; in field, P; in exergue, A.
↙   1.78 g.   19 mm.   AE antoninianus.

This specimen most closely resembles *RIC*, no.
65 (Cohen, no. 117) for Salonina during the sole
reign of Gallienus, except that the Cupid mentioned in *RIC* is not visible on the Stovall coin
(possibly worn away) and *RIC* mentions only a
"P" in the right field, whereas this coin appears
to have that mark as well as an "A" (or possibly
"II") in the exergue.

277

Aurelian: Siscia (third *officina*), A.D. 270–75
(C82/7/17)

Obv.   [I]MP C D AVRELIANVS [AVG]. Radi-
        ate, draped bust of Aurelian r.
Rev.   [CONCORDIA MI]LI. Two Concordiae
        standing facing, each holding a standard,
        between them, a third standard; in ex-
        ergue, T.
↑   3.99 g.   20.5 mm.   AE antoninianus.
        Cohen, no. 51; *RIC*, no. 202.

RIC lists "S" as the only *officina* mark for this
issue, but the mark on the Stovall coin is clearly
"T." This coin belongs to the early part of Aurelian's reign. Period I, see *RIC*, vol. 5, pt. 1,
p. 248.

278

Aurelian: mint uncertain, A.D. 270–75
(C82/7/18)

Obv.   IMP AVRE . . . AVG. Radiate, cuirassed bust of Aurelian r.
Rev.   OR[IENS AVG]. Sol, standing l., with raised r. hand, globe in l.; at foot to l., captive.
↙   3.26 g.   21.5 mm.   AE antoninianus.

No mint mark is visible to enable a specific identification, but *RIC*, nos. 246 and 361 seem the most likely possibilities.

279

Aurelian: Rome, A.D. 270–75
(C82/7/19)

Obv.   SEVERI[NA] AVG. Diademed, draped bust of Severina r.
Rev.   [VENVS FELIX]. Draped Venus standing l., with right hand extended (Mattingly suggests that she may be holding Cupid, but this specimen is too worn for this to be seen), l. hand holding scepter; mint mark is not visible.
↙   1.92 g.   19 mm.   AE denarius. Cohen, no. 14; *RIC*, no. 6.

This coin is dated to the latter part of the reign of Aurelian. Period III, see *RIC*, vol. 5, pt. 1, p. 249.

280

Probus: Rome (seventh *officina*), A.D. 276–82
(C82/7/20)

Obv.   IMP PROB-VS P F AVG. Radiate bust of Probus r., cuirassed.
Rev.   [ADVE]N-TVS AVG. Emperor riding l., r. hand raised, l. holding scepter; at foot, captive; in exergue, [R]*Z.
↙   3.42 g.   22 mm.   AE antoninianus. Cohen, no. 36; *RIC*, no. 155.

281

Probus: Ticinum, A.D. 276–82
(C82/7/21)

Obv.   [VIRTVS] PROBI INVICTI AVG. Radiate bust of Probus l., helmeted, cuirassed, holding spear and shield.
Rev.   SALVS [AVG]. Salus standing r., feeding serpent in arms; mint mark:

[XXIT]

↖   3.63 g.   22.5 mm.   AE antoninianus. Cohen, no. 586; *RIC*, no. 501.

Late Roman Imperial

A number of the Stovall coins from the late Roman Empire belong to what is called the *vota* series. J. P. C. Kent (*RIC*, vol. 8, p. 50) states that the "*vota* are promises made to gods conditional upon receiving specified benefits." These *vota*, with which the emperors hoped to obtain long, successful reigns, were celebrated throughout the Roman Empire, at first in ten-year intervals, later in five-year intervals. In the period of Constantine I and his family, they became a very common reverse type. In the general format for stating their *vota* on coinage, e.g., VOT/XV/-MVLT/XX, the first number represents their *vota soluta*, completed vows for the years they have already reigned, and the second number shows their *vota suscepta*, the vows they undertake for five or ten more years of rule. If only one number is mentioned, it can refer to either category. Theoretically, the numbers given should allow us to date a coin exactly; however, the emperors in this period often celebrated their *vota* well before or well after the correct year or changed the year for the celebration to coincide with that of their fellow rulers. Thus, dating of the *vota* coinage is very problematic. We have generally followed Kent's ideas (*RIC*, vol. 8, pp. 50–54) for their dating in this period, when no specific dating of the coin is possible.

Also, in the late empire mint marks appear on almost all the coinage, indicating the city of mintage with one or a few letters (sometimes preceded by the standard formula SM, for *Sacra Moneta*), and with one letter the *officina* (workshop) in which the coin was struck. The numbering of the *officinae* is based either on the Latin ordinal numbers—P, S, T, or Q, for *Prima, Secunda, Tertia*, or *Quarta*—or the Greek alphabet. For example, SMNA would indicate a coin struck in the first *officina* at Nicomedia, preceded by the standard formula. When information on the *officina* number is legible in the mint mark, it has been noted in parentheses after the city of mintage.

282

Diocletian: Rome, A.D. 292
(C82/7/22)

Obv.   IMP DIOCLE-TIANVS AVG. Radiate bust of Diocletian r., draped, cuirassed.

Rev.   IOVI CO-NSERVAT AVGG. Jupiter stand-
        ing facing, looking r., holding scepter in
        r. hand (*RIC* indicates that he also holds a
        thunderbolt in his l. hand, and that an
        eagle holding a wreath is at his feet, but
        this piece is too worn to detect these at-
        tributes); mint mark not visible.

↑   2.79 g.   22 mm.   AE antoninianus.
        Cohen, no. 242; *RIC*, vol. 5, pt. 2,
        no. 166.

This coin was issued just before Diocletian's reform of the coinage in A.D. 294, by which the antoninianus was abolished.

283

Diocletian: Cyzicus (third *officina*), ca. A.D. 295–99
(C82/7/23)

Obv.   IMP C C VAL DIOCLETIANVS P F AVG.
        Radiate bust of Diocletian r., cuirassed.

Rev.   CONCORDIA MI-LITVM. Prince stand-
        ing r., in military dress, receiving small
        Victory on globe from Jupiter, standing
        l., l. hand holding scepter; below Vic-
        tory, KΓ.

↗   3.94 g.   23 mm.   AE radiate fraction
        (light).   *RIC*, vol. 6, Cyzicus, no. 15a.

284

Diocletian: Cyzicus (first *officina*)
(C82/7/24)

Obv.   [GAL   VAL]   MAXIMIANVS   NOB
        [CAES]. Radiate bust of Galerius Maxi-
        mian r., cuirassed.

Rev.   CONCORDIA MI-LITVM. Type same
        as no. 283 above; below Victory, [K]A.

↓   2.76 g.   21 mm.   AE radiate fraction
        (light).   *RIC*, vol. 6, Cyzicus, no. 18b.

Galerius Maximian appears on coins like this
from most of the Eastern mints; however, judg-
ing from the fact that there are obviously only
two letters in the mint mark and from the way in
which the reverse legend is divided, this coin
could only be from Cyzicus.

285

Maxentius: Aquileia or Rome, A.D. 307–11
(C82/7/25)

Obv.   IMP C MA[XE]NTIVS [P F] AVG. Lau-
        reate head of Maxentius r.

Rev.   CON[SE]RV [VRB SVAE]. Roma, seated
        facing, in hexastyle temple, holding globe

in r. hand, scepter in l.; wreath in pedi-
ment (coin is too worn to see other detail
on temple); no mint mark visible.

↙   4.69 g.   23 mm.   AE follis.

Absence of a legible mint mark on this coin prevents an exact identification. Maxentius minted
coins with these types and legends in Aquileia
and Rome, A.D. 307–11. *RIC*, vol. 6, Aquileia,
no. 121a, Rome, nos. 202a and 258. A hole has
been punched in this coin just before Maxentius's eyes, possibly for mounting in jewelry.

286

Licinius I: Aquileia (first *officina*), A.D. 308–24
(C82/7/26)

Obv.   IMP LICINIVS P F AVG. Laureate bust
        of Licinius r., cuirassed.

Rev.   SOLI IN[VI]-CTO COMITI. Sol, stand-
        ing l., with chlamys over l. shoulder,
        r. arm raised, l. hand holding globe; in
        field, A-F; in exergue, AQP.

↑   2.84 g.   20.5 mm.   AE follis.

This coin is in a good condition, but there are no
coins in *RIC* with which to identify it. *RIC*, vol. 6,
Aquileia, no. 143, comes closest, but it has numerous major differences from the Stovall coin.
We can only be certain that this is a coin of Licinius's, minted at Aquileia. Nothing in the appearance of the coin suggests that it is not authentic, and it seems unlikely that anyone would
imitate such a common type of coin.

287

Maxentius: Ostia, A.D. 309–12
(C82/7/27)

Obv.   IMP C MAX[ENTIVS P F AVG]. Laure-
        ate head of Maxentius r.

Rev.   [AETERNITAS] AVG N. Castor and Pol-
        lux, with chlamys hanging from shoul-
        ders, standing facing each other, each
        holding scepter in outer hand, bridled
        horse with inner hand (stars above their
        heads, which are mentioned in *RIC*, are
        not visible on our coin because of corro-
        sion); no mint mark visible.

↑   5.41 g.   24 mm.   AE follis. *RIC*, vol. 6,
        Ostia, no. 35.

Because of its unusual reverse this coin can be
exactly identified despite its poor condition.

288

Constantine I: Trier (first *officina*), A.D. 310–13
(C82/7/28)

Obv.   CONSTANTINVS P F AVG. Laureate bust of Constantine I r., cuirassed.
Rev.   SOLI INVIC-TO COMITI. Sol standing facing, head to l., chlamys draped over l. shoulder, r. arm raised, l. hand holding globe; in field, T-F; in exergue, PTR.
↓   3.24 g.   20.5 mm.   AE follis.   *RIC*, vol. 6, Treveri, no. 873.

The first letter of the mint mark looks more like an "A" or a "D," but is probably just a badly formed "P."

289

Constantine I: Trier (first *officina*), A.D. 313–15
(C82/7/29)

Obv.   IMP CON[STAN]TINVS AVG. Laureate bust of Constantine I r., draped, cuirassed.
Rev.   MARTI CO[N]-SERVATORI. Mars, helmeted in military dress, standing r., holding inverted spear in r. hand, resting l. hand on shield; mint mark:

$$\frac{\text{T} \mid \text{F}}{\text{PTR}} \cdot$$

↓   4.42 g.   22.75 mm.   AE follis.   *RIC*, vol. 7, Trier, no. 49.

290

Licinius I: Alexandria (first *officina*), A.D. 315
(C82/7/30)

Obv.   IMP C VAL LICIN LICINIVS P F AVG. Laureate head of Licinius I r.
Rev.   IOVI [CONSER]-VATORI AVGG. Jupiter standing l., chlamys across l. shoulder, holding scepter in l. hand, in r. hand, Victory (who, *RIC* tells us, holds a wreath, which is not visible here); to l. eagle with wreath; mint mark:

↘   3.62 g.   18 mm.   AE follis.   *RIC*, vol. 7, Alexandria, no. 10.

291

Constantine I: Rome (first *officina*), A.D. 317–18
(C82/7/31)

Obv.   [DIV]O CONSTANTI[O PIO PRINC]. Laureate and veiled head of Constantius I r.
Rev.   [MEMORIAE] AETERNA[E]. Eagle standing r., looking l.; in exergue, RP.
↖   2.02 g.   16 mm.   AE.   *RIC*, vol. 7, Rome, no. 111.

292

Constantine I: Antioch (first *officina*), A.D. 317–20
(C82/7/32)

Obv.   D N VAL LICI[N LICINIVS NOB C]. Laureate bust of Licinius II l., globe, scepter in l. hand, mappa in r.
Rev.   IOVI [CONSERV]ATORI CAESS. Jupiter standing l., chlamys across l. shoulder, leaning on scepter in l. hand, holding Victory on globe in r. hand, at feet, captive; mint mark:

$$\frac{\mid \text{A}}{\text{SMANT}}$$

↑   1.97 g.   18.5 mm.   AE follis.   *RIC*, vol. 7, Antioch, nos. 28, 29, or 30.

293

Constantine I: Ticinum, A.D. 318–19
(C82/7/33)

Obv.   IMP CONSTAN-TINVS MAX [AVG]. Bust of Constantine I r., wearing laureate helmet and cuirass.
Rev.   VICTORIAE LAETAE [PRINC PERP]. Two draped Victories, standing facing one another, holding shield, inscribed VOT/PR, on altar; on front of altar, a cross; mint mark not visible.
↖   3.56 g.   18 mm.   AE follis.   *RIC*, vol. 7, Ticinum, no. 86.

According to *RIC*, Constantine I issued several coins like this one. But Ticinum appears to be the only mint that put a cross on the altar, as we find on this coin.

294

Constantine I: mint uncertain, A.D. 318–20
(C82/7/34)

Obv.   . . . CONSTAN-TINVS MAX AVG. Bust

of Constantine I r., wearing helmet (laureate?) and cuirass.

Rev.   [VICTORI]AE LAETA. . . . Two draped Victories, standing facing each other, holding shield on altar (any lettering on shield or altar, as well as the mint mark, is unclear).

↖   3.91 g.   17.25 mm.   AE follis.

RIC, vol. 7, indicates that Constantine issued coins with reverse legends beginning as this does at several mints during the period A.D. 318–20.

295

Constantine I: Siscia (third *officina*), A.D. 320
(C82/7/35)

Obv.   IVL CRISPVS NOB CAES. Laureate bust of Crispus l., cuirassed with spear pointing forward, shield on l. arm.

Rev.   VIRTVS-EXERCIT. Standard inscribed VOT/X, a captive sitting on either side; mint mark:

S	Γ
	H
Γ[SI]S✳	

↖   2.04 g.   18.5 mm.   AE follis.   *RIC*, vol. 7, Siscia, no. 130.

Crispus had been Caesar for three years when this votive issue was struck, indicating that the number ten must represent *vota suscepta*. There is a small hole pierced through the coin on the front part of Crispus's cuirass, possibly for mounting in jewelry.

296

Constantine I: Arles?, A.D. 321?
(C82/2/13)

Obv.   CONSTANTINVS IVN NOB C. Laureate head of Constantine II r.

Rev.   CAESARVM NOSTRORVM. Laurel wreath; inside, VOT/./X; in exergue, Q✳A.

↓   3.12 g.   18 mm.   AE follis.

Although nothing comparable is mentioned in *RIC*, this coin is possibly an addition to one group of coins from Arles (ibid., vol. 7, Arles, nos. 239–45), if the mint mark listed there, Q✳A, can be identified with Q✳A (there are no plates for this group of coins). If the Stovall coin is genuine, it would indicate that Constantine II

began to issue VOT X coinage at Arles earlier than indicated in *RIC*, which places his first VOT X issue in A.D. 322 with the mint mark ARLQ. Membership in the group of coins mentioned above would mean that this coin was struck in A.D. 321, in the fourth *officina* at Arles. Although the uniqueness of this coin brings up the possibility that it is a forgery, nothing in its weight or appearance seems to indicate this.

297

Constantine I: Ticinum (second *officina*), A.D. 322–25
(C49–50/9/2)

Obv.   CONSTAN-TINVS AVG. Laureate head of Constantine I r.

Rev.   D N CONSTANTINI MAX AVG. Laurel wreath; inside, VOT/./X X/◡; in exergue, S T.

↓   3.56 g.   18 mm.   AE follis.   *LRBC*, pt. 1, no. 479; *RIC*, vol. 7, Ticinum, no. 167.

298

Constantine I: Rome (fifth *officina*), A.D. 330
(C82/7/36)

Obv.   CONSTANTI-NOPOLIS. Constantinople l., wearing laureate helmet, imperial cloak and holding reversed spear.

Rev.   Victory standing l. on prow, holding spear in r. hand, shield in l.; in exergue, [R]FЄ.

↑   2.30 g.   17 mm.   AE follis.   *LRBC*, pt. 1, no. 536; *RIC*, vol. 7, Rome, no. 332.

This coin may also possibly be an example of *RIC*, no. 333 or 334, having dots between or around the mint mark. Wear on that part of the coin prevents a certain determination, although the coin is most probably *RIC*, no. 332.

299

Constantine I: A.D. 330–31
(C82/7/37)

Obv.   CONST[ANTI]-NOPOLIS. Type same as no. 298 above.

Rev.   Type same as no. 298 above; in exergue, RBЄ.

↑   2.27 g. 18.25 mm. AE follis. *LRBC*, pt. 1, no. 541; *RIC*, vol. 7, Rome, no. 339.

300

Constantine I: Trier (first *officina*), A.D. 330–31
(C82/7/38)

Obv.   CONSTANTI-NVS MAX AVG. Laureate bust of Constantine I r., draped, cuirassed.

Rev.   GLOR-IA EXERC-ITVS. Two cuirassed, helmeted soldiers standing facing each other, each holding a spear in his outside hand, a shield with his inside hand, between them two military standards; in exergue, TRP.

↘   2.53 g. 17 mm. AE follis. *LRBC*, pt. 1, no. 54; *RIC*, vol. 7, Trier, no. 526.

301

Constantine I: Rome (second *officina*), A.D. 330–31
(C82/7/39)

Obv.   CONSTANTINVS IVN NOB C. Laureate bust of Constantine II r., cuirassed.

Rev.   GLOR-IA EXERC-ITVS. Type same as no. 300 above; in exergue, RBS.

↘   1.72 g. 17.5 mm. AE follis. *LRBC*, pt. 1, no. 538; *RIC*, vol. 7, Rome, no. 336.

302

Constantine I: Constantinople (sixth *officina*?), A.D. 330–35
(C82/2/31)

Obv.   [FL IVL] CON[STAN]TIVS NOB C. Laureate bust of Constantius II r., draped, cuirassed.

Rev.   [GLORIA EXERCITVS]. Two soldiers standing facing with two military standards between them; in exergue, CONS(S?).

↓   2.77 g. 17 mm. AE follis. *LRBC*, pt. 1, no. 1007; *RIC*, vol. 7, Constantinople, no. 61 or 75.

303

Constantine I: Siscia (second *officina*), A.D. 334–35
(C82/2/14)

Obv.   CONST[AN]-TINOPOLIS. Helmeted

bust of Constantinople l., wearing imperial cloak, holding a spear.

Rev.   Victory standing on prow l., draped, holding scepter in r. hand, round shield in l.; in exergue, .BSIS.

↙   2.37 g. 18 mm. AE follis. *LRBC*, pt. 1, no. 751; *RIC*, vol. 7, Siscia, no. 241.

304

Family of Constantine I: Constantinople, A.D. 335–41
(C82/2/1)

Obv.   (Legend worn away). Diademed male head r.

Rev.   [GLORIA EXERCITVS]. Two cuirassed, helmeted soldiers with a military standard between them, each holding a shield in his inside hand and a spear in his outside hand; in exergue, CONS. . . .

↖   1.59 g. 15 mm. AE.

305

Family of Constantine I: mint uncertain, A.D. 335–41
(C82/2/2)

Obv.   (No legible lettering). Type not distinguishable.

Rev.   [GLORIA] EXERC-ITVS. Same as no. 304 but no mint mark visible.

?   1.62 g. 14.5 mm. AE.

According to *LRBC*, coins of this type were minted at most of the mints of the period by the following: Constantine I, Constantine II, Constans, Constantius II, and Delmatius; there were also autonomous issues of Rome and Constantinople. They belong to *LRBC*'s period III (A.D. 335–41) for the era of Constantine I. Neither coin has any legible obverse lettering with which to make a more specific identification.

306

Constantine II: Rome (first *officina*), A.D. 337–40
(C82/7/43)

Obv.   [V]IC CONSTA-NTINVS AVG. Laureate bust of Constantine II, cuirassed.

Rev.   VIRTVS-AVGVSTI. Emperor standing l., in military dress, holding inverted spear in r. hand, shield resting on ground in l. (head is no longer visible); in exergue, R♡P.

↘ 1.53 g. 14.5 mm. AE. *LRBC*, pt. 1, no. 580; *RIC*, vol. 8, Rome, no. 4.

307

Constantius II: mint uncertain, A.D. 337–ca. 346 (C82/2/32)

Obv. D N CON . . . P F AVG. Diademed bust of Constantius II or Constans r., draped.

Rev. Laurel wreath; inside, VOT/XV/MVLT/XX; in exergue, . . . S.

↖ 1.77 g. 15.5 mm. AE.

Kent states (*RIC*, vol. 8, p. 51) that Constantius II issued VOT/XV/MVLT/XX coinage from A.D. 337 to 340, while Constans's issues date to ca. 342 and ca. 346. Both Constantine I and Constantine II also issued coins with similar reverses, but the portrait is clearly not of Constantine I, and Constantine II issued this coin only before he was named Augustus. Not enough of the mint mark is visible to identify the specific mint.

308

Constantius II: Nicomedia (fifth *officina*?), A.D. 347–48 (C82/2/3)

Obv. D N CONSTA. . . . Diademed head r., of Constantius II or Constans.

Rev. Laurel wreath; inside, VOT/XX/MVLT/XXX; in exergue, SMN(Є?).

↓ 1.26 g. 14 mm. AE.

This coin belongs to the second group of base billon and bronze coinage on pages 474–75 of *RIC*, volume 8. *RIC* states that both Constantius II and Constans appear on this issue; since the end of obverse legend is obliterated, we cannot determine which of these emperors minted the Stovall coin.

309

Constantius II: Antioch, A.D. 347–48 (C82/2/46)

Obv. D N CONST. . . . Diademed head of Constantius II or Constans r.

Rev. Laurel wreath; inside, VOT/XX/MVLT/XXX; in exergue, SMAN. . . .

↘ 1.42 g. 15 mm. AE. *RIC*, vol. 8, Antioch, no. 113 (Constantius) or no. 115 (Constans).

This coin is probably one of Constantius II, as *RIC*, no. 113 is much more common than *RIC*,

no. 115. No. 115 was struck in all of the fifteen *officinae* operating at Antioch during this period, while no. 113 was struck in only three. Most of Constans's *vota* coinage from Antioch in this period bears the more correct reverse legend, VOT/XV/MVLT/XX, while at the other mints none of his coinage bore the more correct legend.

310

Constantius II: Cyzicus (first *officina*?), A.D. 347–48 (C82/2/33)

Obv. [D N CONS]TA-NS P F AVG. Diademed head of Constans r.

Rev. Laurel wreath; inside, VOT/XX/MVLT/XXX; in exergue, *SMK(A?).

↑ 1.25 g. 15 mm. AE. *RIC*, vol. 8, Cyzicus, no. 64; *LRBC*, pt. 1, no. 1319.

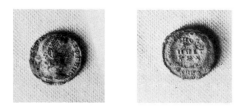

311

Constantius II: Antioch, A.D. 347–55 (C56–57/9/11)

Obv. D N CONSTAN-TIVS P F AVG. Diademed bust of Constantius II r., draped.

Rev. Laurel wreath; inside, VOTIS/XXX/MVLTIS/XXXX; in exergue, ANT.

↖ 1.85 g. 18 mm. AR siliqua. *RIC*, vol. 8, Antioch, no. 108.

312

Constantius II: mint uncertain, A.D. 351–61 (C82/2/12)

Obv. [D N C]ONSTAN-TIVS [P F AVG]. Diademed bust of Constantius II r., draped.

Rev. FEL TEMP [REPARATIO]. Virtus standing l., holding spear in r. hand, shield in l., spearing fallen horseman to l.; in

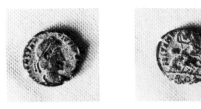

exergue, faintly visible mint mark, not legible.

↓   2.23 g.   16 mm (edge worn).   AE.

313

Constantius II
(C51–52/1/29)

Obv.   [D N C]ONST[ANTIVS P F AVG]. Same as no. 312 above.
Rev.   [FEL TEMP REPAR]ATIO. Same as no. 312 above.
↘   2.57 g.   24.5 mm (edge worn).   AE.

314

Constantius II
(C51–52/1/32)

Obv.   D N CON[STAN]TIV[S P F AVG]. Same as no. 312 above.
Rev.   [FEL TEMP REPARATIO]. Same as no. 312 above, but no mint mark visible.
↓   2.02 g.   17 mm.   AE.

315

Constantius II
(C82/2/34)

Obv.   [D N CO]NSTA[NTIVS P F AVG]. Same as no. 314.
Rev.   [FEL] T[E]MP [RE]PARATIO. Same as no. 314.
↘   1.46 g.   14.25 mm (edge worn).   AE.

316

Constantius II
(C82/2/35)

Obv.   D N CON[STANTIVS P F AVG]. Same as no. 314 above.
Rev.   [FEL TEMP] REPAR[ATIO]. Same as no. 314 above.
↘   2.75 g.   16.5 mm.   AE.

317

Constantius II
(C82/2/36)

Obv.   D N [CONSTANTIVS P F AVG]. Same as no. 314 above.

Rev.   FEL T[EMP REPARATIO]. Same as no. 314 above.
↘   1.64 g.   15.75 mm.   AE.

318

Constantius II
(C82/2/37)

Obv.   (No lettering legible). Bust (diademed?) of Constantius II, Constantius Gallus, or Julian II r., draped.
Rev.   [FEL TEMP REPARATIO]. Same as no. 314 above.
↘   1.67 g.   15.5 mm (edge broken away). AE.

According to *LRBC*, coins of this size and type were struck at most of the mints of the period by Constantius II with Constantius Gallus from A.D. 351 to 354, and by Constantius II with Julian II from A.D. 355 to 361. However, we can specify that numbers 312–17 belong to Constantius II, from the few letters that are legible and the fact that the obverse portrait on these coins shows a diadem. Number 318 is too worn to determine whether the obverse portrait is diademed or not, and thus the specific ruler cannot be identified.

319

Constantius II: (see below), A.D. 355–61
(C82/2/11)

Obv.   D N CONSTAN[TIVS P F AVG]. Diademed bust of Constantius II r., draped.
Rev.   SPE[S REIPV]BLIC[E]. Virtus in military dress, standing l., holding globe in r. hand, spear in l.; in exergue, SM. . . .
↓   1.96 g.   16 mm.   AE.

According to *LRBC*, this coin was issued by Constantius II along with Julian II at almost all of the mints of the period. However, only the following used mint marks beginning with SM: Trier, Thessalonica, Heraclea, Nicomedia, and Cyzicus.

320

Julian II: Cyzicus (first *officina*), A.D. 361–63
(C82/2/38)

Obv.   D N FL C[L IVLIAN]V[S P F AVG]. Diademed bust of Julian II r., draped, cuirassed.
Rev.   [SPES] REI-[PVBLICE]. Julian standing l., helmeted, in military dress, holding

globe in r. hand, spear in l.; in exergue, SMKA.

↘   1.83 g.   15.5 mm (edge broken away). AE.   *RIC*, vol. 8, Cyzicus, no. 123.

321

Valentinian I: Rome (third *officina*), A.D. 364–75 (C82/7/47)

Obv.   D N VALENTINI-ANVS P F AVG. Diademed bust of Valentinian r., draped, cuirassed.
Rev.   SECVR[ITAS]-REIPVBLICAE. Draped Victory advancing l., holding wreath in r. hand and palm in l.; in exergue, R.TERTIA.
↓   1.94 g.   18.5 mm.   AE.   *LRBC*, pt. 2, no. 718; *RIC*, vol. 9, Rome, no. 17a or 24a.

The Stovall coin differs from *RIC*, nos. 17a and 24a, in that they list the mint mark as RTERTIA, whereas here it appears to be R.TERTIA.

322

Valentinian I: Siscia (fourth *officina*), A.D. 364–75 (C82/7/48)

Obv.   Same legend and type as no. 321 above.
Rev.   [SECVRI]TAS-REIPVBLICAE. Same type as no. 321 above; in exergue, .ΔSISC.
↑   1.77 g.   18.75 mm.   AE.   *LRBC*, pt. 2, no. 1277, 1288, or 1302; *RIC*, vol. 9, Siscia, no. 7a or 15a.

This coin is definitely from Siscia; however, wear on the left side of the reverse prevents a definite identification of the mint mark. It could be mint mark ii, v, or x, using the list found in *RIC*, vol. 9, pp. 140–41. *LRBC* says that on this coin Valentinian is merely draped, whereas *RIC* suggests he is draped and cuirassed; the Stovall specimen is worn but appears to be both.

323

Valens: Constantinople, A.D. 364–67 (C56–57/9/12)

Obv.   D N VALENS-P F AVG. Diademed bust of Valens, draped, cuirassed r.
Rev.   Laurel wreath; inside VOT/V; top part of mint mark faintly visible.
↗   1.52 g.   16 mm (edge broken away). AR siliqua. *RIC*, vol. 9, Constantinople, no. 13d.

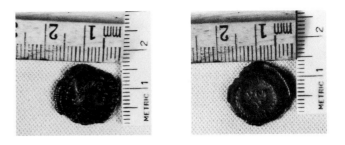

Given the choice of mint marks listed with this issue in *RIC*, the mint mark must be either C.Γ or C.Z, meaning the coin was produced in either the third (Γ) or seventh (Z) *officina* at Constantinople.

324

Valens: Lugdunum (first *officina*), A.D. 367–75 (C82/2/4)

Obv.   (Legend worn away). Diademed bust of Valens or Gratian r., draped, cuirassed.
Rev.   [SEC]VRITA[S] REIP[VBLICAE]. Victory standing l., draped, holding wreath in r. hand, palm in l.; in l. field, palm branch.
↓   1.87 g.   15 mm.   AE.

Because of the unusual mint mark that this issue bears (a palm branch in the left field) we can identify this coin almost exactly, despite its worn condition. The full mint mark for this coin is

OF │ I
̶̶̶̶̶̶̶̶̶̶̶̶
LVGP

, and it was minted within the dates given above either by Valens (*LRBC*, pt. 2, no. 328; *RIC*, vol. 9, Lugdunum, no. 21a) or by Gratian (*LRBC*, pt. 2, no. 329; *RIC*, vol. 9, Lugdunum, no. 21b). *LRBC* mentions no other mint marks for the period which involve a palm branch in the left field.

325

Valens: mint uncertain, A.D. 364–78 (C82/7/49)

Obv.   D N VALEN-S P F AVG. Diademed bust of Valens, draped, cuirassed.
Rev.   SECVRITAS-REIPVBLICAE. Draped Victory advancing to l., holding wreath in r. hand, palm in l.; mint mark not visible.
↓   2.28 g.   17.25 mm.   AE.

LRBC indicates that Valens struck issues like this throughout his reign at most of the mints of the period. Since the mint mark is not visible, no more specific identification can be made.

326

Valens: Rome (first *officina*), A.D. 367–78
(C82/7/50)

Obv.   Same legend and type as no. 325 above.
Rev.   Same legend and type as no. 325 above; in exergue, SM ♥ RP.
↓   2.14 g.   17.75 mm.   AE.   *LRBC*, pt. 2, no. 725 or 730; *RIC*, vol. 9, Rome, no. 24b or 28a.

RIC says that Valens is draped and cuirassed on this coin, whereas *LRBC* states that he is just draped. On the Stovall coin there seems to be some evidence of a cuirass on his r. shoulder.

327

Valentinian II: Antioch (second *officina*), A.D. 378–83
(C82/5/3)

Obv.   D N VAL[EN]TINIA-[NV]S IVN [P F AVG]. Diademed bust of Valentinian II r., draped.
Rev.   VRBS-ROMA. Roma seated l., draped, holding Victory on globe in r. hand, spear in l.; below, cuirass; in field r., star; in exergue, ANTB.
↖   1.91 g.   18.75 mm.   AE.   *LRBC*, pt. 2, no. 2270; *RIC*, no. 9, Antioch, no. 51.

The reverse of Roma on a coin minted in the East indicates that Gratian, emperor of the Western Empire, still had some leadership over Theodosius I, the new Augustus of the Eastern Empire. *RIC*, vol. 9, p. xviii. Valentinian II, the half brother of Gratian, was only nominally the co-Augustus of Gratian, being no more than twelve years old when this coin was minted.

328

Theodosius I: mint uncertain, A.D. 378–88
(C82/7/51)

Obv.   D N THEODO-SIVS P F AVG. Diademed bust of Theodosius I r., draped.
Rev.   [REPARATIO REIPVB]. Emperor standing facing, head to l., raising kneeling woman with his r. hand, holding Victory on globe in his l. hand; no mint mark visible.
↓   5.03 g.   23 mm.   AE.

RIC indicates that coins like this one were issued by Theodosius I at most of the mints of the period, at least from 378 to 383, and at some mints as late as 388. Since the mint mark is not visible, no more specific identification can be made.

329

Arcadius: Cyzicus (third *officina*?), A.D. 388–92
(C82/2/39)

Obv.   [D N] ARCADIVS P F AVG. Diademed bust of Arcadius r., draped, cuirassed.
Rev.   SALVS [REIPVBLIC]AE. Victory standing l. (less worn examples also show she holds a trophy and drags a captive, and there is a ₽ in the l. field); in exergue, [S]MK(Γ?).
↙   1.30 g.   13 mm.   AE.   *LRBC*, pt. 2, no. 2570; *RIC*, vol. 9, Cyzicus, no. 26c.

African

(FREDERICK L. BROWN)

Abbreviations used in bibliographical references:

Mazard   Jean Mazard, *Corpus Nummorum Numidiae Mauretaniaeque* (Paris, 1955).

Müller   Ludvig Müller et al., *Numismatique de l'ancienne Afrique*, 3 vols. (Copenhagen, 1860–62; reprint: Chicago, 1977).

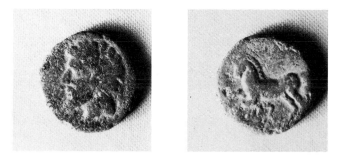

330

Numidia, 202–ca. 118 B.C.
(C84/4/16)

Obv.   Laureate head l., with pointed beard, possibly that of Micipsa or Masinissa.

Rev.   Horse galloping l., without halter; below, top portion of two Punic letters visible, probably the equivalent of MN, as found on many Numidian coins.

↑   16.57 g.   26.5 mm.   AE.   Compare Mazard, no. 23; Müller, vol. 3, Numidia, no. 25.

There is great uncertainty as to the significance of the bearded head which appears on Numidian coinage in the second century B.C., some scholars feeling that it portrays a god, such as Hercules or Jupiter, others that it represents individual rulers. Mazard (pp. 23–24) feels that the great diversity of portraits probably represents distinct rulers, but he does not identify each coin with a specific ruler. The two-letter legends which appear on many issues may represent the first and last letter of various Punic words, in this case, MN for Micipsan or Masinissan; although these letters may have been adopted by other Numidian rulers. Ibid., p. 32. Mazard (p. 25) feels that the horse type must be the symbol of a Phoenician god, analogous to the Roman Mars, who was likely called Hadad or Ba'al.

331

Numidia, ca. second century B.C.
(C84/4/18)

Obv.   Laureate head l., with rounded beard and larger nose than no. 330.

Rev.   Same as no. 330 above, but no lettering visible.

↑   14.25 g.   25.5 mm.   AE.

Neither Müller nor Mazard illustrates a Numidian coin on which the obverse portrait has a nose as large as the one on the Stovall coin; however, the similar type and style clearly indicate it belongs to the same period as no. 330.

332

Carthage, ca. 200–146 B.C.
(C51–52/1/4)

Obv.   Head of Tanit l., wearing wreath of corn and an earring.

Rev.   Horse trotting r.; below, Punic equivalent of letter *A*; to r., pellet.

↑   15.62 g.   27 mm.   AE.   Müller, vol. 2,
Carthage, no. 246.

333
Carthage
(C51–52/1/1)
Obv.   Same as no. 332 above.
Rev.   Same as no. 332 above (but Punic letter
       less clear, no pellet visible).
↑   16.02 g.   28 mm.   AE.   Probably Mül-
       ler, vol. 2, Carthage, no. 245 or 246.

334
Carthage
(C51–52/1/2)
Obv.   Same as no. 333 above.
Rev.   Same as no. 333 above.
↗   18.93 g.   29.5 mm.   AE.   Probably
       Müller, vol. 2, Carthage, no. 245 or 246.

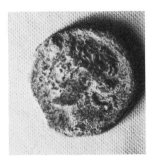 

335
Carthage
(C51–52/1/3)
Obv.   Same as no. 333 above.
Rev.   Same as no. 333 above.
↑   21.15 g.   27.5 mm.   AE.   Probably
       Müller, vol. 2, Carthage, no. 245 or 246.

336
Carthage
(C51–52/1/5)
Obv.   Same as no. 333 above.
Rev.   Same as no. 333 above.
↑   17.73 g.   26 mm.   AE.   Probably Mül-
       ler, vol. 2, Carthage, no. 245 or 246.

337
Carthage
(C51–52/1/6)
Obv.   Same as no. 333 above.
Rev.   Same as no. 333 above (but any letter
       once visible has been worn away).
↑   18.13 g.   27.5 mm.   AE.

338
Carthage
(C51–52/1/7)
Obv.   Same as no. 337 above.
Rev.   Same as no. 337 above.
↑   19.25 g.   28 mm.   AE.

339
Carthage
(C51–52/1/8)
Obv.   Same as no. 337 above.
Rev.   Same as no. 337 above.
↑   18.08 g.   27.5 mm.   AE.

340
Carthage
(C51–52/1/9)
Obv.   Same as no. 337 above.
Rev.   Same as no. 337 above.
↑   18.83 g.   27.5 mm.   AE.

341
Carthage
(C51–52/1/10)
Obv.   Same as no. 337 above.
Rev.   Same as no. 337 above.
↑   20.44 g.   27.5 mm.   AE.

342
Carthage
(C51–52/1/11)
Obv.   Same as no. 337 above.
Rev.   Same as no. 337 above.
↑   16.59 g.   27.5 mm.   AE.

Although these coins are in different states of
wear, their style clearly indicates that they all
belong to the same period, probably the same
issue. They all belong to Müller's group B.IV for
bronze coins of Carthage. The dates above are
given by G. K. Jenkins and R. B. Lewis for a coin
of similar style. *Carthaginian Gold and Electrum
Coins* (London, 1963), pl. 28.15.

The goddess on the obverse is almost certainly Tanit, one of the chief deities of the Car-
thaginians; the wreath of corn may indicate that
she was associated with Demeter, whose worship
was introduced into Carthage in 396 B.C. Ibid.,
p. 11. The horse on the reverse may refer to any
of several deities. The Punic letter visible on
some of our coins is probably the mark of an unknown moneyer or of the mint. Müller, vol. 2,
p. 128.

GLOSSARY OF TERMS
(PRIMARILY FOR POTTERY)
(See following chart)

Alabastron: A perfume jar with narrow neck, flared lip, and rounded bottom.

Amphora: A two-handled vessel for storing liquids and solids; in the neck-amphora the neck is set off from the body.

Apotropaic: A term applied to objects or designs supposed to avert evil.

Aryballos: A small perfume jar with rounded body and narrow neck.

Biga: A chariot pulled by one pair of horses (so quadriga = the same with four horses).

Chiton: A lightweight, sleeved dress or tunic worn by both men and women.

Crater: A large bowl with wide mouth and broad body, used for mixing wine and water. The bell crater is named from its resemblance to an inverted bell, the volute crater from the volutes at the ends of its handles.

Epichysis: A type of small oinochoe or jug with a high, narrow handle and neck upon a body shaped like a reel.

Exergue: A term used primarily in numismatics, indicating that portion of the field below the base line of the main decoration.

Gorgoneion: The face of a Gorgon.

Himation: A heavy mantle or cloak, draped over the body, worn by both sexes.

Hydria: A water jar, so designated owing to the presence of its three handles for lifting and pouring.

Kantharos: A drinking cup with two vertical handles and deep bowl.

Kotyle: Also known as a skyphos.

Kyathos: A kind of ladle with a deep cup and a very high handle.

Kylix: A drinking cup with two handles, a shallow bowl, and a tall foot; the komast cup takes its name from the drunken dancers painted on it.

Lekythos: A slender vase with one handle and a narrow neck, used for oil and unguents and offerings for the dead.

Miltos: A red ochre used as a type of paint.

Oinochoe: A pitcher of one handle, used in ladling wine from craters into drinking cups, often with trefoil mouth.

Olpe: A type of slender oinochoe with a continuous curve from the foot to the lip.

Pelike: A type of amphora with a distinct base, broad mouth, and bulbous lower body.

Peplos: A heavy sleeveless overgarment, worn by women.

Phiale: A low, flat saucer without handles.

Plastic Vase: A vase made in the shape of a human or animal figure, or some other natural object, giving a three-dimensional aspect.

Polos: A cylindrical headdress, or pillbox hat, usually worn by a goddess.

Protome: The upper half of a human figure, or the forepart of an animal.

Provenance: A term that refers to the area where an object was found; to be distinguished from "origin," the place where it was made.

Pyxis: A small jar or box with lid, used for storing cosmetics, medicines, and toiletries.

Reserved Area: The area on a vase deliberately left in the color of the clay.

Skyphos: A deep drinking cup with a low base and usually with two horizontal handles.

Slip: A term designating a coating of clay applied to a vessel before firing, invariably different in color and texture from the clay of the vessel itself.

Stele: An inscribed stone slab.

Thyrsus: A staff ornamented with ivy and vine leaves, carried by devotees of the god Dionysos.

Wash: A term indicating a thin slip.

Amphora (Panathenaic)

Pelike

Neck Amphora

Column Krater

Volute Krater

Calyx Krater

Stamnos

Bell Krater

Lebes

Hydria

Hydria (Kalpis)

Psykter

Oinochoe

Oinochoe

Oinochoe (Chous)

Loutrophoros

Kylix

Kylix

Skyphos

Stemless Kylix

Skyphos

Kyathos

Kantharos

Squat Lekythos

Lekythos

Pyxis

Pyxis

Pyxis

Lekanis

Aryballos

Alabastron

Lebes Gamikos

Select Bibliography

For the reader's convenience are gathered here the bibliographical entries listed at the beginnings of the major sections in this catalogue.

Pottery

Åström, Paul. *The Swedish Cyprus Expedition.* Vol. IV, pt. 1. *The Middle Cypriote Bronze Age* (Lund, 1957).

————. *The Swedish Cyprus Expedition.* Vol. IV, pt. 1. *The Late Cypriote Bronze Age* (Lund, 1972).

Beazley, J. D. *Attic Black-figure Vase-painters* (Oxford, 1956).

————. *Attic Red-figure Vase-painters.* 2d ed. (Oxford, 1963).

————. *Paralipomena: Additions to Attic Black-figure Vase-painters and to Attic Red-figure Vase-painters* (Oxford, 1971).

Birmingham, Judy. "The Chronology of Some Early and Middle Iron Age Cypriot Sites," *AJA* 67 (1963): 15–42.

Coldstream, J. N. *Greek Geometric Pottery* (London, 1968).

Cook, R. M. *Greek Painted Pottery.* 2d ed. (London, 1972).

Dikaios, Porphyrios, and Stewart, James R. *The Swedish Cyprus Expedition.* Vol. IV, pt. 1. *The Stone Age and the Early Bronze Age in Cyprus* (Lund, 1962).

Furumark, A. *The Mycenaean Pottery: Analysis and Classification* (Stockholm, 1941).

Gjerstad, Einar. *Cypriot Pottery from the Neolithic to the Hellenistic Period* (Mâcon, 1932).

————. *The Swedish Cyprus Expedition.* Vol. IV, pt. 2. *The Cypro-Geometric, Cypro-Archaic, and Cypro-Classical Periods* (Stockholm, 1948).

Myres, John. *Handbook of the Cesnola Collection of Antiquities from Cyprus* (New York, 1914).

Payne, H. G. G. *Necrocorinthia: A Study of Corinthian Art in the Archaic Period* (Oxford, 1931).

Trendall, A. D. *The Red-figured Vases of Lucania, Campania, and Sicily.* 2 vols. (Oxford, 1967).

————, and Cambitoglou, A. *The Red-figured Vases of Apulia.* Vol. 1 (Oxford, 1978).

Vessberg, Olof, and Westholm, Alfred. *The Swedish Cyprus Expedition.* Vol. IV, pt. 3. *The Hellenistic and Roman Periods* (Lund, 1956).

Young, R. S. *Late Geometric Graves and a Seventh-century Well in the Agora. Hesperia,* Supplement 2 (Princeton, N.J., 1939).

Terra-cottas

Bailey, Donald M. *A Catalogue of the Lamps in the British Museum.* 2 vols. (London, 1975–80).

————. *Greek and Roman Pottery Lamps.* Rev. ed. (London, 1972).

Bell, Malcolm, III. *Morgantina Studies.* Vol. 1. *The Terracottas* (Princeton, 1981).

Higgins, R. A. *Catalogue of the Terracottas in the Department of Greek and Roman Antiquities, British Museum.* 2d ed., 2 vols. (London, 1968).

————. *Greek Terracottas* (London, 1967).

Howland, Richard. *Greek Lamps and Their Survivals.* Vol. 4. *Athenian Agora* (Princeton, N.J., 1958).

Perlzweig, Judith. *Lamps of the Roman Period.* Vol. 7. *Athenian Agora* (Princeton, N.J., 1961).

Szentléleky, Tihamér. *Ancient Lamps* (Budapest, 1969).

Vessberg, Olof, and Westholm, Alfred. *The Swedish Cyprus Expedition.* Vol. IV, pt. 3. *The Hellenistic and Roman Periods* (Lund, 1956).

Glass

Auth, Susan H. *Ancient Glass at the Newark Museum* (Newark, N.J., 1976).

Hayes, John W. *Roman and Pre-Roman Glass in the Royal Ontario Museum: A Catalogue* (Toronto, 1975).

Isings, C. *Roman Glass from Dated Finds* (Groningen, 1957).

Smith, R. W. *Glass from the Ancient World: The Ray Winfield Smith Collection* (Corning, N.Y., 1957).

Coinage

Babelon, Ernest C. F. *Description historique et chronologique des monnaies de la république romaine*. 2 vols. (Paris, 1885–86. Reprint. Bologna, 1963).

Cohen, Henry. *Description historique des monnaies frappées sous l'empire romain communément appelées médailles imperiales*. 8 vols. (Paris, 1880. Reprint. Graz, 1955).

Crawford, Michael H. *Roman Republican Coinage*. 2 vols. (Cambridge, 1974).

Grueber, H. A. *Coins of the Roman Republic in the British Museum*. 3 vols. (London, 1910).

Hendin, David. *Guide to Ancient Jewish Coins* (New York, 1976).

Hill, P. V., and Kent, J. P. C. *Late Roman Bronze Coinage A.D. 324–498* (London, 1965).

Kindler, Arie. *Coins of the Land of Israel* (Jerusalem, 1974).

Mattingly, Harold, et al. *Coins of the Roman Empire in the British Museum*. 6 vols. (London, 1923–62. Vols. 1–4 reprinted [vols. 3 and 4 with alterations]. London, 1965–68).

——. *Roman Imperial Coinage*. 10 vols. (London, 1926–81).

Mazard, Jean. *Corpus Nummorum Numidiae Mauretaniaeque* (Paris, 1955).

Meshorer, Ya'akov. *Jewish Coins of the Second Temple Period* (Tel Aviv, 1967).

Müller, Ludvig, et al. *Numismatique de l'ancienne Afrique*. 3 vols. (Copenhagen, 1860–62).

Poole, Reginald, et al. *A Catalogue of Greek Coins in the British Museum*. 29 vols. (London, 1873–1927. Reprint. Bologna, 1963–65).

Reifenberg, A. *Ancient Jewish Coins*. 2d ed. (Jerusalem, 1947).

Reinach, Theodore. *Jewish Coins* (London, 1903).

Sydenham, Edward A. *The Coinage of the Roman Republic* (London, 1952).

Index

Classical Antiquities,
designed by Bill Cason, was set in various sizes of Baskerville by G & S Typesetters. Text and color section were printed offset on 80-pound Warren's Flokote, the text by McNaughton & Gunn, the color section by University of Oklahoma Printing Services, with case binding by John H. Dekker & Sons.